T0128177

CONSTANTINE

Helena—Nicaea—Dead Sea Scrolls

JOHN MENCH

WESTBOW
PRESS®
A DIVISION OF THOMAS NELSON
& ZONDERVAN

WestBow Press books may be ordered through booksellers or by contacting:

WestBow Press
A Division of Thomas Nelson & Zondervan
1663 Liberty Drive
Bloomington, IN 47403
www.westbowpress om
1 (866) 928-1240

ISBN: 978-1-9736-4506-1 (sc)
ISBN: 978-1-9736-4507-8 (hc)
ISBN: 978-1-9736-4508-5 (e)

Library of Congress Control Number: 2018913502

Print information available on the last page.

WestBow Press rev. date: 11/14/2018

DEDICATION

Dedicated to my wife, Rose, who for thirty-four years, focused our lives around Jesus' message and to my second wife, Ann, who encouraged me for the last twenty years. Her illness provided me with the time to write and her love of life encouraged me to tell my stories. God's grace to both of you.

CONTENTS

Acknowledgement

To my friends who after reading my book gave me critical guidance and loving care.

INTRODUCTION

The Foundation of Christianity

In an effort to stimulate your imagination, I have written a series of books concerning the formation of the Christian Church.

Our understanding of Christianity was probably formed when we attended Sunday school. Hopefully, what we learned was based on the principles of the Bible. The Bible's New Testament provides us with a disjointed series of stories about Jesus. The stories are incomplete and have caused me to be concerned about the incidents not preserved in history. Some will say they are a figment of my imagination.

After reading the books, I encourage you to form and record your imagination about the unrecorded events.

My books were written as fiction related to history. In my opinion, history concerning any specific topic in ancient times is fiction. The amount of written history that is accurate is pure speculation. The amount of fiction that is contained in written history is based on several items:

1. elapsed time (from event to now)
2. government influence (the winners of war write history)
3. greed (writing to make money)
4. perspective (being human)

When you read a history book, you are reading a written perspective that has been deemed acceptable by your generation and your environment. Most history books are the perspective of well-paid victors.

Introduction - Constantine

This story takes place during the third and fourth centuries. The Roman Empire grew by taking control of land in adjacent areas. The politics and economy of the empire made it necessary to expand. Constantine's story begins in Britain where the Roman Empire had deployed a large contingent of troops. Constantine's father, Constantius Chlorus, was a great warrior in the Roman army. He was a career soldier and very proud of his military position. His service took him to the eastern part of the empire where he met Helena. Constantine was a son of this marriage. Much of the action of this story occurs in the area of Nicomedia.

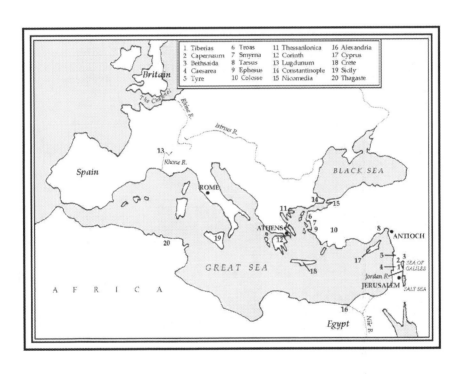

1 Tiberias	6 Troas	11 Thessanlonica	16 Alexandria
2 Capernaum	7 Smyrna	12 Corinth	17 Cyprus
3 Bethsaida	8 Tarsus	13 Lugdunum	18 Crete
4 Caesarea	9 Ephesus	14 Constantinople	19 Sicily
5 Tyre	10 Colosse	15 Nicomedia	20 Thagaste

CHAPTER 1

CONSTANTINE'S CHILDHOOD

The eastern section, of the Roman Empire, became more important and exerted a greater influence on the total empire than the western portion. The cities grew and many highways built. The empire's government was divided and the Christian Church felt the same pressure. Each experienced an East versus West situation. The economy weakened due to its dependence on slave labor and a change in the climate. The climate change adversely influenced the growth of food and the location of the people. Politics were unstable and it wasn't uncommon to have a new emperor every few months. Some countries like Britain accepted gifts from the empire and joined with the Romans. The Roman Empire was constantly at war because many countries tried to take back land that had become part of the empire when the Roman army occupied the territory. The barbarians continued to cause problems along the Rhine and Istrius Rivers.

The Roman military commander, Maximian, was with his junior officers. They engaged in boisterous discussions concerning the river campaign.

"The Rhine River was a successful campaign for you," Maximian said. "The treasure you captured will be put in our treasury. The commanders in Rome will be pleased."

"We fought long and hard for the empire," Constantius said. "I have delivered two hundred prisoners to your guards."

He held up two fingers and waved them.

"You are a great warrior," Maximian said. "I will reward you with an assignment in Britain. It should be good for your career."

Constantius looked at him and nodded approval.

"How will I get to Britain?" he asked. "I would prefer to sail."

"You will go by ship," he said. "You will sail to Smyrna and then transfer to a ship going to Rome. In Rome you will transfer to another ship."

"The trip sounds involved," he said. "It is a very long journey."

Maximian allowed Constantius to choose five soldiers to accompany him.

Constantius hoped for a successful tour which would result in a promotion. After a month of sailing, Constantius arrived in Britain.

It was a rainy, cloudy, dismal day, when he visited the king. The King had decided he liked the protection provided by the Roman military, and King Cole and Constantius quickly became good friends. They regularly met and discussed the army's progress. The king on many occasions brought his daughter, Elene, to dinner, so she could learn to know Constantius. He thought Elene would make Constantius a good wife. Eventually, Constantius became cautiously friendly with the king's daughter.

"It is a good day to be inside," the king said.

He pointed at the heavy rain pounding on the castle walls.

"It seems to continually rain in Britain," Constantius said. "Many of our men are engaged with the enemy, but I decided it was the perfect day to visit with you. I was sure your castle would be warm and dry."

He looked at the king and smiled.

"How are the men doing?" he asked. "Are we safe?"

"Yes," he said. "We are making progress. We will defeat Allectus; it is just a matter of time."

Constantius' answer pleased King Cole. He stroked his beard, paused and then invited Constantius to dinner. He made it very clear that Elene would join them. Acknowledging the king's cooks were much better than the army's cooks, Constantius gracefully accepted the invitation. They enjoyed a meal fit for a king. After the meal, they adjourned to the library. It wasn't long before King Cole excused himself.

Elene and Constantius went for a walk in the lavish gardens of the palace. He immediately noted the scent of flowers filled the air.

"It is nice to see you," Elene said. "Do you think you will be here for a long time?"

"As soon as my men are successful, they move me," he said. "I have never remained in one location for an extended period of time."

"That is too bad," she said. "Britain is a beautiful place. I think you could learn to like it here. I could help you."

"It is necessary for me to be where the empire needs me," he said. "They don't ask me, they tell me."

"I guess that is the life of a warrior," she said. "I have never traveled very far. How do you like the yellow flowers?"

She picked a flower and placed it under Constantius' nose. His eyes watered, and he sneezed.

Blinking his eyes repeatedly he said, "They are fine, my horse likes to eat them. I must go now, please excuse me."

Elene didn't understand Constantius' comments about his horse eating flowers, and she was concerned about him leaving so abruptly.

Constantius jumped astraddle his horse, waved to Elene, and returned to his troops. Sergeant Yorkshire approached him and advised that the troops made slow but steady progress.

The next day, the fighting was fierce.

"Send more troops to their left flank," Constantius said. "We can block their escape route."

He stood and looked directly at his sergeant.

"They are well entrenched," Sergeant Yorkshire said. "Several men have been wounded today."

Constantius walked directly before the sergeant.

"I will visit with the wounded," he said. "You block their escape."

"I will lead the men to the left flank," Yorkshire said. "We will make our enemy pay for what they did."

"I don't think they can withstand our line much longer," Constantius said. "Send a scout to the front and then report back to me."

After he sent a scout to the front, the sergeant departed. His men engaged in hand-to-hand combat with the enemy. The weapons, of the

Roman army, were newer than their enemies and Constantius' forces make significant progress. The enemy began to retreat. Their path was blocked and they were beaten badly. The sergeant returned to Constantius with good news.

The next day, Constantius visited with King Cole to inform the king of his armies progress.

"I expect Allectus to surrender tomorrow," he said. "I may not be able to return to see you again."

The king was surprised by Constantius' remark.

"We will miss you," he said. "Where will you go?"

"I don't know," he said.

He surmised he would probably take his army to Gaul.

"I will get Elene, so you can say goodbye," King Cole said. "I am sure she will want to see you."

After a few moments, the king returned with Elene. She was dressed in her best clothes, but she had a tear in her eye and a frown on her face.

"Must you go?" she asked. "I am so sad; I don't know what I will do without being able to see you."

"Parting is always difficult, maybe someday I will return," Constantius smirked.

Constantius kissed Elene on her forehead and returned to his troops. She was heartbroken, but understood Constantius' first priority was the empire.

The following week, after Allectus' surrender conditions were completed, Constantius had him restrained in leg irons and sent to the army commander in Rome. The remaining officers of the enemy's troops were interrogated. A few were considered radical and put to death.

Two week later, Constantius was in his tent when he saw a soldier approach.

"Sir, a messenger is here to see you," Markus said. "Should I escort him into the tent?"

"Yes," Constantius said. "Bring him to me. He probably has news about where we are going."

The messenger marched to Constantius and stood at attention.

"At ease, soldier," he said.

"I bring you congratulations from Rome," the messenger said. "I have a written message for you."

After Constantius perused the message, he dispatched the messenger, who returned to Gaul. Constantius' orders were to take most of his troop and march to Gaul. The troops that remained would complete Allectus' surrender. Many of Allectus' troops decided to join the Roman Army.

That evening Constantius stood tall, as he addressed his troops.

"You have done a fine job," he said. "We have been ordered to Gaul."

He read part of the message to his troops. They asked very few questions.

After he addressed the troops, he returned to his quarters.

"Sergeant Yorkshire is here to see you," Markus asked. "I will show him in."

"I am to remain in Britain," Yorkshire said. "King Cole's daughter sure was nice. It is too bad you must leave her behind."

Constantius explained to sergeant Yorkshire that talking with King Cole and being nice to his daughter were part of his job. He further explained he had no particular connection with Elene, and that he was certain he would find a girl in Gaul.

"I wish you the best," Yorkshire said. "When do you depart?"

"We will leave the day after tomorrow," he said. "Markus, prepare the men to move."

"Is this an urgent move?" Markus asked. "What will our pace be?"

"It is not urgent," he said. "We will march for eight hours each day."

Markus departed the tent.

Constantius didn't see King Cole or his daughter again. Constantius thought the new headquarters, in Gaul, would be in Lugdunum a town on the Rhone River. When they arrived at the great channel, the troops built a large fire, played games, and rested as they waited for Roman ships to ferry them across the water.

"I'm not much of a sailor," Markus said. "I will be glad when we reach Gaul."

The Roman sailors joined the soldiers, sitting around the fire, waiting for dinner.

"Give the sailors a good meal," Constantius said. "They probably don't eat anything but fish. Give them chops for dinner."

"That is a good idea," Markus said. "It is always good to have friends in the fleet."

That evening the soldiers and the sailors swapped stories while they ate a meal of chops and roots. Constantius listened to soldiers sing songs about marching. Then sailors sang songs about life on the sea. Eventually, the fires went out and the troops went to sleep.

In the morning, the soldiers boarded the ships.

"I think I will stand here by the railing," Markus said. "I ate too many chops."

"Sergeant, make sure the men are secure," Constantius said. "Sometimes this can be a rough ride."

He looked at Markus and smiled. Constantius enjoyed sailing across the channel. Markus spent his time standing at the ship's railing being nauseous. When the ship docked, he quickly recovered, and the troops disembarked. Markus introduced Constantius to the new sergeant assigned to them. He had requested to leave Britain and just joined the troops. His name was Pointus.

"Is everything ready to start our march to Gaul?" sergeant Pointus asked. "With whom should I communicate?"

"I will take a few men and proceed to Lugdunum," Constantius said. "I want you to establish camp north of Lugdunum. When you break camp, we will probably travel east."

He pointed east and asked for his horse.

"Yes, sir," Pointus said. "We will see you. Have a safe journey."

Constantius went to Lugdunum. He met with his commander and was told his troops wouldn't be stationed in Lugdunum; their assignment would be to eliminate the revolutionist along the river. He wasn't surprised. The area around Lugdunum had been peaceful for several years.

Two weeks later, he and his troops headed east. They fought the local terrorist every day. They successfully cleared the river, and after two months they reached the Istrius River (Danube). When they were twenty-five miles from the Great Black Sea, they encamped. The troops rested, built large fires, and cleaned their weapons. Constantius informed Pointus they could plan on staying at the location for at least a week.

After a few days, Constantius and Markus went to the town of Naissus.

"It will be good to be stationary for a while," Constantius said. "I am looking forward to eating and sleeping at an inn."

"Not marching will be good," Markus said. "Thank you for bringing me along."

"Your job is to escort me," he said. "You are allowed to have a little fun." He looked at Markus and smiled.

They decided to stay at the Inn with the large sign that advertised, "Good Food and Wine". They entered the Inn and sat at a table.

"Hello, soldiers," she said. "My name is Helena. I will bring a meal to you."

"Hello, Helena," Constantius said. "Bring us the best dinner you are serving. You can join us for dinner."

"I will bring you dinner," she said. "My father will not allow me to eat with you. You are our guests."

Helena departed to get their food. Constantius and Markus watched her every move. They discussed how young and beautiful Helena appeared. Constantius commented that he was certain he would like this area better than Britain. They came to the conclusion, if Helena's father allowed her to see them, she was old enough. When Helena served them dinner, Constantius told her he would like to see her after dinner. She replied that she would be working for two more hours, and then she would meet him for a glass of wine. Constantius looked at Markus and smiled. They ate very slowly and drank several glasses of wine.

Later that evening Constantius and Helena shared a bottle of wine.

"How long have you worked here?" Constantius asked. "Is Naissus your home?"

"We moved here, from Nicomedia, when I was young," Helena said. "My mother, brothers, and sister help father with the inn. It is a family business."

"I have been in the army most of my life," he said. "Someday, I hope to settle down. Come over here and sit next to me."

Constantius winked at her and motioned for her to come closer.

"Sir," she said. "Be good, this is my home. So whether you eat or drink or whatever you do, do it all for the glory of God. (1 Corinthians, 10, 31, NIV)"

Constantius paused for a moment. He considered her message cute.

"May I see you tomorrow?" he asked. "We have a few days away from work."

"I will wait for you in the park," she said. "I will see you tomorrow."

The next day, Constantius went to the park. He waited and waited, Helena never appeared. He was very disappointed. The following day, Constantius went to the Inn. Helena explained her father wouldn't allow her to see him.

She looked at him and said, "As you know, we consider blessed those who have persevered." (James, 5, 11 partial, NIV)

She smiled at Constantius. He didn't hear her, but he saw the smile. They very rapidly became good friends. Constantius visited the Inn whenever possible. Things progressed very rapidly. Soon, they decided to get married. It took a while, but Helena's father learned to like Constantius. After a short courtship, Helena and Constantius were married. They lived in a small house in town. The legion was permanently stationed at the juncture of the Great Black Sea and the Istrius River. Constantius was, on several occasions, rewarded for his military successes.

Constantius spent as much time as possible with Helena. After dinner, he planned to deliver good news to her.

"I have been promoted," Constantius said. "The army has been good to us."

"I like it better than I thought," Helena said. "I was afraid you would be gone every night."

"I am sure they will send me into battle," he said. "However, things are peaceful in this part of the empire."

"I still have problems sleeping," she said. "Maybe I will get used to it."

"I am sure you will," Constantius said. "I don't think about the dangers."

Helena took Constantius' hand and rubbed it. She put her arm around him.

"I want to have a baby," she said. "We should start a family."

"Not yet," he said. "We haven't been married long enough to start a family."

"Sure we have," Helena said. "When they send you away, I don't want to be alone."

"I am not going anywhere," he said. "We will have plenty of time."

"Do you want a son or a daughter?" she asked. "I think I want a son."

Constantius looked into her pleading eyes.

"I don't want anything right now," he said. "I am too busy with my troops."

Helena stood. She looked directly at him.

"I hope it is a boy," she said. "I am sure you will like a boy. He will be just like you."

Constantius became alarmed by her manner.

"Are you trying to tell me something?" he asked. "Are we going to have a baby?"

She ran her fingers through her long, dark hair and looked at Constantius.

"Yes, I haven't told anyone," she said. "I wanted to tell you first."

Constantius was happy, conflicted, and in mild shock.

"Don't tell anyone," he said. "I want you to wait for a little while. I need to tell my commander."

"You don't want me to tell anyone?" Helena asked. "I want to send my mother a message."

He hesitated for a moment and then looked at Helena.

"Tell your mother," he said. "When it is time, maybe she can come and help you."

"Didn't they teach you how to love a baby?" she asked. "It is useful information. There is no fear in love. But perfect love drives out fear; because fear has to do with punishment. The one who fears is not made perfect in love." (1 John, 4, 18, NIV)

Constantius hear her loud and clear. He paused and looked at her.

"I know you will need an attendant," he said. "I will hire an attendant to help you and the baby. I will find one as soon as possible,"

He looked at her and took her in his arms and kissed her. She gave him a big hug.

"Good," she said. "That will give us time to train the attendant."

Constantius hired Helena an attendant named Ruth. Several months passed, Helena told Constantius her time was soon. He sent a soldier to bring Helena's sister, Chara, to care for her. They greeted each other, and she updated Helena concerning the family. Helena introduced Chara to her attendant, Ruth and showed her to the sleeping area that had been prepared. Ruth inquired if Chara had experience in helping with childbirth. She looked at Ruth and smiled.

"Yes," she said. "I have helped deliver many babies. I have three older sisters and ten nieces and nephews."

The following week, Helena became restless. Another week passed, Helena was finally ready to give birth.

"Chara, I think it is my time," she said. "Get my attendant ready to help me."

"Ruth and I are ready," she said. "It is up to you."

Helena pushed but nothing happened. Ruth became worried. Chara held her hand and talked with her. After a few false alarms, Constantine was born. He was born on February twenty-seventh, in the year two hundred and seventy-two, a date marked in history.

"You hoped for and delivered a boy," Chara said. "You and the baby are fine."

Helena waited for Constantius to return. Her prayer had been answered; she had a healthy baby boy. Constantius came home late that evening. Ruth greeted him and then went to Helena.

"Your husband is home," she said. "Hold the baby and I will escort him to you."

She returned with Constantius. He looked at the baby and smiled.

"He is wonderful," Constantius said. "He will be a great emperor."

"You have grand ideas," Helena said. "He is just a little baby boy."

He took her by the hand.

"I have news," he said. "I am being sent west along the Istrius (Danube). I will be gone for a few months."

"I don't want you to go," she said. "I just had our baby."

"I don't want to go either. I will be back as soon as possible."

"Do you have to go?" she asked. "I need you."

"I don't have any choice," he said. "I am a warrior."

"You can be a warrior when he is older, can't you?" she asked. "I knew this would happen."

"I am sorry," he said. "I will see you in a few months."

"Are you certain you have to go?" Helena asked. "Don't you want to stay with your little boy?"

"I do want to stay with you, but the empire called," he said.

Helena was disappointed and worried about Constantius' safety. She looked at him with tears in her eyes and pouted.

"Chara and Ruth can take care of me," she said. "I hope you are successful. I will miss you."

Constantius kissed her forehead.

He and several of his troops headed west to combat the barbarians.

After a few evenings, as they sat around the campfire talking, Constantius inquired if any of the troopers had experience with new born babies.

"Yes, I have younger sisters," Markus said. "You get used to the sound after a while."

"I was hoping he might be less noisy in two months," Constantius said. "I would rather fight barbarians than listen to him cry."

"He will be a lot different when we return," he said. "Did you talk with sergeant Pointus?"

"No, does he have children?" he asked.

"Yes, he has five children," he said. "He spends a lot of time away from home."

"That is probably why he is a sergeant," Constantius said. "He got a promotion after each child because he was fighting the empire's enemy."

Markus looked at Constantius and they both laughed.

Helena depended on her Christian faith to give her strength while Constantine was away from home. She remembered her mother praying for strength to deal with her father and family. When Constantius returned home, he spent the week days with the troops but was home every weekend.

"I am glad you are able to spend time with us," Helena said. "We missed you."

"I hope to be home for a while," he said. "We drove the barbarians away from the river."

"Would you like to hold, Constantine?" she asked. "Hold your arms like this."

11

Helena formed a cradle with her arms. He stretched out his arms and Helena placed Constantine in his arms. Constantius smiled at his son.

"I got him," he said. "He sure is small."

"He will grow up," she said. "You were once this small."

"I guess," he said. "I don't remember."

"Would you like me to take him?" Ruth asked. "I will hold him. It is almost time to feed him. We will see you in a few moments."

Constantius went outside and looked at the stars. He thought about his many blessings. He considered the possibility that Helena's God had blessed them with a healthy son.

The next morning, Constantius enjoyed breakfast with Helena.

"Constantine is sleeping," she said. "Ruth is with him. He is sleeping much longer each night."

"You must be sleeping better," Constantius said. "I know he woke you every time he woke."

"Yes, I am sleeping much better. Ruth cares for him, except for his feedings."

Several months passed, and Constantine grew rapidly. Helena studied her scrolls of Christian writings. She enjoyed telling Constantine stories about Jesus. Ruth helped with the house work but spent most of her time with the infant.

One evening when Constantius arrived home, he was in an especially good humor.

"Helena, I have good news," Constantius said. "I am being named Governor of Dalmatia. We will be moving. You will be living in a great home with servants."

"I will travel anywhere with you," she said. "May I take Ruth with me?"

Constantius agreed. She talked with Ruth.

"We are going to relocate," Helena said. "I want you to go with us."

"Where are you going?" Ruth asked. "This is my hometown."

"Dalmatia, we will have a large house," she said. "We will have plenty of room for you."

"I don't think I want to leave home," she said. "I know everyone in town."

"Constantius is going to be a governor," she said. "It is an important position. You would be the aid of the governor's wife."

Ruth looked at the floor.

"I am sure you will be able to find someone to work for you," she said. "I will remain at home. Thank you for asking me to accompany you."

"You must go with me. I won't know anyone," Helena said.

"You will hire a good attendant," she said. "You will learn to know her."

"Please come with me," she said. "It is important to me."

"Being close to my home is important to me," Ruth said. "I am sorry to see you go. I will have to find a new job."

"I will miss you," she said. "Whoever we hire, they won't be as good as you have been to us."

The hugged each other.

Soon, they moved to Dalmatia. Constantius was now primarily an administrator. He was not required to lead warriors. His friend, Diecletian, a fellow warrior was named co-emperor and controlled the Eastern Roman Empire. Maximian was emperor of the Western Roman Empire.

Constantius spent most of his evenings at home with Helena.

"I love our new house," Helena said. "I would appreciate a personal attendant."

"We have servants to do everything," Constantius said. "Are you sure you need a personal attendant?"

"Did you bring Markus and sergeant Pointus with you?" she asked. "I didn't bring Ruth."

"Yes, they came with me," he said. "I understand the point you are making. I will get you an attendant."

He looked at Helena and shook his head.

Constantius sensed Maximian didn't like his wife. He considered her to be from a low background. He continually told Constantius he should marry his daughter.

"You must divorce that woman," Maximian said. "That innkeeper's daughter will ruin your career."

"I love Helena and our son," Constantius said. "He is a wonderful child."

"Do you want Helena or do you want to marry my daughter and be emperor?" he asked. "Theodora is a fine lady. Everyone would be proud of you and her."

Constantius knew he had a serious problem. He wasn't sure what to say. He hesitated.

"It doesn't seem fair," he said. "Helena is a good wife."

"Life is not always fair," Maximian said. "Helena doesn't fit into the circle of the other wives. The other wives make frequent trips to the temple. She doesn't want to be with them."

"She worked all her life," Constantius said. "The other ladies have never worked."

"Exactly," he said. "I would like to see you be emperor."

Constantius said he needed some time. Maximian told him the matter was urgent and wanted an answer. Maximian ended the conservation and walked away.

After a worrisome week, Constantius talked with Maximian.

"I believe I understand," he said. "Tell Theodora I will marry her. I must keep my boy."

"That is no problem," he said. "Theodora and the servants will raise him."

"What are you going to do about Helena," Constantius asked. "I need to take good care of her."

"She can go to Diocletian's court, or she can go home," Maximian said. "Either way the empire will make sure she has an attendant and receives good care. At home she will be with her kind of people."

After Constantius went home, he sat in the living area of the house. Helena started to talk with him. He didn't give her a chance. He told Helena, he and Constantine would never be emperors if he didn't marry Theodora. He explained how the empire was always first in his life. She voiced her concern, but decided not to interfere with the possibility of Constantius becoming emperor. She explained, she and Constantine would say a prayer for him. Helena grieved and cried for several days. Then she went home. She wasn't well received. She seemed out of place and decided to go to Diocletian's court.

Constantius spent very little time with his son. Theodora instructed the servants to take good care of the child.

"I want him to have a good education," Theodora said. "Find a tutor for him."

"That won't be a problem," the servant said. "Several tutors already come to the palace."

"I want him to speak perfect Latin," she said. "If we start to teach him now, he won't have to unlearn bad habits."

"Yes," he said. "I will have a tutor talk to you tomorrow."

The following morning a tutor came to see Constantine.

"Hello," Loctus said. "I have come to meet Constantine. I am looking forward to teaching him."

Theodora looked at him.

"I wanted to speak with you," she said. "Choosing a tutor for Constantine is an important task."

Theodora made certain Loctus had at least ten years of experience tutoring young men. She explained the importance of Constantine leaning to speak and write perfect Latin. She also made sure Loctus understood that Constantine would someday be an emperor.

"Show me something you wrote," Theodora said. "I must be sure you are the correct teacher."

"I don't have anything with me," Loctus said. "I can write something for you."

"That will be fine," she said. "Sit down at the desk, I will return in a few moments."

Loctus took a seat. A servant gave him ink, a stylus, and a parchment.

Loctus wrote Theodora a letter. After Theodora read the letter, she hired Loctus. He remained Constantine's tutor for many years. When Constantine was eight years old, he began his military training.

"Loctus, what are we studying today," Constantine asked. "Are we going to study Roman history?"

"Yes," Loctus said. "It is important that you understand the history of the Roman Empire. I am sure you will defend it when you are older."

"I will be like my father," he said. "He is a great warrior."

"He was a very great warrior," he said. "Now he is a good administrator. The job he has now is very political."

Constantine wasn't sure he liked Loctus' comment. He looked at him for a few moments.

Constantine was educated in the best Roman Military tradition. His stepmother, Theodora, made certain that he studied with the best tutors and attended the best classes. Constantine was educated in Latin, Latin literature, and how to be successful in the Roman military. One of his Latin language teachers was a Christian scholar. He taught Constantine more about the Christian religion including the prayer Jesus taught the disciples. They would take educational walks to visit the churches and the temples. He studied Greek, but he never became fluent in Greek. Constantius constantly reinforced the importance of Constantine's education. The servants understood Constantius' position. They tolerated Theodora's attitude.

"Ensure he is fed and sent to class," Theodora said. "His father insists he study."

"Yes Theodora," the attendant said. "We will make certain he attends class."

"When he returns home, his tutor will be here," Theodora said. "His tutor will review his lessons with him."

"Where is his father?" the attendant asked. "When will he be home?"

"I don't know," she said. "He will be home when my father wants him to be home."

Constantius was appointed Caesar by Diocletian. As Constantine aged, he dreamed of serving with his father. He often thought of his mother and the message of Christian love she had taught him.

"When will I be able to serve with my father?" he asked. "When will he be home?"

"I expect him home very soon," Theodora said. "I don't know how long he will remain with us."

The following week, Constantius arrived home. Constantine smiled from ear to ear. He wanted to impress Constantius with the education. He recited several passages from current Roman edicts and then told Constantius about Jesus' resurrection. Constantius praised him for his education, but warned him about the empire's position against the Christian religion.

"When will I be old enough to serve with you?" Constantine asked. "I want to be a warrior."

"You are still a little young," Constantius said. "Maybe you can join me in another year."

"I feel like I am a prisoner," he said. "Am I ransom to ensure you return home?"

Constantius was surprised by his comment. He looked at Constantine.

"No," he said. "Next year, I will ask for you to join my troops."

Constantius was again needed as a warrior. The situation along the rivers was serious. When he was sent to Gaul to control the barbarians, the family relocated. Constantine attended Diocletian's court, in Nicomedia. He was allowed to attend a church that taught Jesus' message as recorded by John. He was impressed with the knowledge and attitude of the priests. He lived the life of a future emperor. He and his stepmother were seated in the living area of their new house.

"When will father be home?" Constantine asked. "I want to talk with him."

"It seems like that is all you ask me," Theodora said. "I don't know."

"I am sorry," he said. "He has got to get me out of here."

"I don't think Diocletian will allow you to go with your father," she said. "I think he might allow you to serve with someone else like Galerius."

"I don't appreciate Galerius," he said. "But I will fight with anyone."

Constantine wanted away from his stepmother and the court. He sensed he was being watched at all times. Many understood that he would be emperor someday. Most were jealous of his position.

When Constantine's father returned home, Constantine talked with him.

"You have to rescue me," he said. "If you wait, they might kill me."

Constantine began to fear for his safety. His father listened carefully. Finally, he was convinced a real threat existed. He was able to convince Diocletian to allow Constantine to travel with the army.

CHAPTER 2

CONSTANTINE SERVED WITH HIS FATHER

After years of Constantine pleading to be allowed to travel with the army, Constantine's father gained permission for Constantine to join Galerius' army. Constantius used the fact that Diocletian granted his request to impress upon Constantine how important it was to do whatever was necessary to keep the empire his utmost priority and his personal feelings subordinate. Diocletian visited Constantine at his military quarters and informed him the he was going to inspect the fortification in Caesarea. Constantine would travel with Diocletian's guard and provide protection for the emperor.

When Diocletian arrived in Caesarea, he went to the military fortification at the harbor which was his home for the next few days. The troops rested and the emperor inspected the retirement center and the fortification.

The next day, the emperor rode in a carriage along the streets of Caesarea, so the people would have an opportunity to see him. The entourage started in the military center where the streets were lined with people hoping to see the emperor or a future emperor. Eusebius of Caesarea sat on the porch of his mother's house in the retirement center, and they watched the procession. One of the soldiers noted the priest's robe and waved to him.

"Do you know who that is," Eusebius asked. "He is very young and can't grow a beard."

"It might be Constantine," Dianna said. "I know his mother is a Christian and is in exile at Diocletian's court in Nicomedia."

Eusebius looked at her.

"All of us that live in the retirement center were given a list of the important people we might see," she said. "Not many of the soldiers are Christians. I am certain he waved to you because of your robe."

"I know Constantine's mother's priest," he said. "We were in school at the same time in Antioch. His name is also Eusebius."

"Two Eusebius," she exclaimed as a large smile appeared her face. Eusebius ignored his mother's attempt at humor.

"I will say a prayer for him," he said. "The empire needs a Christian emperor. Someday, maybe, we will have freedom of religion."

They continued to watch as the soldiers marched into the distance.

After Diocletian returned home, he assigned Constantine to fight the barbarians along the Istrius River.

"It is time you to start your military career as an officer," he said. "I am going to send you to the river to fight. Nickus will be assigned as your aid."

"I am looking forward to being an active military officer," Constantine said. "I will do my best."

Nickus was a tall, clean shaven, young man with clean boots. He planned to spend his life in the Roman military and was eager to serve with Constantine.

"I have heard the Istrius valley is beautiful," Constantine said.

"Yes, the river valley is beautiful," Nickus said. "However, the fighting can be anything but beautiful."

"You are a good soldier," he said. "I will learn military strategy from you. I am lucky to have you with me."

"It is my honor, sir," he said. "I would be glad to serve with you in any campaign. We will rid the river valley of the barbarians."

Constantine and Nickus sailed to the military fortification at the juncture of the Istrius River and the Black Sea. When they joined the troops there, Sergeant Josh awaited them. He had prepared the troops for a long, hard fight. He was experienced and had sent advanced scouts along the river to determine the locations and the number of barbarian tribes.

After three days of marching, a scout joined them for dinner.

"A tribe of barbarians is living in a town about twenty miles west of us," he said. "They have terrorized the people in the area. Give me twenty men, and we will block their northern and western escape routes."

Constantine agreed with the plan and assigned twenty men to the scout. The next morning, the scout and his men departed.

The troops broke camp and started to march west along the river. They planned to engage the barbarians on the morning of the second day. When the sun rose, the troops marched into town where they came upon a great amount of activity. People were quickly loading wagons and heading out of town. Constantine entered a small shop.

"I am Constantine," he said. "I have been sent to rid your town of the barbarians. I need someone to work with me."

The shopkeeper stared at Constantine for a moment and decided that the protection of the Roman army would be better than living with the barbarians.

"I will work with you," he said. "They have destroyed my shop and stolen all my goods. If you hurry, you will be able to catch them. They are still loading the wagons they stole from us."

The troops rounded up those who were trying to flee. They were mostly old men and women. Constantine knew they weren't the major source of the problems. Sergeant Josh informed him the young men had already fled. Twenty men on horseback followed the barbarians' trail. The scout and his men surprised the fleeing barbarians and killed many of them. The others turned back, but encountered troops on horseback who killed most of them. The few who survived surrendered and they were taken back to town, where they were turned over to the townspeople and put in prison to await trial. The Roman soldiers became heroes.

After Constantine drove the barbarians from the river, he returned home. After a few days later, Diocletian visited him. He was ordered to help the troops protect the eastern frontier of the empire.

"Sergeant Josh, get the troops prepared for a long march," Constantine said. "We are going east."

"We can be ready in two days," he said. "Where are we going?"

"We are going to sweep the eastern frontier," he said. "This assignment is going to require a lot of dedication."

"We are better prepared than we were for our last long march," he said. "We have a few additional wagons and horses."

Two days later, the troops headed east. Nickus led the way. Constantine traveled with them.

"We will have to discuss our trip home," Constantine said. "Maybe, we will take a ship."

After the troops marched for a few months, they stopped in Antioch before heading further east and then south. Nickus and Constantine planned to have the troops rest for a week. Each day, a few soldiers were given the day off to shop and visit the town. Nickus employed an historian to educate Constantine concerning the area.

Nickus and Constantine were in their tent.

"Did your tutor tell you about Antioch and Paul?" he asked. "Antioch was close to his home in Tarsus."

"I am sure he did, but I probably didn't pay close attention," Constantine said. "Tell me about Paul."

"Jesus' apostle, Paul, used Antioch as a home base for several of his missionary journeys," he said. "He was a member of the church in Antioch."

"I remember now. My mother mentioned him," he said. "Paul was the one who saw Jesus after He was resurrected."

"That's right," Nickus said. "His encounter with his childhood friend made a lasting impression on him."

"My mother, bless her, made a lasting impression on me," Constantine said. "I hope she is being treated well."

"There is a lot of Christian history in this area," Nickus said. "Do you want me to bring the historian with us?"

"Yes," he said. "When one learns about a location while living there, he better understands what he is told."

Nickus paid the historian, Nichlos, to accompany them for several months. After visiting each area, Nichlos would discuss religion and language with Constantine and Nickus. They enjoyed their lessons.

"Most of this land, east of the Jordan River, is not heavily populated,"

Nickus said. "This is probably due to lack of water and fertile land. If you travel far enough, you would reach the Euphrates River."

"That is an area that was populated before written history," Nichlos said. "Abraham journeyed from that area."

"We can't go that far east," Constantine said. "Our assignment is to secure this frontier. We claim this territory, and so does our Persian enemy."

"I will ensure we have plenty of water," Nickus said. "I will get the troops ready to move."

They entered Mesopotamia and engaged a small army that was protecting the Persian frontier. They caught the enemy by surprise. As the enemy soldiers sat by a fire, the Roman soldiers slaughtered them. Most of the enemy never tried to flee. Constantine didn't chase those who did flee. He wasn't interested in taking prisoners. They remained in the area for a week. The enemy didn't return. When Nickus informed Constantine they had completed their assignment in the area, Constantine decided it was time to march south.

Eventually, they reached the area located just east of the Jordan River. Constantine visited the town of Auranitis and was surprised to find a large church. Nichlos explained the area was primarily Christian, and that the Roman Empire hadn't enforced religious persecution upon the townspeople. They camped in this area for several days before deciding to visit the church. They saw a priest kneeling at the prayer rail.

"Hello," he said. "Can I help you? We don't see many Roman soldiers."

"I saw your church and decided to visit," Constantine said. "My mother told me many stories about Jesus."

"This is a very old church," he said. "You are welcome to pray."

"I will just watch you," he said. "My father has warned me to stay distant from the Christian church. I must be careful."

The priest blessed them.

It was a very dry, but beautiful area. The town was located near several springs, and fruit trees were abundant. Constantine had a wagon, loaded with fruit, delivered to his troops. After the troops rested, they moved towards the southern end of the Sea of Galilee.

The troops established a camp, while Constantine visited the Roman fortification in Tiberias. He was surprised the Jordan River was almost dry.

"I thought this would be a very large river," Constantine said. "From my mother's stories about Jesus, it sounded much larger."

"The weather has been very dry," Nickus said. "The watershed has not received much rain this year."

He picked up a clump of dirt and squeezed it into a cloud of dust. He blew it out of his hand.

"I guess that is why they built the fortification on the Sea of Galilee," Constantine said. "It is a great sea."

"It doesn't go dry," Nickus said. "It is a good source of water and fish. The fortification was temporary to protect from invasion from the east."

When they reached the fortification, they were greeted by the local commander, Anthony. He took them to his office.

"I am sure our problems will be held at bay for a while," he said. "The presence of your army is a great help."

Constantine smiled.

"I received your message and thought I would stop and meet your daughter, Minervina," he said. "Could she join us for dinner tonight?"

"She will be with me," he said. "We will eat at seven. I have quarters prepared for you."

Nickus wanted to know more about Minervina, but Constantine didn't offer any information. In preparation for dinner, they shaved and cleaned their boots. At sunset, they departed for dinner.

"Good evening," Anthony said. "I have had our cook prepare a special meal of fish and roots. I hope you like it. This is my daughter, Minervina."

Minervina stood and bowed to the men. Constantine and Minervina greeted each other and decided to meet after dinner. Minervina indicated that her father had told her about him.

"I don't usually eat this well," he said. "When you are moving an army, it is highly unlikely to enjoy a meal like this one."

After dinner, Constantine and Minervina discussed their future. As had been planned, they agreed to marry, and Minervina would relocate to Nicomedia with him. She admitted that she was very apprehensive about leaving her father and journeying to a place she had never visited.

The next morning Constantine met with Anthony.

"I am so glad you sent me a message," Constantine said. "I have talked with your daughter, and we agreed to be married. I don't have much time before I need to leave Tiberias. Can you have us married in the next few days?"

Anthony smiled.

"Military men are always in a hurry," Anthony said. "Yes, I will have the priest marry you."

"That is fine," he said. "I will be sailing next week."

"Will Minervina be going with you?" he asked. "I am going to miss her."

"Minervina will be sailing to Nicomedia, but not with me," he said. "I have a large house there and many servants. I am sure she will be happy."

Constantine stayed with Minervina for several days. He wished Nickus God's speed and had him return to the troops. He prepared them to march to Caesarea.

Nickus informed Constantine that he had scheduled two ships from Caesarea for the troops. Constantine joked about paying for their voyages using booty.

Nickus looked at Constantine and smiled.

After Constantine completed his assignment on the frontier, he expected to be promoted.

"I think the frontier is safe now," Constantine said. "Send a message to Diocletian. Tell him we are coming home."

"The messenger is on his way," Nickus said. "I am ready to go home."

Three days later, Constantine and Minervina were married. They remained on the Sea of Galilee for several days. Then they sailed separately to Nicomedia. When Minervina reached Nicomedia, a carriage met her and took her home.

"Welcome, Minervina," a servant said. "We have been waiting for you. We have everything prepared."

Minervina didn't know what to say. Her new home was much larger than her father's quarters in Tiberias. She didn't want to look at the servant.

"Thank you," she said. "My husband should arrive this afternoon."

The servants unloaded the carriages and took Minervina's belongings to her rooms.

That evening, Constantine joined her.

"I have been granted a week of leave time," Constantine said. "I will be with you the entire week. Maybe, some of the time, I will be gone during the days."

Minervina held out her arms.

"Come here," she said.

Constantine smiled and embraced her.

"I want you to meet Judge," he said. "He is my military attendant. He will live with us. The slaves work for him."

"Did you say he is going to live with us?" Minervina asked. "Is he going to manage the house for us?"

"Yes, dear," he said. "He will help us with anything we might need."

"Thank you," she said. "The slaves make me feel uncomfortable. Judge reminds me of father's attendant."

"Don't worry," he said. "I want you to be at ease."

"Will you hire a female attendant for me?" she asked. "I have always had an attendant."

"We will have Judge," he said. "Do you think you will really need an attendant?"

Minervina looked at the floor. Constantine sensed her disappointment.

"A proper lady always has an attendant," Minervina said. "Father made sure I always had an attendant."

Constantine realized he didn't have any choice. He had Judge locate an attendant.

"The following evening, Constantine told Minervina about the new attendant.

"Her name is Uniona," he said. "She will start tomorrow."

"If you need anything, just ask," he said. "Someone will do it for you."

"I am glad you will be home," she said. "I may need another hug."

She smiled at Constantine.

"Next week, Nickus will be here. He will give us a tour of the town," Constantine said. "I will take a day away from work to be with you."

Minervina became excited. She batted her eyes and looked at Constantine.

The following week, they enjoyed a sunlit breakfast on the patio. It was a warm and breezy day. Constantine watched as Nickus arrived.

"I have a carriage," Nickus said. "I know the town fairly well."

"Show us the wall and the aqueduct," Constantine said. "Then take us to the Royal Villa and the mint."

"That will take most of the day," he said. "We better get started."

It was a beautiful day, and the newlyweds were in love. They enjoyed the carriage ride. Occasionally, they looked at a building. Minervina was impressed with Nicomedia. The only other large town she could remember was Jerusalem. That evening, Constantine invited Nickus to dinner.

"The servants have prepared a fine dinner for us," Constantine said. "You were a great tour guide."

"Thank you," he said. "It is good to be home. Thank you for dinner."

"I will see you tomorrow," he said. "We need to write a few more reports regarding our assignment to the frontier."

"I will be at the office," he said. "I have already written most of the reports."

A few weeks later, the local Christian church that overlooked the royal palace was destroyed. Constantine was aware that his father ignored the edicts of persecution against the Christians. He was told that many Christians, who refused to sacrifice animals to Jupiter, were burned alive. He felt powerless and sent a message to his father.

Constantius
Emperor of the Roman Empire

God bless you
I have returned to Nicomedia.
   I am appalled at the persecution of the Christians.
   The church was destroyed and many believers have been burned.

I am not looking forward to being expected to enforce
the edict.

Please ask for my transfer to your command.

Constantine

Nickus found Constantine in his office and told him Diocletian was
out of control.

The next day, Constantine heard Diocletian talking with the guards.

"Imprison the priests," Diocletian said. "Burn the scriptures and bring
me everything of value you find in the church."

A few days later, the guard reported to Diocletian.

"We have destroyed many buildings," the soldier said. "The treasure
is in your palace."

Constantine was abhorred by this activity, but did nothing. He could
not be involved. He feared Diocletian and felt impotent during the great
persecution.

One evening, Constantine was in a restaurant when a stranger
approached him.

"So, you think you are a great warrior," he said. "The really brave
warriors fight lions in the arena."

Constantine knew that the man had too much to drink. The man
continued to challenge his bravery.

"That is how they earn their living," Constantine said. "I am a Roman
military warrior. I could destroy one of their lions, bare-handed."

Smiling, the man realized that Constantine took the bait.

"I will be there tomorrow with all my friends," he said. "We will see if
you really are a great warrior."

Constantine understood he had been duped. He was not happy.

"You don't have to fight just because of him," Nickus said. "He was
full of wine."

Constantine explained to Nickus it was now a matter of pride. He said
a prayer, asking for protection.

"I have given him my word," he said. "Wish me well."

The next day, Constantine made his way to the arena. He was

announced as the great Roman warrior, who would fight the lion without any weapons. Constantine waved to the jeering crowd.

"Are you ready?" the arena announcer asked.

Constantine signaled to the arena master.

"Turn the lion loose," Constantine said. "This one will not survive."

"Good luck," the arena announcer said. "This is not the lion's first challenge."

"It will be his last," he said. "Send him my way."

As Constantine pointed to heaven, a large lion rushed at him. Constantine avoided its charge and suddenly jumped on its back. He grabbed the lion by its neck and broke it with his bare hands. The lion fell limp to the ground. Constantine dismounted it, put his foot on its back, and looked out at the crowd.

"This is how a Roman soldier handles his enemies!" he yelled.

They cheered wildly for Constantine and threw flowers at his feet. He waved to the crowd.

"Well done," the announcer said. "This was his last trip to the arena."

"Just in a day's work," Constantine said. "Do you have any barbarians?"

"No," he said. "We do have a few Christians."

"Not funny," Constantine said. "Maybe you should fight a lion."

The arena master sent a maiden to place a wreath around Constantine's neck. She kissed his cheek. Nickus escorted him out of the ring.

"No more lions," Constantine said. "He was very large."

"Yes he was," Nickus said. "He has killed three armed gladiators."

"Now you tell me," he said. "I am glad I didn't know that."

"This is going to make you very popular," he said. "But I recommend staying away from lions. You made your point."

That evening when Constantine returned home, Minervina awaited him. "Our neighbor told me you really enjoyed the wreath ceremony at the arena," she said. "If that lion had killed you, you wouldn't have known your son. I know you are a warrior; you need to be a smart warrior."

She looked at him with her large, dark, sad eyes. Suddenly, he understood what she said.

"You are going to have a baby?" Constantine asked. "I mean, we are going to have a baby?"

"Now you have it," Minervina said. "He will be here in about four months."

"We have a lot of planning to do," he said. "I will have the doctor at the clinic come and visit you,"

"I will go to the clinic," she said. "You might hire another attendant. Our son will need one."

"Will you need anything else?" Constantine asked. "Judge will make arrangements for you to interview several women. You can choose the one you like best."

"Have Uniona interview her," she said. "She will have to work with her."

"We will find an attendant tomorrow," Constantine said.

"Good," she said. "That will give Uniona time to train her."

Sara, the second attendant, was a quick learner and easy to train. She quickly became part of the staff.

The time for Minervina to give birth approached.

"Is everything ready?" Minervina asked. "I think it won't be long before I am ready. I feel something strange."

"Lie down on the bed," Uniona said. "I will get Sara."

"Something is wrong," she said. "Get the doctor from the clinic and send one of the slaves to tell Constantine I am having problems."

Minervina was doubled over with pain.

"Stay calm," Sara said. "Everything will be all right."

When the doctor arrived, Minervina was unconscious. He worked on her for a long time. The baby was finally born, but Minervina never regained consciousness. Constantine arrived and went directly to Minervina.

"How is my wife, doctor?" Constantine asked. "I want to see her."

"I couldn't save her," the doctor said.

Constantine looked at the doctor in disbelief.

"I loved her so much," he said and began to sob.

"You have a baby boy," the doctor said. "It was a very difficult birth."

"I have a boy?" Constantine asked through his tears. "Is he healthy?"

"Yes," the doctor said. "He will need constant care."

"I will find someone for him," he said. "We have many servants."

"You need to find someone to breast feed him," the doctor said. "Milk, from a woman who is nursing, will be the best food for him for a while. Did you select a name?"

"Yes, his name will be Crispus," Constantine said. "Thank you, doctor."

"I will check on you every day," he said. "If I am busy, I will send one of my nurses."

The doctor packed up his equipment and returned to the clinic.

"Judge, check with the servants and see if any of them are nursing," Constantine said. "I will pay her to feed my son."

After a short time, Judge returned. He had found a young slave who was nursing. He introduced Julia to Constantine.

"Hello Julia," Constantine said. "I need you to feed my son. His name is Crispus."

"It will be an honor for me to nurse him," Julia said. "Shall I take him to my quarters?"

"No," he said. "Judge will prepare a room in the main house for you and the baby. Have you worked for the empire long?"

"All my life," she said. "My father, your cook, also worked for your father. He made meals for you when you were very young."

Constantine turned to Judge.

"Judge, bring her father to me," he said. "I want to talk to him."

After a few moments, Judge returned with the cook.

"You wanted me, sir," he said. "I have food in the oven."

"How long have you worked for my family?" Constantine asked. "Your daughter is going to feed my son."

He thought for a moment. He didn't want to admit he couldn't keep track of time.

"I don't know," he said. "I worked for your father and mother before you were born."

"What is your name?" he asked. "I would like to call you and Julia by your names."

"They call me Chop," he said. "I think that is because I prepare all the meat. I don't let anyone else handle the meat."

"It is nice to meet you, Chop," he said. "I will talk with you later."

"Your mother was a good cook," Chop said. "She taught me how to make many of the meals I now cook for you."

Constantine promoted Julia to assistant attendant and gave her father a bonus. Chop was already an important part of the family and Julia was charged with taking care of Crispus. Judge helped her when he was needed.

Diocletian became very ill and resigned. However, it was Galerius who was promoted, not Constantine.

Galerius considered Constantine a threat and sent him on several dangerous missions. He hoped Constantine would be killed. Galerius called Constantine into his chambers and gave him new orders.

"The last time you were sent to the Istrius River," Galerius said. "Some of the barbarians hid from you in the swamps. They, again, are making the river area unsafe."

"We weren't able to kill all of them," Constantine said."

"You allowed them to escape and now they are causing problems," he said. "I want you to do the job correctly this time."

"They know the swamp," Constantine said. "We are unfamiliar with that area."

"It is time you learn about it," he said. "Take your troops to the swamp and don't return until you've killed all of them."

Both men stood.

"I will leave tomorrow," Constantine said. "We will destroy them."

"Don't be afraid to get wet," Galerius said. "It will do you good."

Constantine and his troops returned to the Istrius River area. They sailed to the fortification near where the river flowed into the sea. As they encamped along the river, Nickus and Constantine sat in their tent and planned their maneuvers.

"We are going to have to track them down," Constantine said. "We need to kill all of them."

Their scouts had arrived at the river several days before to survey the area. Nickus informed Constantine of their findings.

"The barbarians live on some swampy low land on the south side of the river,"

Nickus said.

"Just as I thought," he said. "We killed those who went north."

"We know more about them this time," Nickus said.

"Take some men and go north of them," he said. "If they flee in your direction, kill them. I want bodies."

"Yes, sir," he said. "We will be ready."

"They will be sorry they have made it difficult for me," he said.

He picked up his sword and pointed it at the sky.

The battle was long. Constantine and his men defeated the barbarians in hand-to-hand combat. He sent the head of the barbarians' leader to Galerius. When Constantine returned to Nicomedia, he was greeted as a hero by all, but Galerius, who insured that Constantine would not be allowed to live the life of a hero.

Two weeks later, he was sent to fight in Egypt. He and his troops gathered at the port, preparing to board their ship.

"We are soldiers," Nickus said. "We are ready to sail, I think!"

"You can stand at the ship's rail and feed the fish," Constantine said. "Soldiers are good at feeding fish."

"Very funny," he said. "I will be there."

It was a rough journey for the soldiers; however, Constantine was quite sea worthy, never getting seasick. He joined his men on deck and talked with them, trying to improve their spirits. Eventually, they reached the coast of Egypt. A local Roman soldier met them.

"I am sure you enjoyed the journey," he said. "Have your troop march a few miles south. They will find our troops waiting for them."

Nickus located Constantine in the crowd of troops.

"I will take care of getting the troops ready," Nickus said. "You can go with him."

"I will see you tonight," Constantine said. "I am sure the troops will be glad to be on dry land."

The sea weary men joined with the local Roman army.

After a week, they marched toward the rebel forces. A scout reported that the rebels were camped just across a field. Constantine swiftly ordered the attack. His men charged the rebels. They beat them badly before the rebels knew what had happened. The troops gathered all the valuables and turned the prisoners over to the local army.

"You have an excellent army," the Egyptian commander said. "I am glad they sent you to help us. The last troops they sent were of little help."

"We are warriors," Constantine said. "Would you acknowledge my men?"

The Egyptian commander spoke eloquently to Constantine's troops, thanking them for their service.

One evening, Constantine was in his tent when a sergeant approached.

"Sir," the sergeant said. "There are fifteen of us who would like to remain with the Roman Army here in Egypt. Will you grant us permission?"

Constantine became defensive.

"Why do you want to leave us?" Constantine asked. "Are you dissatisfied?"

"We don't have families of our own, and we like it here," he said. "It also eliminates traveling back by ship."

Constantine smiled, understandingly.

"Yes," he said. "I will tell Nickus to complete the necessary paperwork."

Constantine was able to negotiate a trade with the local army leader. Fifteen men from the Egyptian Roman Army sailed back to Nicomedia with Constantine.

When Constantine arrived in Nicomedia, he was again recognized as a hero. His father, fearful that Constantine would be killed, requested that he be allowed to fight in Britain. Eventually, Galerius granted the request. Constantine wasted no time and joined his father in Gaul.

"You will be safer in Britain," Constantius said. "Men fight with honor. Barbarians and animals have no honor."

"I am glad to be with you," Constantine said. "When do we go to Britain?"

"We will cross the channel before the end of the month," he said. "My troops are headed there now. After we make camp, I want to talk with you."

That evening, Constantius talked at length with his son about using the empire's coins as a political tool. He explained that not many people have the opportunity to see an emperor, but they did use coins. Everyone liked commemorative coins. The image on their coins was their emperor;

therefore, one side of all coins would depict an accurate likeness of the emperor. The other side would depict an event or God that was popular with the people.

"The people will feel like you represent them," Constantius said. "And the coins will help build your legacy. Coins should make people feel proud."

Constantine understood and agreed to follow his father's advice.

The troops crossed the channel without incident, and Constantine and his father continued to York. Constantine spent a year with his father, learning his military strategies. They often discussed their victories and their failures.

"It is very difficult to fight the Picts," Constantius said. "They will fight hard and then suddenly disband. A month later, they join together again at a different location. They are a difficult enemy. They fight bravely."

Later that evening while sitting around the camp fire, Constantius explained to Constantine how important it was that he wasn't baptized. When Constantine questioned him, his father told him that the Roman Empire was a pagan empire. People would consider his baptism an affront to the empire. Constantine understood. Constantius knew that his Christian wife, Helena, had wanted Constantine to be baptized, but Constantine obeyed his father. He valued his father's opinion and lived by it, even when he didn't fully agree. Then, they discussed the Great Persecution. Constantius wasn't in favor of persecuting the Christians, but he was a Roman Emperor and bound by the edict. He cautioned Constantine to always remember that he was a Roman officer before being a person.

Constantine complained about the cold weather.

"I don't like this weather," he said. "It is difficult to stay warm. I need a new coat."

"We will stay here for a while," Constantius said. "Find a town and purchase a new coat. Bring one for me. I don't feel like riding."

Constantine and Nickus went into town.

"I see some coats in this shop," Nickus said. "Let's go inside."

They dismounted and walked into the shop.

"It looks like they have what we want," Constantine said. "Remember we need one for father. I think we should also purchase a few wool blankets."

"We want to purchase three woolen coats," Constantine said to the shopkeeper. "How many do you have?"

"We don't have any," the shopkeeper said, not looking up. "We are out of coats."

Constantine knew the shopkeeper wasn't telling the truth, but he wasn't sure why the man was trying to mislead them.

"I saw several coats. We looked before we came into your shop," he said. "Why don't you want to sell to us?"

"I don't sell coats to Roman soldiers," he said. "I sell them to our local people."

Constantine became agitated.

"I want to purchase three coats from you," Constantine demanded. "If you won't sell them to us, my troops will destroy your store, and your coats will become spoils of war."

A worried look appeared on the shopkeeper's face. He looked at his wife, she looked at the floor. The shopkeeper left the floor and brought back an arm load of coats.

"I am sure you will find something you'll like," he said. "Here, try this one."

"I will find one for your aid," the storekeeper's wife said. "He is not very large."

"I also need one for my father. I will take as many blankets as you can spare."

After they paid for their goods, the shopkeeper explained that the last group of soldiers who came to his store didn't pay for the things they took. Constantine reached into his pocket and took out a handful of silver coins and gave them to him. The shopkeeper was happy.

"I know that not all Roman soldiers are dishonest," he said. "Can I help you load everything onto your horses?"

After they loaded the coats and blankets, very little room remained.

Later, Constantine told his father about the incident at the shop. His father slowly put on his coat and laid a blanket on his lap.

"I have been cold and not feeling well," he said. "These feel nice."

Constantine was pleased that his father loved his gifts.

"Did you hear that some of the soldiers we captured have joined us?" Constantius asked.

"They are good soldiers," Constantine said. "We will make them fine Roman soldiers."

The weather remained rainy and cold. The troops didn't see the sun for many days and had become discouraged. Constantine purchased several sheep and had the men build a large fire. They roasted the meat and ate roots. The good food and comradery helped the group's morale. They didn't look for engagements with the enemy, but they did protect the area.

A month later, Constantine was asleep in his tent when Nickus woke him.

"Your father has died. I will inform the troops."

"What happened?" Constantine asked. "I thought he was getting better."

"He has been very ill," he said. "He didn't want me to tell you. He didn't want you to worry about him."

Constantine looked away. Tears began to flow down his face.

"We have to make arrangements to have a proper burial," Constantine said. "Can you handle that for me?"

"It will be an honor, sir," Nickus said. "I am sure all the troops will want to help."

Constantius received a military burial at the encampment.

A few days after Constantius was buried, Constantine was declared emperor by his father's troops.

The news spread quickly throughout Britain and Gaul. The people didn't question Constantine's rule. Nickus suggested that they inform Galerius of Constantius death. A messenger was dispatched to Rome.

"Take this message to Galerius," Constantine said. "Tell him I have become emperor and am commanding Constantius' troops."

When he received Constantine's message, Galerius was furious. He considered sending his troops to seize Constantine, but knew that war was not an appropriate response. He was fully aware that Constantine was very well-respected. He granted Constantine the title of Caesar and sent him a gift containing robes. Galerius' acknowledgement persuaded many others to accept Constantine's rule and power. Constantine now ruled the western part of the empire.

CHAPTER 3

EMPEROR CONSTANTINE

The western region of the Roman Empire included Britain, Gaul and Spain. Constantine commanded a massive army and expelled the Picts from Britain's territory. Following this, Constantine's popularity grew rapidly. He gained confidence in his position, and he granted religious freedom to the Christians who were persecuted. Eventually, he returned their personal property that had been seized. He knew that his actions were in violation of the Roman edict of persecution, so Constantine kept these activities to himself. He took time to pray and gave thanks for his mother's influence during his earlier life. Remembering his father's advice, he made no public announcement of being a Christian and remained unbaptized. The other emperors took no action against him or his position regarding religious persecution. He began a building program in the western region of the empire that included the construction of churches, highways, and aqueducts. He prayed for protection and guidance.

One evening while in their quarters, the soldiers discussed a strategic military plan.

"If we work closely with the bishop, we can easily control his district," Constantine said. "If we do this properly, we can bring prosperity and peace to a great number of people. They all love the bishop, and he has guided their beliefs for a long time"

Nickus looked at Constantine.

"He has set a good example for us," Nickus said. "How long are we going to remain in Britain?"

"Until we have restructured our troops, and they are in complete control of the territory," he said. "I hope it doesn't take long."

"We have started repairing the highway network," he said. "That will make it much easier for us to use our carriages and wagons."

"I hated to destroy so much of the system,' he said. "Now, we will rebuild it so it is better than when it was new."

"Some of our troops have started south," Nickus said. "How many of our troops are going to serve with the local troops?"

It was a politically sound move to reinforce the local army. They were proud to be able to keep the peace. They were a good army, and Constantine wanted them to remain his friend and show allegiance to the Roman army.

"I am looking forward to returning to Gaul," Nickus said. "We should be able to travel in about a month."

"Don't wish your life away," Constantine said. "We will be there soon enough, but it will probably be a temporary assignment. I don't expect a permanent post for several years."

Constantine, the new emperor, and most of his troops went to Trier in Gaul. It was the capital city for the northwestern portion of the empire. He liked the area and was very pleased to be able to be home. He looked forward to playing with his son.

"It is good to have you home, sir," Judge said. "I have everything prepared for you."

"How is my son?" Constantine asked. "How big is he?"

"He has grown and is quite large," Julia said. "I brought him to see you."

Constantine smiled at his housekeepers. When he saw his son, he motioned to him and then held out an arm.

"Come here, my boy," he said. "I am your father. You are doing a fine job, Julia."

Crispus ran into Constantine's arms. They embraced each other.

"Thank you," she said. "Judge has been a great help. People respect him. He doesn't have to say things twice."

Constantine explained that Judge was accustomed to getting things done. He had been in the army for several years and only needed to issue an order once. He looked at Judge.

"Does Crispus have a tutor?" he asked. "He is old enough now to learn Latin."

"We are teaching him Latin," Judge said. "Maybe, I should hire a tutor."

"I think that would be a good idea," he said. "You can't start to learn too early."

"Yes, sir," he said. "I will take care of that."

Judge realized he should have thought of a tutor and immediately employed one.

"I will make certain he has time to play," Julia said. "He plays with my daughter."

Constantine smiled at Julia.

"That is good, Julia," Constantine said. "How is your father?"

"He is getting a little slower," she said. "He still loves to cook for us."

Judge walked over to Constantine.

"Sir, I have a message for you," Judge said.

Constantine took the message and read it.

"Judge, send for Nickus," he said. "We have some work to do."

One hour later, Nickus appeared.

"You sent for me?" Nickus asked.

"The Franks are invading the territory," Constantine said. "Get the troops ready."

"Yes, sir," he said. "We will be ready by morning."

The next morning, Constantine talked with his troops. He explained that they would have to earn respect, just as his father's army had.

"The Franks think that because I am a new emperor, I don't have the power to eradicate them," he said. "We will to teach them a lesson."

During the next six months, Constantine's troops fought the Franks. They defeated them badly and captured two of their kings. The kings were sent back to Trier and put on public display. Loaded with the spoils of war, Constantine's troops proudly marched home. Nickus reminded Constantine of proper protocol.

"We will need to make an appearance at the welcome home celebration," Nickus said. "Everyone wants to see you."

"If you can, make it brief," Constantine said. "I want to see my son."

After celebrating their triumph, Constantine headed home. Nickus went to the amphitheater. The celebration continued for two days. Judge met Constantine at the door of the house.

"Your son is beginning to write Latin words," Judge said. "He is a very quick learner. The tutor comes and works with him twice a week."

"Good job, Judge," Constantine said. "My son needs to prepare to be emperor."

Judge looked at Constantine.

"Did you hear about the two kings you sent to us?" he asked. "They were killed at the games yesterday."

Constantine gasped and a frown appeared on his face.

"That should not have happened," he said. "All I wanted to do was to discourage their followers."

"Nickus told me that the situation got out of hand," he said. "The crowd actually demanded that they be killed."

"Have someone send my condolences to their families," Constantine said. "I don't want to incite their followers. Have Nickus handle the message,"

A message was sent to the two royal families, explaining that their kings were killed due to a riot at the amphitheater. The message was never answered. Constantine visited Nickus at the military headquarters.

"I want to make our city as great as Rome," Constantine said.

"We have captured many slaves," Nickus said. "I will put them to work."

Constantine thought for a moment.

"Start by building another aqueduct," he said. "We will need more water for the thousands that will want to live in Trier."

"I will build the largest water system," he said. "Trier will be the envy of every city in the western empire."

"I remember the Roman baths," Constantine said. "Build a public bath. Make it large and available to the masses."

"That is a good idea. We should build things everyone will enjoy," Nickus said. "Everyone likes a hot bath."

"Don't forget our army," he said. "We need to reward them."

"I will also build new quarters for our troops," he said. "That will increase morale. I will include a large room for them to read and relax."

"That's the spirit," he said. "Give half of our troops a day away from duty. Give the other half a day next week."

"Yes, sir," Nickus said. "Then I will enlarge the wall around the city." Constantine thought for a moment.

"I want new gates with our army's insignia on each one," he said. "I want those who visit our city to know who we are."

After the public projects were built, the construction of a large, self-contained palace began. Twenty buildings made up the palace complex. Everything the emperor and his staff needed would be provided within the palace walls. Matching stones were used to construct each building. It was a grand project.

After dinner one evening, Constantine, his son, and his staff discussed the new palace and the new public parks.

"I love the new public parks," Julia said. "Crispus chases all the animals."

"I am glad you like them," Constantine said. "Judge suggested I have them built."

"The new library at the university was needed," Crispus said. "Someday, I will study at the university."

"My next project is to expand the university," he said. "We will need to find more professors."

"I could teach military logistics," Nickus said. "I mean, after I get too old to fight."

"I didn't see you standing there, Nickus," Constantine said. "I hope you are keeping our troops busy. The men are happiest when they are busy."

"Yes, the troops are very busy," Nickus said. "I think we should improve a few of our neighboring towns as well."

"I agree," Constantine said. "Meet with their town committees. Build them new waterways and parks."

"I would like to start in Arles," he said. "They have supplied our army with many troops."

Constantine nodded agreement.

"That is fine," he said. "I also want you to build a large church."

"That is a great idea," Nickus said. "That will let everyone know you are a good man."

"Many will think I have become a Christian," he said. "How is my mother?"

"The last I heard, she was well," he said. "She loves you very much."

"Someday, maybe she can be part of my family," he said. "Send her a message. Tell her I love her."

They listened to the sounds of the river and the boats.

Constantine knew that it was not the proper time to bring his mother to Trier. He sent her several messages each year. When Nickus appeared, Constantine was at work in his office.

"Many of the people are comparing you favorably to your father," Nickus said. "Your popularity is growing. I think your public building projects are helping us."

"I understand Rome has minted a coin with my likeness," Constantine said. "I am going to have our mint produce a coin with God reaching down and touching my raised hand on the reverse side. I will be driving my chariot."

Nickus thought for a few moments.

"Be careful, sir," he said. "We don't want to alienate the people."

"Right," Constantine said. "The coin won't say which God I am touching."

"That should make everyone happy," he said. "The troops will like that coin. Why don't you make a coin with them on it?"

"Great idea," he said. "People, who can't read, especially appreciate new coins."

The different Roman mints produced many coins celebrating Constantine, his family, and his troops. At the time, the silver coins that were in circulation were overvalued. Constantine agreed to revalue the silver coins and produce a gold coin, called the 'solidus.' He thought that would restore faith in the monetary system. Constantine and the Director of Mints discussed how to control inflation and restore public faith in their monetary system. The director told him that when the intrinsic value of the gold in the coin is equal to the face value of the coin, inflation will stop and faith will be restored. Constantine listened carefully and agreed to allow him to try his plan.

Nickus always carried a few such coins everywhere they traveled. He gave Crispus one of the coins. Constantine had just finished dinner with Julia, Judge, and his son. Crispus looked at his father.

"I like this coin," he said. "It has your likeness on it."

"That is because I want everyone to know who the emperor is," Constantine said. "Some people can't read, but they can recognize images."

"Did all the emperors have coins made with their likeness?" he asked. "That would be a lot of coins."

"If they were emperor long enough to have a die made, the coins were produced," he said. "My collection contains coins that depict almost every emperor."

Crispus wanted to see Constantine's coin collection.

"I think I will start my own collection," he said. "Yours will be my first coin."

Constantine smiled at Crispus.

"How would you like to go to Spain with me?" Constantine asked. "I have never taken you with me on my travels."

"Really, father?" he said. "I would love to go to Spain. Where, in Spain, will we be going?"

"My conference is in Barcelona," he said. "I must inform several people that you will be accompanying me."

"Can Julia and my tutor come with us?" Crispus asked. "I'm sure they would like to see Barcelona."

"I hadn't planned on taking them," he said. "We will be using a military boat."

"I must continue my lessons," he said. "I know they wouldn't be a problem."

"It will take a considerable amount of extra work to take a woman with us," he said. "But I think it could be arranged."

"Have Judge take care of it," Crispus said.

Constantine reminded Crispus that Judge was responsible for

maintaining the house. Other soldiers performed other duties for him. He suggested his aid might be able to make the arrangements.

"Thank you, father," he said. "I will tell Julia."

"I will have Nickus make all the necessary arrangements," Constantine said. "We will leave next week."

Constantine told Nickus that he expected a soldier to be posted with his family at all times.

The following week, Constantine, his army escort, and his family departed for Barcelona. Making their way by carriage, they traveled over land to the river. They planned to take a boat along the Rhone River and then take a ship to Barcelona. Constantine introduced Crispus and Julia to the army troops.

"This is a special river boat," Constantine said. "My father had it built. I have used it several times."

"Originally, it was a fighting vessel," Nickus said. "We have built new river boats that are better prepared for fighting."

"This boat is prepared for use by the emperor," Constantine said. "It has very nice quarters. Each cabin has a mate assigned to help the guest."

"We will take special care of you, Julia," Nickus said. "We aren't accustomed to traveling with a woman. I will post a guard outside your cabin door."

Nickus showed Julia to her cabin.

"I guess I am staying with my tutor," Crispus said. "Why do I have to stay with him?"

"Your father is working," Nickus said. "You can't stay with him."

"I could stay with Julia," he said. "Looking after me is her job."

"Julia is staying by herself," he said. "Maybe you could stay alone."

Nickus looked at Crispus.

"I will stay with my tutor," he said.

"You will be able to observe the valley from the deck," Nickus said. "I will always have guards posted to protect anyone who wants to be on the deck."

"Our crews are well-trained as boatmen and as soldiers," Constantine said. "When I travel on the rivers, they are always with me."

"I have one stop planned. We will stay for about a day and a half," Nickus said. "We will restock the boat and visit the town."

"Where is that?" Crispus asked. "I want my tutor to tell me about the town before we arrive."

"It is Lugdunum," he said. "I think you will like the town."

They proceeded west to the Rhone and then proceeded south. The weather was warm and the river was smooth. Crispus and Julia sat on the main deck and looked at the valley. Their mate stood close by.

"This river valley is beautiful," Crispus said. "I'm enjoying being with father on his trip."

"I feel a little funny," Julia said. "I am the only woman with all these men."

"You don't have to worry," he said. "Father and I will protect you."

Julia looked at Crispus and smiled.

"Is anything wrong?" Nickus asked. "Would you like a glass of water?"

"Everything is fine," she said. "Yes, I would like a glass of water."

"Mate," he said. "Bring the lady some water."

The tutor was standing on the ship's deck, with his brush in his hand, painting a picture of the river valley.

"How do you create a painting when the scene is constantly changing?" Crispus asked.

"It is a composite of what I am seeing," he said. "It is nothing exactly, but it is everything generally."

Crispus hesitated for a moment.

"I think I understand the concept," he said. "I want to be a warrior, not a painter."

"Painting puts your mind at ease. It is a very restful hobby," the tutor said. "It is good for the soul."

"There's a small town," Crispus said. "I see the church. People are standing on the bank waving at us."

He jumped to his feet and pointed at the bell tower.

"You can wave," Nickus said. "They are our friends and recognize our boat."

Crispus waved to everyone. The boat continued to move down the river during the night. Soldiers walked along its bank, just ahead of the boat. The only sound was the boat cutting through the water. The light from the moon and the stars reflected on the river. Each morning, the air was filled with the aroma of the cook's breakfast. Crispus rubbed his stomach.

"Breakfast is ready," the cook said. "I have a table set on the main deck for you and your family, sir."

"Thank you," Constantine said. "Eggs, fish, fruit, and hot bread are what I call a real breakfast."

Constantine waited while Crispus blessed their meal.

"I am very glad you brought us along," Crispus said. "When will we arrive in Lugdunum?"

"We will be there tomorrow, late afternoon," Nickus said. "We will tour the town the next day."

The following day, it rained. Crispus spent most of the morning with his tutor. Julia joined them and slowly learned to read. The following afternoon, they docked in Lugdunum. Constantine talked with Crispus about Lugdunum.

"This town was devastated by a battle and never fully recovered," Constantine said. "With my building program, I have been able to help them with many rebuilding projects and a few new buildings."

"My tutor told me that Lugdunum was a great city when Irenaeus was bishop," Crispus said. "He also told me about the church."

"Nickus will show you the church," he said. "It was one of our rebuilding projects. I am going to have lunch with the priest."

"It takes a lot of supplies to support a boat like this," Crispus said. "Everyone needs fresh water."

"They will unload the trash tonight," Nickus said. "Tomorrow they will load our supplies."

"I am glad you don't throw the trash in the river," Crispus said. "I know some of it does go in the river."

"We do what we can," he said. "The local school trains boatmen on the proper methods of managing a boat."

"Nickus, post a few guards on the main deck," Constantine said. "I will treat everyone who goes ashore to dinner at the restaurant that overlooks the dock."

The guards were posted, and everyone else went ashore. Crispus held on to Julia by one hand and his tutor by the other. The soldiers had cleaned and dressed for dinner. They were an impressive group.

The restaurant owner saw them approaching.

"Good evening, sir," the restaurateur said. "Will you and your party be dining with us?"

"Yes," Nickus said. "Give the men all the food they want, but only two glasses of wine. Give me the bill."

"Yes, sir," he said. "I notice you have a woman with you."

"Julia is the attendant for the emperor's son," Nickus said. "She is your most important guest."

"Yes, sir," he said. "I understand. We will take very good care of her. Does she drink wine?"

"I don't know," he said.

"Excuse me, Miss," he said. "Would you like a glass of wine?"

"No, thank you," Julia said. "I would like a glass of goat's milk, and bring one for Crispus."

"Thank you, Miss," he said. "Dinner is being prepared."

It was a pleasant evening. They listened to the sounds of the rivers and the boats. The group ate slowly and talked for a few hours. When they returned to the ship, they sat on the main deck and watched the town slowly become dark. The next morning, they rose early. Nickus posted a different group of guards, and the restaurant served everyone eggs and chops. The aroma of the cooked meat filled the air.

After breakfast, a carriage with guards arrived to take Nickus, the tutor, Julia, and Crispus for a tour of the town.

"All the new buildings along the river are part of Constantine's building program," Nickus said. "Many of them contain government offices for this smaller province."

"What made the province smaller?" Crispus asked. "The battle didn't do that."

Nickus looked at Crispus.

"The empire redefined the provinces," he said. "As a result, many provinces became smaller."

"Are we going to the church?" Julia asked. "I would like to say a prayer of thanks. I have never had such a wonderful experience."

"Yes," Nickus said. "It is our next stop. Constantine is visiting with the priest."

They climbed out of the carriage and stretched their legs.

"It is a nice church," Crispus said. "What is the building next to the church?"

"It is a school," he said. "It has been an important school for many years. They teach you a skill. Then you can get a good job."

Julia remained at the church and school for several hours. Later, they traveled to the mint. After they toured the mint, they returned to the boat.

"I got a brand new coin with Constantine's likeness for each of us," Nickus said. "It will remind us of today."

He displayed a hand full of new shiny silver coins.

"May I have one?" Crispus asked. "They are pretty."

Nickus flipped him a coin.

"Julia, catch your coin," he said.

He flipped Julia a coin. She caught it and looked at it.

"Thank you," she said. "I will never forget today."

"Are we going to eat at the restaurant?" Crispus asked. "They have great food."

"Yes," Nickus said. "First we will go aboard and dress for dinner. I will change the guards. When Constantine returns, we will eat dinner."

When Constantine arrived, a boatman called everyone to dinner. The group paraded to the restaurant.

"Two glasses of goat's milk," he said. "See, I remembered."

"Thank you," Julia said. "What are you cooking for us?"

"We are serving lamb," he said. "It is fresh, and my cook has been preparing it all day. We also have made several different breads for you."

"That sounds great," Crispus said. "I love hot bread."

Crispus looked at Julia and said, "Your father makes really good bread."

"Your father is a cook?" the restaurateur asked. "It is a good job."

"Yes," she said. "He is the emperor's cook."

"That is a really good job," he said. "I hope you like our food."

"You do a nice job," Crispus said. "That is why father brought us to your restaurant."

Constantine walked to Crispus' table and showed him a scroll.

"The priest gave this to me," Constantine said. "He said it belonged to Irenaeus and thought John, the apostle, might have written it."

"May I see it?" the tutor asked. "John didn't write, but he used the same scribe for most of his later years."

"Read us a verse," Crispus asked.

"In in beginning was the Word, and the Word was with God, and the Word was God," (John, 1, 1, NIV) the tutor said.

"Tell me what you think," Constantine said. "I am going to put it in my library."

"It is old," he said. "We have been using codices for a hundred years. It looks like the real thing to me."

"It was nice of the priest to give it to you," Crispus said.

"We are good friends," he said. "Enjoy your dinner. I will see you tomorrow aboard the boat. We will be traveling downstream."

After a few days, they reached the Great Sea. Constantine saw a Roman Military ship.

"Hoist his flag. The emperor is coming aboard," the captain said. "Mate, greet our guests."

The ship sailed for Barcelona. The sea was calm. The wind was still. On two occasions, it was necessary for the sailors to row the ship towards the wind. The captain apologized for their delay. It became a long, hot trip. Everyone was restless. When they reached the dock, the group quickly disembarked.

"I have made arrangements for us to stay at the fortification," Nickus said. "They will take good care of us."

"Are you going to show us Barcelona?" Crispus asked. "You are a good tour guide."

"No," he said. "I will be with your father."

"I almost forgot that this is a business trip," Crispus said. "I hope everything goes well for you."

"Justus, a local army sergeant, will show you the town," he said. "He knows the area very well."

The next morning after breakfast, several guards and the group went on tour.

"I will ride in the carriage with you and Julia," the sergeant said. "Your father told me your names. Call me Sergeant. I will help you board the carriage."

"It is a little high for me, but I can climb aboard," Crispus said. "Have you lived here long?"

"I have been here for seven years," he said. "The Commander of the fortification and I have served together for a long time."

"Nickus and my father have been together for a long time," he said. "I guess you understand the Commander."

"First, take a good look at our harbor," he said. "It is deep and large. We are blessed with a great harbor."

"I see churches," Crispus said. "We like to visit churches."

"I will show you a church that was started by the apostle Paul" he said. "The building is newer, but the church is very old."

"I thought the building was the church," Julia said. "What are you saying?"

"The people who worship the Christian God have been here for a long time," he said. "They represent the church. The building is about twenty-five years old."

Julia looked at the sergeant and blushed.

"Yes," she said. "I understand."

They toured the city for three days. Each day, Julia visited a different church to pray. On the third day, Constantine ate dinner with Crispus, the tutor, and Julia.

"I hope you enjoyed the city," he said. "Tomorrow we will board the ship."

"The city is great," Crispus said. "I think you would like the sergeant."

"I know him," he said. "He is a good soldier."

"How was your conference?" Crispus asked. "What did you talk about?"

"I agreed to allow them to build a new library using tax money," he said. "It was a successful meeting."

After breakfast the next morning, they boarded the ship and started their journey to the Rhone River. One hour after they departed Barcelona, the wind stopped blowing.

"Sailors, man the oars," the captain said. "The wind isn't helping today."

"Without wind, it is going to take much longer," Constantine said. "They will inform us of our new schedule."

Constantine scratched his head and walked away.

"Rowing reminds me of marching in the rain," Nickus said. "If you want to move forward, you have to do it."

After three hours, the sails captured some wind, and the ship began to increase its speed. The crew trimmed the sails.

"If the wind stays in our sails, we will get back on schedule," the captain said. "I am sorry for the delay."

The captain was worried that the emperor would be upset. The crew worked diligently to insure everyone was as comfortable as possible. When they arrived at the Rhone River, the river boat awaited them.

"Captain, your men are good oarsmen," Constantine said. "You sail a tight ship. I look forward to sailing with you again."

"Thank you, sir," he said. "It was our honor."

Crispus walked to Constantine and pointed.

"Our boat is waiting," Crispus said. "Where are we going to stop during our return journey?"

"I thought you might like to see Vienne," Nickus said. "It is just south of Lugdunum."

When they boarded the boat, they were greeted by the crew. Their cabins were prepared and fresh fruit awaited each traveler.

The oarsmen were in place for the upriver journey.

"Welcome," the boat captain said. "We have everything in order."

"We want to spend a day at Vienne," Nickus said. "No other stops will be required for us."

"Tell me when everyone is aboard," the mate said. "We are ready when you are."

That evening for dinner, a special grape wine was served. Goat's milk was served to Julia and Crispus. Crispus looked at his father's wine glass.

"I will be glad when I am allowed to drink wine," Crispus said. "I am the only man with goat's milk."

"I am old enough to drink wine," Julia said. "I prefer goat's milk."

"I will have goat's milk with you," Crispus said. "Do you know anything about Vienne?"

They passed many boats that were going south. A few of the heavily laden boats that were heading north heaved to and allowed their boat to pass. It was evening, and the family sat on the deck and enjoyed the stars and moonlight.

"You have a good job, father," Crispus said. "I didn't know you had boats like this."

"I don't wade through the swamps, fighting hand-to-hand any longer," Constantine said. "I allow the younger men that pleasure. This job is more of an administrative job."

"When necessary, we do the fighting," Nickus said. "We are always ready."

"I noted you always have guards posted," Crispus said. "I feel well protected."

"It is part of our job," he said. "Did you notice that a boat is traveling just ahead of us?"

Crispus stood and looked over the bow of the boat. He pointed at the boat in the distance.

"Are you talking about that boat?" he asked.

"Yes," he said. "It always leads our boat on the river. It carries additional troops."

"It doesn't look like a military boat," he said. "I would have never guessed."

"That is the idea," Nickus said. "It was your father's idea. We have encountered barbarians on more than one occasion."

"I enjoy looking at the moon," Julia said. "It is peaceful."

They docked at Vienne during the night. When everyone awoke for breakfast, they learned it was being served on the dock. They disembarked and sat at their tables watching boats go up stream. Soon Nickus arrived.

"Vienne isn't as large as Lugdunum," Nickus said. "I want you to note the communal style of life. They grow large public gardens."

"Do they have churches?" Crispus asked. "Julia and I will spend some time at the prayer rail."

"They have churches," he said. "One of the largest churches was once a temple. During your father's building campaign, it was converted to a church."

"I want to go into that one," he said. "It will have special meaning to us."

"Julia, I am going to purchase a barrel of olive oil for your father," Nickus said. "This area produces the best oil available."

"He will appreciate that," she said. "He might even cook you a special meal."

Nickus looked at her.

"I was counting on that," he said.

They spent a pleasant day touring and then returned to the dock for dinner. After dinner, they boarded the boat. It had been a long day. The boat headed north and passed Lugdunum while everyone was asleep. The following morning, breakfast was served on deck. The sun shone, and a mild wind blew. The crews on the southbound boats waved greetings as they passed. After breakfast, Crispus and his tutor reviewed a lesson.

"I want you to write about your tour of Vienne," the tutor said. "Write it in Latin. After I have corrected it, I want you to read it to me in Greek."

"Can you do that?" Julia asked. "That sounds very difficult."

Crispus looked at her and smiled.

"Yes," he said. "I can do it. After I read it, he will help me write it in Greek."

"You have to learn a lot to be an emperor," she said. "Can I listen?"

"Sure, just don't laugh," he said. "We have been studying history recently. I might be a little rusty."

After the lesson, it started to rain. They remained below deck for the rest of the day. Candles were provided for reading. Eventually, the boat returned to Trier.

"I hope you had a pleasant journey," the captain said. "I look forward to our next journey."

"I must go to the office," Constantine said. "I might not be home tonight."

Nickus looked at Julia and Crispus.

"I will have a carriage take you home," Nickus said. "A wagon will make a delivery to the house. I will have the driver ask for you. Your father's oil will be on the wagon."

"Thank you," Crispus said. "I enjoyed the trip."

"I want to thank you for taking me along," the tutor said. "I have only read about Barcelona. I had never been there."

"Me too, I have never traveled. Let me know the next time you are coming to the house," Julia said. "We will have a special dinner prepared for you and Constantine."

A month later, Nickus came to dinner. Constantine started to think of himself as the only emperor. He knew it would be a struggle. It would take time, and it would probably result in civil war. He met with Nickus.

"Our army will never be the largest," Constantine said. "It must be the best army."

"What do you want me to do?" Nickus asked. "We are ready to serve."

"I want you to purchase the most advanced weapons," he said. "The men need to practice with the new equipment. I want them to become accustomed to using it."

"I have seen a new club," Nickus said. "I will get one and show it to you. I think you might like it."

"I want you to train them physically and mentally," he said. "We must be better at fighting and better at planning."

"I will increase our marching routine," he said. "Marching is good exercise for the mind and the body."

"Our enemy has a large cavalry," Nickus said. "We need to train a cavalry."

"Not just a cavalry," Constantine said. "We need the best cavalry. Purchase one hundred of the best horses and build a large stable."

"I will need someone to lead our cavalry," Nickus said. "I will determine our best horseman."

"I also want a spiritual leader to be part of our army," he said. "Send a message to the bishop. Ask him for a priest who is a good horseman and wants to be in the army."

"A priest in the army?" he asked. "I haven't heard of that."

"It is going to be part of our superior strategic plan," he said. "We will be physically and mentally prepared for hardship. It is a Christian trait."

Nickus smiled at Constantine.

"I am going to find someone to strengthen our navy as well," Constantine said. "We will be better than our enemy in every endeavor. I will have to develop a new symbol for our army."

Constantine and Nickus had a new vision. They went to work building and improving their army. They didn't know when or how things might transpire, but they would be prepared. They prepared to out fight and out think any enemy.

The first building constructed was the new stable. They built new quarters for the cavalry adjacent to the stable. The horsemen needed to be close to their mounts at all times. They would be required to endure additional strength training, and they would receive additional pay. Nickus took a special interest in the cavalry. He checked every horse before it was purchased. When one hundred horses had been purchased, Nickus asked Constantine to inspect them.

"They are beautiful," he said. "Now you have to train them to be accustomed to carrying a warrior who is swinging a club."

"The training has started," Nickus said. "Please, visit with us in a month."

"Make the men into warriors," Constantine said. "Train them diligently."

It was a time of turmoil within the empire. Galerius made decisions, but had trouble enforcing them. He depended on Severus to command his army and to control his rivals.

CHAPTER 4

CONSTANTINE AND MAXENTIUS

Constantius had consummated an alliance with Maximian. They respected each other as co-emperors and the Roman Empire expanded very rapidly. After Constantius died, Constantine was named an emperor by his troops. Maxentius wasn't named an emperor. He claimed to be an emperor, but Galerius and others refused to recognize him. He became offended and felt he hadn't been treated fairly. It became necessary for Galerius to threaten him.

"I am a true emperor," Maxentius said. "Constantine is living on the reputation and work of his father."

Galerius looked at him with distain. He pounded on his desk.

"You must recognize the Roman structure," he said. "If you don't, I will have you destroyed."

Galerius dismissed Maxentius.

A few days passed, before Galerius assigned an army leader, Serverus, the job of bringing Maxentius under control. Serverus lead his army against Maxentius.

"This shouldn't be much of a battle," Severus said. "We should be able to capture him without much resistance."

"The men are restless," the sergeant said. "They aren't happy about having to fight Maxentius."

"Get our troops ready to fight. His army isn't very large," he said.

"When we bring Maxentius back as a captive, I am sure everyone will be promoted."

"Most of our men were once commanded by his father," the sergeant said. "They are still loyal to Maximian and don't like the idea of fighting his son."

"They are in the Roman Army," Severus said. "They are not part of his family or part of Maximian's army."

Severus was very proud of his position in the Roman army. He refused to acknowledge how popular Maximian had been. Severus' only thought was that Maxentius wasn't named an emperor and assumed the role. Severus wanted to defeat Maxentius and prove to Galerius that he was a great warrior.

Before two days passed, the sergeant brought Severus bad news.

"Our army has refused to fight," he said. "They are going to take us captive and put us in prison."

"I am in command," Severus said. "Tell them to return to their posts."

"They don't recognize your authority," he said. "They won't obey any orders I give to them. The situation is not good."

Severus couldn't believe what he was told. He was taken captive by his army and delivered to Maxentius.

Severus' troops elected a spokesperson to communicate with Maxentius.

"We decided we don't want to fight against you," the trooper said. "We all know your father, and we respect him."

"You are welcome to join my army," Maxentius said. "I will talk to my father and see if he will join us."

Galerius' position of power was now being threatened. Maximian, Maxentius' father, went to Gaul to confer with Constantine. When he arrived in Trier, Nickus greeted him.

"We have heard your son is causing Galerius many problems," he said.

"He is trying to cause trouble," Maximian said.

He paused for a moment. He looked at the floor.

When Nickus knocked on the door, Constantine was at work in his office.

"I have a friend of your father's and his daughter to see you," Nickus said.

Constantine motioned to Nickus to bring them in.

"Come in and have a seat," he said. "He will see you."

"My name is Maximian, I knew your father very well," he said. "This is my daughter Fausta."

"You came a long way to see me," Constantine said. "I am sure you must have something very important to discuss."

"My son, Maxentius, is a little out of control and saying things that are not correct," he said. "He feels threatened by your success."

"I have heard that he doesn't like me," Constantine said. "Galerius is the one who doesn't recognize him. The people here don't really know or care much about him."

"He is a bit of a hot head," he said. "I have tried to teach him patience, but he has his own agenda."

Constantine stared at Maximian. He wondered why his daughter had come with him.

"I heard your troops have joined with his troops," he said. "Galerius thought they would be loyal to anyone he assigned to lead them."

"I would like you and my son to have an understanding like your father and I once had," he said. "We weren't good friends, but we weren't enemies. We were both officers in the Roman Army."

"What do you propose?" Constantine asked. "I see your son didn't bother to come with you."

"No, he isn't with me," Maximian said. "I still have a lot of troops that are faithful to me. I have brought my daughter, Fausta."

"Welcome to Gaul," Constantine said. "I hope you will enjoy your visit."

Constantine looked her over very carefully.

"I want you to support, Maxentius," he said. "In return, I will give you my daughter in marriage. That will bring peace between you and Maxentius."

Constantine was still looking at Fausta and was not listening to what Maximian said. Suddenly, he realized what Maximian had proposed.

"That is an interesting offer," he said. "Fausta, do you know I have a son?"

She raised her head, and with her large brown eyes she stared at him.

"Yes, I know," she said. "They told me about you before they brought me to you. I could give you more sons."

Constantine was overcome by her beauty.

"When can you marry?" he asked. "I am interested in more sons, and I have plenty of room for you."

"I will marry you now, as my father wishes," she said. "I want to be away from Italy."

Constantine looked at Maximian, and then he turned to Fausta.

"Are you sure you would like living here with me?" he asked. "You must know all about army soldiers."

"Yes," she said. "I have given this a lot of thought. We can have a good life."

"I accept your offer," Constantine said to Maximian. "I will marry your daughter, but don't expect me to do much for your son."

"Marrying my daughter will show your support of my son," Maximian said. "That is all my son needs."

"Fausta and I will be married next week," he said. "I will contact the priest. Please stay for the wedding."

"I am not much for church weddings," Maximian said. "I want to return home and tell Maxentius that you are going to support him."

"Father, please stay for my wedding," Fausta said. "I don't want to be alone."

"You agreed to marry him if I brought you along," he said. "I need to go back to see your brother."

Fausta tried to convince her father to stay for her wedding, but he refused. He didn't want to be labeled as a Christian sympathizer.

The following week, Fausta and Constantine were married. Now, she was away from Italy and her family quarrels. She hoped she would learn to love Constantine. Constantine wrote Maxentius a letter of recognition.

While relaxing at home, Fausta and Constantine discussed the house staff.

"Judge is the head of my household staff," Constantine said. "He is also in the Roman Army. He will make certain you receive the best care. If you need anything, ask him."

She looked at Judge.

"Welcome to Trier. I have been with Constantine for a long time," Judge said. "It is my privilege to attend to your needs."

Constantine put his arm around his son.

"This is my son," he said. "His name is Crispus. His attendant is Julia. Julia and her father are considered part of my family."

Fausta greeted Crispus and Julia. She embraced Crispus.

"I am looking forward to learning to know you." Crispus said. "Your father knew my grandfather."

"I have one more person for you to meet," Constantine said. "This is Nickus, he runs the army for me."

Chop entered the room.

"Dinner is served," he said. "I am the cook. Call me Chop."

Fausta looked at Chop and smiled.

"You must be Julia's father," she said.

Constantine nodded.

"I will try to remember everyone's name," she said. "I am looking forward to being with you."

After Fausta and Julia learned to understand each other, they became a family. They enjoyed dinners together. Constantine and Fausta decided to start their own family. Constantine was busy with the military and politics, but they often ate breakfast together.

"I will be busy at the office today," Constantine said. "I may not be home for dinner. Don't wait on me. Please pass me the eggs."

"Pass me the burned and scraped bread," Crispus said. "I can see Chop didn't make breakfast."

Julia looked at Crispus and smiled.

"Crispus, we should all be thankful for what we have," Julia said. "We are all very blessed."

"I will take care of the bread problem," Judge said. "From now on it will be hot, but not burned."

Constantine went to the office and the others went about their daily routines. The tutor arrived at ten o'clock.

"What is the lesson for today?" Crispus asked. "Am I going to be reading or writing?"

"Both," the tutor said. "I will be here most of the day. We will start with a little religion."

"Which religion?" he asked. "Father seems interested in the Christian religion."

They spent the next hour discussing when Easter should be celebrated. When dinner time arrived, Constantine was not home.

"Dinner is ready," Chop said. "Should I have it served?"

"Yes," Judge said. "Constantine instructed us not to wait on him. He is busy at the office."

"Dinner will be on the table in a few moments," he said. "You can round up the troops."

Judge gave him thumbs up. When Constantine returned home, they had already finished dinner and were seated in the living area. He asked for a cup of tea and joined the family.

"I have decided to have an economic conference at the mint in Lugdunum," Constantine said. "I plan to leave tomorrow and will return in three months. I am taking my artist and engraver with me."

"May I go with you?" Crispus asked. "We can take my tutor."

"Not this time," he said. "I am going to be very busy."

"We won't be a problem," he said. "I could learn a lot."

"No, Crispus," he said. "You stay here with Fausta and Julia. I will arrange for your tutor to come more often while I am away."

"Are you sure I can't go with you?" Crispus asked.

"I am certain," he said. "No more discussion."

Crispus understood and looked at the floor. He knew from past experience when to be quiet. It wouldn't benefit his cause if he angered his father. Fausta looked at Constantine and smiled.

"Our family might be larger went you get home," she said. "I will try for a son."

"I wish I could stay with you," Constantine said. "I can't change this trip. It involves too many people."

"I also wish you could be with me," she said. "I understand. You are a busy man. I'll be fine. Save the empire."

He kissed Fausta's forehead.

"I can't be here, but I can make sure you have plenty of help," he said. "Judge will have everything arranged for you."

"I will be fine," she said. "Maybe you can be here the next time." She blew a kiss to him.

After Constantine left for Lugdunum, Fausta consulted with Judge.

"I would like a doctor to examine me," she said. "The army probably doesn't have baby doctors."

"We have baby doctors," Judge said. "The wives of the soldiers have babies. I will find you the best baby doctor."

"I don't want to go the army base," she said. "Can you arrange for him to come here to see me?"

"Certainly, he will do whatever the emperor's wife desires," he said. "I will bring him to see you."

Two weeks later, the doctor arrived and checked Fausta. She was fine, and the baby was doing well.

"I like the doctor," Fausta said. "I didn't think about the soldiers' wives having babies. He seems very knowledgeable."

"He has helped deliver many babies," Judge said. "He will take good care of you."

Constantine, Nickus, an artist, and an engraver boarded the boat. The next morning, they headed to Lugdunum. The second boat was loaded with troops. Nickus conducted drills with them each day. They were trained to be warriors who arrived by boat instead of on foot. Constantine and Nickus discussed strategy.

"I don't want to send troops to Italy," Constantine said. "I want to use our resources to help our people."

"I can plan a few more trips for us," Nickus said. "Do you want to send troops to Britain?"

Constantine thought for a moment.

"That's not a bad idea," he said. "It's been a long time since I've been there."

"You could stay at home for a while and then take some troops with you to Britain," he said. "When you come home, you could return with the troops that desire to return to Trier."

When they docked at Lugdunum, Constantine visited with the priest at the local church. When an emperor visited, it was very good for the priest's popularity.

"Come in," the priest said. "It is always good to see you. What brings you to Lugdunum?"

"I am having some new coins designed," Constantine said. "I have an artist with me. I will be spending my time at the mint."

"Would you like to stay at the church with us?" he asked. "We have an extra room."

"I can dine with you on occasion," he said. "My guards and I will be staying on the boat. Would you like to visit with us?"

"Yes," he said. "I have seen river boats that carry cargo, but I have never seen a military boat."

"Come to dinner tomorrow evening at seven," Constantine said. "We have a very good cook. Our boat is not a freight barge."

The priest looked at Constantine and smiled.

"I understand," he said. "I will see you at seven."

Constantine told the cook they would be having a guest for dinner the next evening. He was adamant about having the best food available. That evening, Constantine talked with the priest again.

"I want you to help me," Constantine said. "I left my wife at home."

"Military men often leave their wives at home," the priest said. "Kneel and pray with me."

Constantine repeated what the priest said, "May the Lord keep watch between you and me when we are away from each other." (Genesis, 31, 49, NIC)

When they finished, the priest ensured Constantine he was not the first one to ask for God's blessing during an absence.

"While I am here, she is going to have a child," he said. "When I planned this trip, I didn't know she was with child."

"She will be fine," the priest said. "Pray daily and send her a message. I will pray for you."

The next day, Constantine and Nickus rode in a carriage to the mint.

"I would like to meet with the director of the mint," Constantine said.

"He won't be in today," the guard said. "He will be here next week."

"Get an artist for me," he said. "Didn't the director receive my message?"

"Yes, he did," he said. "He is home with his wife. She is having a baby. He chose to be with her. He was certain you would understand."

The manager of the mint arrived and spoke with Constantine.

"We have several artists," he said. "One specializes in coins for the emperors."

"Bring him to me," he said. "I brought my artist with me. We can talk coins."

A few moments later, the artist arrived.

Constantine and the two artists discussed new coins for several days.

"I want several new coins with my likeness on them," Constantine said. "One of them will have our new army symbol on the reverse."

"I can draw the coins," the mint's artist said. "Your artist can help me. The problem is getting all the engraving accomplished."

"I can help with that," Constantine's artist said. "I brought an engraver with me."

"He can start working on the new coin dies as soon as the artwork is completed," Constantine said. "I will bring him with me tomorrow."

"That will be a great help," the manager said. "Our engraver is slow, and we are always waiting on him."

"Would you like to join us for dinner?" he asked. "We are dining on board at seven o'clock."

"I would be honored," he said. "I look forward to seeing your boat."

They returned to the boat, shaved and dressed for dinner. A guard escorted the priest to Constantine's office at about fifteen minutes before seven.

"I came a few minutes early so you could give me a tour," the priest said. "This is a beautiful boat."

"I will be with you in a few minutes," Constantine said.

"I apologize. I am early," he said. "I love your boat."

"I am very pleased with it," Constantine said. "It is my home away from home. The other boat carries our guards and troops."

Soon, the manager of the mint arrived. He knew the priest, and they exchanged greetings.

Constantine and his guests toured the boat. He showed them one of the estate cabins, the large library, and the area used for relaxation. He didn't take the priest to the functional areas used to store oars and supplies.

"This library is first class," the priest said. "If you every need any blank codices, our school produces them."

"Have them send one hundred to the mate," Constantine said. "He will pay for them. We like to help the economy of the towns that we visit."

The priest was surprised and blessed Constantine's generosity.

"I think dinner is ready," he said. "We are eating on deck. I asked my military assistant to dine with us."

"Do you want me to bless the food?" the priest asked. "Is everyone a Christian?"

"I don't know," he said. "They either work for me or are my guest. Bless the food."

The ship's cook had visited every merchant at the market and purchased the best ingredients available. The dinner was superb. After dinner, the priest returned to the church. The manager of the mint talked with Constantine for several hours.

The next day, Constantine's engraver went to the mint.

"I will start engraving the obverse of the blank die," he said. "I don't need the artist to draw a picture of you. I know what you look like."

"I have to draw his picture," the mint's artist said. "We keep drawings for our records."

"You can draw his picture after we leave," he said. "I want to get started."

"If he is not here, I can't see him," he said. "I want an accurate likeness. It will only take a few days."

"We are designing several different reverse planchets," he said. "Draw them for me. I will draw all the obverse likenesses."

"You draw," he said. "I will engrave. Don't bother to give me your drawings of Constantine, just put them in your file."

"What is the problem?" Nickus asked. "You haven't started engraving."

"He is the problem," he said. "He wants to draw five pictures of Constantine."

"Artist, draw the reverse of coin one," Nickus said. "I will have our artist draw five likenesses of Constantine."

"Thank you," he said. "I will get started on the reverse at once."

"You will have to make several planchets of each reverse," the mint's manager said. "The dies break with use."

"After he finishes the reverse, I need about half a day and you can start minting coins."

"I want a barrel full of each style of coin," Nickus said. "I will pay you for the labor. I have the bullion for you to produce the coins,"

"Do you have copper, silver or gold?" the mint manager asked. "I am glad you brought the bullion. That solves many problems."

"I have mostly gold and silver," he said. "I don't have any copper."

"We will put the silver coins in circulation," Constantine said. "We will give the gold coins away as presents."

The manager of the mint looked at Constantine.

"That is very generous of you," he said. "We can have your troops bring me some bullion, starting tomorrow."

Constantine was careful to order both pagan and Christian symbols for the reverse of the coins. He was skillful at using his likeness on the coins as a political tool.

"How long will you require minting the coins?" Constantine asked. "How can we help?"

"You could have some of your soldiers help strike the coins," he said. "That would be a great help."

Soon, the director of the mint returned to work. His wife had delivered a baby girl.

After two months, the five barrels of coins were aboard the boat. An agreement was reached between Constantine and the mint's director. The mint would receive bullion, and they would ship coins to Trier. Their labor would be paid with bullion. One hundred gold coins of each type was struck and given to Nickus. The priest and the mint manager were invited on board the boat for a farewell dinner.

"I consider this a very successful trip," Constantine said. "The coins have been minted, and we have been able to help the school and the clinic."

"I want to thank you," the priest said. "You are a great emperor. You love your people. I am sure your wife loves you."

"I thank you for the help of your engraver," the mint manager said.

"I have a present for you," Constantine said. "I have five coins, one gold coin of each type that we had minted,"

"Thank you," the mint manager said. "I will treasure them."

"I will keep one," the priest said. "May I sell the other coins to help the needy in our church?"

"Yes," Nickus said. "They are for you. Do with them as you please."

"I hope you enjoy your dinner," Constantine said. "We will depart later this evening."

Constantine was edgy. He thought of Fausta and prayed for her comfort and safety. He also prayed for his mother. He knew she would be pleased she would have additional grandchildren.

When it was time for Fausta to deliver the baby, the doctor brought several helpers with him. He tried to comfort Fausta.

"We will take good care of you," the doctor said. "We have a lot of practice delivering babies."

"I don't see any women," Fausta said. "May I have my attendant with me?"

"Certainly," he said. "We don't want her to do anything, but she can be here with you."

After the baby was born, a doctor agreed to stay with Fausta for two weeks.

One week later, Constantine's boat docked in Trier. The men looked forward to being home. Constantine and Nickus talked as they disembarked.

"Give me about a month, and I will be ready to leave for Britain," Constantine said. "It will be a while before I go to Italy."

"I will see you in the office tomorrow," Nickus said.

Constantine looked at Nickus.

"I am going to take tomorrow away from work," he said. "I should have another son by the time I get home."

"I hope everything went well for your wife," he said. "I'll see you the day after tomorrow."

"I will be there," Constantine said. "I'll have a carriage driver take me home. Load the number two boat with barrels of silver bullion and send it to Lugdunum."

"I will take care of that," Nickus said. "I will fill the treasury with silver coins. I will send a freight barge down the river to the sea. Then, we will put the barrels of bullion on a ship and have it delivered to the Rhone River. It will be transferred and taken to the mint. That way our boats will be available. I will send guards with the bullion."

When Constantine arrived home, his family awaited him. Nickus had sent Judge a message.

"I see a carriage," Crispus said. "Father is home."

"I want to talk with him," Fausta said. "I will show him his new son."

"It is good to see you," Constantine said. "I missed you. Do you have news for me?"

"Yes," she said.

She looked at Julia.

"Bring Constantine his son," she said. "First, swaddle him carefully."

Julia brought a baby, wrapped in clothes, and put him in Constantine's outstretched arms.

"We have a son," Constantine said. "I prayed it would be a boy. Next, we can try for a girl."

"What are you going to name him?" Fausta asked. "Constantine II?"

Constantine looked at Fausta and smiled.

"I like Constantine II," he said. "That is a fine name. I am sure he will make a fine emperor."

"I missed you," Fausta said. "Tell us all about your trip."

"It was mostly a business trip," he said. "I did take time to visit with my friend, the priest. I have presents for everyone."

Crispus moved to his father's side.

"Did you bring me something?" he asked. "I like presents."

"I have five gold coins for you, and I have five gold coins for my wife," he said. "Hold out your hands."

They cupped their hands and Constantine put five gold coins into them.

"The coins have your likeness on them," Crispus said. "They are very nice. I won't spend mine."

"I have some silver coins for you and Fausta to spend," he said.

Constantine looked at Judge.

"Get Julia and her father," he said. "I am going to give each of them five silver coins."

When Judge returned, Constantine instructed him to give one silver coin to each member of the staff.

After everyone received their gifts, Constantine and Fausta relaxed in the living area.

"The doctor did a fine job, but I didn't like being alone," Fausta said. "I want to increase the size of our family."

"Me too," Constantine said. "I will be home about a month. Then I am going to take some troops to Britain."

She looked at Constantine and batted her eyes.

"That should be long enough," she said.

She put her arm around Constantine. He smiled back and filled their wine glasses.

"Here is to our larger family" he said.

The next morning, they slept late. Constantine was awakened when Judge knocked on the bedroom door.

"Sir," Judge said. "Chop is about ready to start making lunch. Do you want breakfast?"

Constantine told Judge to inform Chop that he had brought him a barrel of olive oil. Then he ordered breakfast.

"We will have hot bread and goat's milk," he said. "Have Chop put our food on the table."

Fausta and Constantine entered the dining area, holding hands.

"I hope you enjoy your breakfast," the servant said. "Thank you for the coin."

"You can spend it however you want," Constantine said. "It is real silver. Don't allow anyone to cheat you."

"I need a new pair of sandals," she said. "I should get the sandals and some copper coins in change."

"That's the idea," he said. "Tell the others what I just told you."

"I will," she said. "Thank you."

The next day, Constantine noticed several of the servants were wearing new sandals.

Constantine was at the office during the day, but was home every night. They discussed where he would go next.

"Several of our troops have requested to return to Britain," Constantine said. "I will take them to my friends and bring back those who are ready to return to Gaul."

"You haven't been there for a while," Crispus said. "Don't you like Britain?"

"It has been a while. I served there with your grandfather," he said. "I like Britain when it is not raining."

He looked at Crispus and smiled.

"What area are you going to visit?" Crispus asked. "You will have to cross the channel."

"The territory near Hadrian's Wall," he said. "Yes, we will be crossing the channel. This time I am only taking a few of my troops."

"Is it another economic conference?" Crispus asked. "Do they mint Roman coins?"

"No," he said. "It is more of a relief or building mission."

"Is Nickus going with you?" he asked.

"Yes," Constantine said. "He goes everywhere with me. He provides my guards."

"How long will you be gone?" he asks. "We will miss you."

"Probably about two or three months," he said. "A smaller group moves much more quickly than an army. Son, you sure have a lot of questions."

Crispus realized that his father was getting tired of answering his questions.

"I will miss you, darling," Fausta said. "When you return, I might have good news for you."

"I hope you do," he said. "I like good news."

Constantine gave his wife a great hug.

The following day, Nickus came to dinner and they completed the plans for their trip. Three months later, Constantine was on his way to Britain. They took carriages and horses to make their journey less cumbersome.

"Mount up, men," Nickus ordered. "Four guards will ride before us and six will ride behind us. The troops will ride in the rear."

"I will ride in the carriage," Constantine said. "I may choose to ride a horse at some point."

Nickus moved the troops into position.

When they arrived at the channel, a ship waited for them. They had to blindfold many of the horses to load them.

"I wonder if that will work for troops," Nickus said. "Some of them can be more difficult than a horse."

Constantine laughed and smiled at Nickus.

"You have my permission to try it," he said. "Blindfolded troops marching aboard ship would be a funny sight."

As it crossed the channel, the ship rocked and rolled. When it docked, the horses were unloaded first. Then the guards and troops disembarked.

"We have been joined by two of our troops from Britain," Nickus said. "They will return with us. Six of you will be staying."

"Yes, sir," the soldier said. "It is our turn for a tour in Britain."

They visited two fortifications on their way north. After two weeks, they reached their destination.

"Governor," Constantine said. "I have brought money to give to the church. Take me to the priest."

"Follow my carriage," the Governor said. "They will be glad to see you. They can always use money."

"Welcome," the priest said. "Many of our members need heavy clothes before the cold weather arrives."

"I have a box of silver coins for you," Constantine said. "It should help."

"We don't use Roman coins," the priest said. "Did you say silver?"

They remained in Britain longer than planned. The return trip took three weeks. Nickus had been in contact with Judge, and Crispus watched for Constantine's carriage

"We have another son," Fausta said. "What will his name be?"

A great smile appeared on Constantine's face.

"I want to name him after my father," he said. "Constantius II."

"I know your father would be proud," she said. "Maybe, our next child will be a girl."

Constantine smiled and kissed Fausta.

"I also have good news," he said. "The church that we helped build is doing well, and we were able to supply some relief for the poor members."

"This is wonderful," she said. "Crispus is doing very well with his lessons."

"Can you write Greek?" Constantine asked his son. "Learning Greek is important."

"I am getting much better," Crispus said.

"I am ready for a few home cooked meals," Constantine said. "How are Julia and her father?"

"Julia is fine, but her father is not doing well," Fausta said. "I retired him. His assistant is now the head cook, and Julia is caring for him."

"Did she move into his quarters?" He asked. "I want them both to be happy."

"Yes," she said. "She is living with him in the slave's quarters."

"I checked on her," Judge said. "She has everything she asked for."

"Take good care of both of them," he said. "Do you need an attendant?"

"No," Fausta said. "Julia sent me a slave to be my attendant. She is doing fine. I am pleased with her."

"Dinner is served," he said. "Good day, sir. They call me Chop II."

"I am planning to take you, Crispus, and his tutor to Cologne," Constantine said. "I will also be taking an expert in building bridges. Their new bridge will be near the Rhine River, but crosses a smaller river."

She put her head on Constantine's shoulder.

The following day, Maximian knocked on the door. Constantine wondered why Maximian would be coming to see him.

"How is married life treating you?" Maximian asked. "Do you have any children?"

"It is great," he said. "We are working on the family."

"I need a job," he said. "I am finished with my son."

Constantine was curious; he wanted to know what had happened between them. Maximian explained that his son had stopped taking advice and was at odds with the entire eastern empire. Constantine thought for a few moments and responded.

"You can work for us," he said. "Nickus will put you to work."

Constantine and Nickus were suspicious of Maximian's motives, but decided to help him. Nickus prepared Maximian to lead a small number of troops against the Franks. He and his troops marched to an area west of the Rhine River. Constantine and his family boarded the boats for their trip to Cologne. Fausta was impressed with the boat.

"I didn't expect the boat to be this grand," Fausta said. "I thought it was a fighting vessel."

"The other boat is the fighting vessel," Constantine said. "When we fight, we take boat number two."

They enjoyed their journey to Cologne. Fausta, Crispus and the tutor toured the town while Constantine and his builder discussed a new bridge with the local politicians. While they were in Cologne, Galerius made some major changes in the Roman political structure. He tried to demote Constantine and Maximian. The new system didn't work because of Constantine's popularity. One of Constantine's coins depicting him and the sun God became well-known. This surprised him. As they sat on the deck, the sun shone brightly.

"It was the coin I liked the least," Constantine said. "We produced it to satisfy the pagans. They love the sun and identify with Apollo."

"We Christians like it because of the implication of monotheism," Crispus said. "It is liked by all your people."

"Maximian is again supporting his son," he said. "I shouldn't have helped him."

"You can't blame him,' Nickus said. "I hope we don't have to kill him."

While Constantine was away, Maximian told everyone that Constantine was dead, and that he was his replacement. When Constantine returned home, he discovered that Maximian had turned against him. Two months later, they located him. As soon as the troops realized Constantine was alive they turned against Maximian.

"When you capture him, bring him to me," Constantine said. "You might not have to kill him."

"I will capture him tonight," he said. "He thinks he is safe hiding in town, but the leader of the town remembered the help you gave them. They are going to allow my troops in at the town's back gate at midnight."

That night, Nickus and his troops entered the town through the back gate and found Maximian sleeping. He didn't have time to resist. Nickus grabbed him by his curly beard. He looked at Nickus in disbelief. He was bound and taken away.

"Kill me! Please kill me!" Maximian pleaded.

"I have promised Constantine I would deliver you to him," Nickus said.

Maximian struggled and tried to free himself.

Early the next morning, Nickus brought a tired and bound Maximian to Constantine. Constantine looked at him with disgust.

"You betrayed my trust," he said. "I don't care if he is your son."

"I deserve to die," he said. "Allow me to die with dignity."

"You have given me no choice," Constantine said. "I will have you imprisoned, and if you haven't killed yourself before I visit tomorrow, you will be hanged in public on the town square."

Maximian thanked Constantine for not making a public display of him. He committed suicide that night.

Those who benefited from Constantine being emperor in the western region started a campaign that suggested that he should be the only emperor of the Roman Empire. Constantine liked the idea, but he liked his new daughter, Constantina, even more. Constantine hugged his wife.

"I am fine," Fausta said. "I understand Maxentius is going to oppose you. Are you going to fight him?"

"He will make things difficult for a while," he said.

Maxentius went about raising taxes on the people of Italy and building his army in northern Italy. The situation grew very difficult for the people as they feared invasion and paid great taxes. As time passed, Maxentius became very unpopular. It was time for Constantine to attack.

"We will take care of him," Nickus said. "He is much less a warrior than his father."

"I will show them what a great army is all about," Constantine said. "I will take one quarter of our army to capture Segusium."

After Constantine captured Segusium, many in northern Italy rejoiced and helped his army. The gates of Milan were opened to him. After he secured the town, he and his troops rested for a month.

"I could learn to like Milan," Constantine said.

"I like the Rhine River valley," Nickus said. "Milan is nice to visit."

He thanked the people of Milan and had a barrel of silver coins distributed to those who helped. Then they marched south.

"You have done a fine job with the cavalry," Constantine said. "Their cavalry is no match to ours. It is just a matter of time."

"When their large army is defeated by a few of our troops, it discourages them," Nickus said. "Our men are better prepared both physically and mentally."

Constantine's army marched toward Rome. They continued to show patience.

During this time, Maxentius was openly mocked by the people. His army was discouraged and restless. They couldn't wait any longer. They built a temporary structure to cross the Tiber River and attacked Constantine's troops. Constantine's cavalry, wearing their new emblazoned armor, easily split the line of Maxentius' troops and forced them into the Tiber River. Constantine's army's armor shone brightly in the sunlight.

"Charge!" Nickus commanded. "Kill them! Drown them! They are helpless. This is what we came to Italy to accomplish."

Maxentius' troops were confused and tried to escape, but they were completely surrounded. The men were stunned by the efficiency of Constantine's troops. Many bodies floated down the Tiber River. People gathered along the river bank and cheered Constantine's troops. It was no contest. Constantine's troops slaughtered Maxentius' army.

"All in a day's work," Constantine's troop hollered. "Our new armor with our battle symbol gave us spirit."

They waved to those along the edge of the river.

"It was a good idea to give each of our men a coin and new armor for their victory charge," Nickus said. "I wondered why you had us bring the coins and armor all this way."

"Our men were invincible," Constantine said. "They deserve to have a good time. Prepare for a grand entrance into Rome. I want the local people to see our troops. I want them to see a real army."

The soldiers groomed themselves, cleaned their armor, combed their horses, and then entered Rome. They were greeted by a cheering and crying crowd.

After a few days, Constantine negotiated with the senate. He showed compassion for the followers of Maxentius. He had Maxentius' head put in a box and sent to his enemy in Egypt. Statues of Constantine were erected throughout Rome. Constantine insisted that the arches and statues contain both pagan and Christian symbols. The arch commemorating Constantine's victory at the Battle of the Milvian Bridge was built. It contained Christian symbols. When it was dedicated, he allowed sacrifices to the pagan Gods while he thanked his Christian God. Constantine tried diligently to please everyone. A large campaign to remove Maxentius' statues and his name from monuments and buildings began.

Constantine's present to the commander of his enemy in Egypt was delivered.

"You have received a box," his aid said. "It is from Constantine."

"I wonder what he is sending me," the king of Egypt said. "He is not my friend, even if we are part of the eastern empire."

"He can't scare us," the aid said. "Our country is greater than his."

"He is a great ruler," the king said. "I don't want to fight him."

"I will open it for you," he said.

He opened the box and gasped. He dropped the box.

"It is a head," he said. "I will read you the message."

"A head?" the king asked. "Whose head would he send to me?"

King of Egypt

> May the sun always shine on you.
> > I am sending you the head of Maxentius.
> > He chose to fight my army.
> > If you chose to fight, I will put your head in a box.
> > I look forward to receiving your letter of recognition.
>
> Constantine

"I think he has been fairly clear," the aid said. "Do you plan to oppose his rule?"

The king didn't hesitate.

"No," he said. "Send him a letter of recognition. I like my head on my shoulders."

His aid thought for a moment.

"I don't think we should just give in," the aid said. "He is a long way from us."

"He has been building and training his army for years," the king said. "He is a patient man. He doesn't fight men; he fights time."

"It sounds like you are afraid," the aid said. "He is just bluffing."

"He doesn't bluff," the king said. "He prepares. Do you want to lead our army against him?"

The aid sensed the king felt cornered. He coughed.

He didn't want to be sent to fight against Constantine, so he changed his tactics.

"Maybe you are correct," the aid said. "He has always been a just ruler. He likes to build as we do."

"He even appreciates libraries," the king said. "We are far away and won't cause him any problems."

The king and his aid spent the next hour rationalizing their good decision not to fight Constantine. They concluded that peace was the best choice for them.

The King of Egypt acknowledged Constantine's rule. The emperor focused his attention on other problem areas.

Constantine was now in a position to arrange for his mother to be a part of the imperial court. He met with Nickus and discussed her return.

"I will send for her," Nickus said. "No one is going to give us any problems."

"I wish I could have helped her sooner," he said. "She has always been my rock."

He looked at the sky. He saw a cloud shaped like a cross and said a silent prayer.

When Constantine returned home, he announced to Fausta the he had sent for his mother, and that she would be living in the palace. Within a few weeks, the troops had located Helena. She was pleased and ready to return to her son. They packed her belongings, put her into a carriage, and took her to the palace. Constantine, Fausta, their two sons, Constantine II and Constantius II, and their daughter greeted her.

"We will try to help you adjust to our family and life style," Fausta said. "I will help in any way I can."

"I am sure we will have some awkward moments," she said. "I have lived through many of them."

Constantine thought it was time for the east to become part of Constantine's Roman Empire. Constantine's mother urged him to meet with Licinius in Milan. After many long and difficult discussions with Helena and Nickus, Constantine, in the year three hundred and thirteen met with Licinius. They discussed many political issues. After most of these issues were agreed upon, Constantine insisted they create a written understanding that they both would issue. It was to be a document that gave those living in the Roman Empire freedom of religion. He insisted that the Christians would no longer be persecuted. Constantine was certain that the edict was politically sound and would increase his popularity. He also realized it would please his mother, and he desperately wanted to please her. He felt poorly that he allowed her to be kept in the emperor's court for such a long period of time. When the written agreement was sent out, the eastern version wasn't exactly like the western version. Christian bishops throughout the Roman Empire read the agreement to their congregations. The agreement marked a great achievement for Constantine.

In the year three hundred fourteen, Emperor Constantine convened a meeting of Christian bishops at Arles. Constantine used this council to put an end to the problems concerning Donatists in Northern Africa. They insisted the previous two councils were flawed and not valid. Like the previous councils, Constantine condemned the Donatists and the material they used.

As the years passed Licinius didn't keep his part of the agreement and began to persecute Christians. Constantine was not pleased with Licinius' decision to ignore their agreement. He ordered Nickus to prepare the army to fight.

"If a man isn't willing to follow an understanding, it really isn't an understanding," Constantine said. "He shouldn't have given me and the people in the eastern portion of the empire his word. We will have to teach him a lesson."

Constantine's army marched against Licinius' army.

"When we defeat this lying rebel, there will only be one emperor," Constantine said. "I will be glad to have peace."

"You can leave the fighting to me and our troops," Nickus said. "It is time for you to rule and enjoy your family."

Constantine's army won victory after victory.

"His army will destroy us," Licinius' commander said. "We don't have much of chance of defeating him."

Licinius became furious.

"If you can't handle our army, I will find someone who wants the job," he said. "Our army is larger than his army."

"Size isn't everything," he said. "His army is skilled and ready to fight. Our army is fat and lazy."

Licinius walked away.

Finally, after the battle of Chrysopolis, Licinius and his commander surrendered. The meeting took place in Nicomedia. Constantine allowed them to live as private citizens for a few years, and then he had them killed. Licinius wasn't Constantine's only problem. He often lamented that religious differences caused major divides among people and were often carried over into politics. Although he tried to appease the greatest number of his followers, he did take strong stances against those who consistently opposed his definition of the orthodox Christian Religion.

After Constantine conferred with his mother's priest, Eusebius, he felt compelled to squelch the efforts of the Christian Arius of Alexandria.

"North Africa seems to be at odds with my understandings," Constantine said. "I wish they could solve their internal problems and settle their differences with our church."

"Some of their bishops have illegal church properties and writings," Eusebius said. "Arius uses John's writings as the foundation of his beliefs. He isn't a bad person; he just interprets scripture differently than the most orthodox."

"They don't even know enough to celebrate Easter on the proper day," Constantine said. "I will straighten them out."

The power of the orthodox Christian church was becoming evident. The church in North Africa decided to bury their non-orthodox scrolls and icons. They put them in jars and either hid them in caves or buried the jars deep in the sand. They continued their beliefs in secret, but professed mainline religion. Constantine was convinced that producing a written understanding was important. His mother's ideas were represented at many church counsels where the future direction of the church was being decided. She firmly believed that Easter should be celebrated on Sunday.

Later, Constantine went to see the pope.

"Hello, Sylvester," Constantine said. "We have made a lot of progress. Not everyone agrees, but we are moving forward."

"You are a great emperor," Sylvester said. "Why have you taken time to visit with me?"

"I am not feeling well," he said. "I don't have the energy I once had. I itch and my skin flakes."

"It sounds like leprosy," he said. "I don't think anyone can cure leprosy. I don't know of any cure for leprosy."

"I want you to pray for me," he said. "Maybe your prayers can cure me. If you cure me, I will help the church, and specifically, your office."

"Kneel with me," he said. "I will put my hands on you and ask the Lord to cure your illness. I can only ask. He must do the curing. Have you been baptized?"

"No, not yet," he said. "I am not ready. I will be baptized just before I die."

"What if you are killed?" he asked.

"I plan to wait," he said. "I want to be baptized just before I die. Then all my sins will be washed away, and I won't have time to sin."

"That is strange logic," the pope said.

"Please understand me," he said. "I am not ready to be baptized."

Constantine excused himself.

The pope was puzzled by Constantine's ideas about baptism. He quietly wished Constantine well and prayed daily for him.

CHAPTER 5

CONSTANTINE'S NEW CAPITAL – CONSTANTINOPLE

Constantine was certain he had resolved the religious problems between the eastern and the western regions of the empire. He planned a new capital to signify that the Roman Empire was politically united and was in the process of determining its location. Rome was too far from the frontier, and it was home to many who lived by manipulating politics. He considered several cities, but insisted on a city with a strategic location. When Constantine's enemies surrendered, it was as if the pagan gods had surrendered. Churches became a greater priority of Constantine's building program and the persecution of Christians was stopped. After Helena returned to the imperial court, her Christian religion influenced Constantine. He legalized Christianity, but remembered that many of his followers were pagan. He appeased them by observing the day of the sun. Many churches began to teach the lessons of Jesus on Sundays. His new capital would have a mint greater than Nicomedia.

Constantine considered the city of Byzantium and met with Nickus.

"I am considering Byzantium as the new location for the capital," Constantine said. "It is well situated and is an easy sail to the Istrius River."

He looked at Nickus for approval. Nickus looked at the floor.

"What do you think?" he asked.

"I am not in favor of it," Nickus said. "The location is good, but Nicomedia, Smyrna or Ephesus would be better accepted."

Constantine became defensive.

"Ephesus' harbor has been a problem," Constantine said. "Smyrna might satisfy our needs, but its harbor is not nearly as good. Byzantium has a great harbor."

"I agree. Byzantium has good potential," he said. "But, why not start with a great city and make it better?"

"I like the layout," Constantine said. "It is styled like a Roman city."

"You are about to make a mistake," Nickus said. "I don't want to be part of the process that makes Byzantium our capital."

Constantine was stunned. He stood and approached Nickus.

"I don't understand your position," Constantine said. "We have worked together a long time."

"I am trying to be as straight forward as I can," Nickus said. "You need to seek more information before making such a decision."

"I am willing to do that," Constantine said. "I understand that this is a very important decision and will influence many lives."

"I have visited many cities with you," Nickus said. "Byzantium would be my last choice for the new location of the capital. I think the capital of the empire should be more centrally located."

Nickus explained to Constantine that he didn't want to cause problems. He had planted his roots in the western portion of the empire and he considered it his home. He also explained that he was getting older and hoped to start a family.

"Send me back to Gaul," Nickus said. "I will remain faithful and lead the army of the west."

Constantine hesitated. He rubbed his hands together.

"I could do that for you," he said. "You have served the empire well."

Nickus walked to Constantine and shook his hand.

"I will miss you," he said. "You won't be disappointed in me."

"I am disappointed in your decision," Constantine said. "Goodbye, my friend. God go with you always."

Constantine worried that he might be making the wrong decision. He valued Nickus' opinion, and his departure was a blow to his confidence.

He contacted the chief of the navy in the east part of the empire, Captain Gruffus. They met in Constantine's office.

"I want you to visit several cities for me," he said. "I have chosen you because you have sailed the seas for many years. I want you to evaluate several harbors for me."

"It would be an honor to work directly for you," he said.

"I want a written report concerning the suitability of the harbors," he said. "I don't want you to tell me about them from your experience. This is important enough to have you spend the next six months sailing and gathering data for me. Having current information will allow me to make the best decision."

"Where do you want me to go?" he asked.

"Byzantium, Ephesus, and Smyrna," he said. "Bring me a detailed written report.

Captain Gruffus sensed that his findings were very important to Constantine. He met with his first mate, and they loaded their ship with supplies and sailed.

Nickus returned to Gaul. His spirit was low, but he remained faithful to Constantine. They stayed in contact with each other. Constantine didn't want to lose the services of Judge, so he met with him and discussed Byzantium.

"I want to relocate our capital city," he said. "My mother has convinced me to call the new city Constantinople. What do you think of the name?"

"I like the name," Judge said.

"I think Byzantium would be a great location for a new capital city," he said. "What do you think?"

Judge hesitated.

"I really haven't thought about it," he said. "You decide where the capital should be located; I want to be involved with the design and fixtures for the palace."

Constantine was pleased with his answer.

"I will ensure the master builder talks with you about the palace and includes your ideas," he said. "Make certain we have ample room for many attendants and servants."

"Yes, sir," Judge said. "I will write down my ideas. We can make the new palace more efficient than what we have had in the past."

"I hope you like Constantinople," Constantine said. "If you need anything, just ask for it."

"I'm not going anywhere," he said. "I'm not sure what was bothering Nickus. Have you chosen his replacement?"

"No. Do you have any suggestions?"

"I know of a young man who would be a good liaison," he said. "You could trust him to do whatever you need accomplished."

"Have him come and see me," he said.

"His name is Yesus," Judge said.

"That is a good name," he said. "I think I will like him."

The following afternoon, Constantine talked with Yesus. He asked about his family and his military career. Yesus was straight forward and quick with his answers. Constantine was impressed. Before the afternoon was over, Constantine chose Yesus as his liaison to the military.

"Your first job is to have the aqueduct system improved," Constantine said. "Right now, it can't supply enough water for the expanded city."

"I will talk to a builder," he said. "Aqueducts are always being built or repaired."

"After Constantinople becomes the capital, many people will move there," he said. "We will build a city where everyone will want to live."

"We have seven hills. That is a good start," Yesus said. "I think this is an excellent location for the new capital. It is on the trade route between east and west."

Constantine was impressed with Yesus knowledge of the area.

"We will need a new palace and many buildings," Constantine said. "This will be the major government city."

"I will have a grand street designed," Yesus said. "It will be lined with great buildings and trees. I will have the street constructed so wide, fire won't be able to jump across it. Whenever a fire starts in the older cities, they are not safe."

"I want several large public parks," he said. "We will need a public library."

"I will commence with the construction," Yesus said. "This will be like building an entirely new city."

"Expanding old buildings and constructing new ones is always exciting," Constantine said. "Ensure the palace has large, very hot, baths."

"Yes, sir," he said. "I will ensure the palace's fortification system has many towers."

"I like towers and domes," he said. "Provide quarters for twenty troops in a separate building on the palace grounds."

Yesus thought for a moment.

"We could give a piece of land to anyone who could afford to move to Constantinople and develop the land," Yesus said. "We could provide public gardens for food and gardens for flowers."

"Giving away land is a good idea," Constantine said. "That will bring rich people to the capital. They will like chariot racing. Build an arena that will seat one hundred thousand people."

Constantine hesitated. He looked at Yesus.

"The pagan temples can be a source of building materials," he said. "I have seen several doors I like."

"I will have doors and ornaments from the temples throughout the empire sent to us," Yesus said. "That will reduce construction time."

Everywhere Constantine looked, new buildings were under construction. The sound of construction was like music to his ears. He walked the new streets and scrutinized the buildings projects. He was especially intrigued by the new palace and anticipated its completion. He took Judge on a tour of the construction site.

"Builder, when will the new palace be completed?" Constantine asked. "I am ready to move in. I spend too much time in my carriage."

Judge answered Constantine.

It will be a few more months," he said. "They have incorporated many of my ideas. I hope you like them."

After they toured the palace, Constantine went to his office. Captain Gruffus returned from his trip and presented his report to Constantine. The report stated that Byzantium had the best harbor. The report contained many pages of facts and figures. When the sailors departed, Yesus entered Constantine's office. He inquired about the sailors and then changed the subject.

"Have you seen Judge recently?" Yesus asked. "He indicated Crispus is spending a lot of time with Fausta."

"I am sure they are packing for the move to the new palace," he said. "Everyone is very busy."

"Part of the new palace is completed," Yesus said. "We relocated some of the furnishings to the new palace."

"I desire mostly new furnishings," Constantine said. "Tell Judge to choose whatever he likes."

The palace was finished, and the royal family relocated. The name of the city was officially changed to Constantinople, and the work continued. One evening after dinner in the new palace, Constantine thought he saw Crispus and Fausta in a compromising situation and confronted Crispus.

"Son, what were you doing with Fausta?" Constantine asked. "She is my wife."

"I know," Crispus said. "She is closer to my age than she is to yours."

Constantine grew very angry. Crispus' answer stabbed him like a sword.

"We brought four children into this world," he said.

Crispus looked at Constantine and smiled. Constantine was furious.

"Her next child will be mine," he said.

Constantine summoned a guard. He realized he had to control himself.

"Do you realize what you are saying?" Constantine asked. "How many people know about this?"

Crispus realized he was in serious trouble.

"I don't know," he said. "A few of the staff might suspect something."

"You have disgraced me, my son. I want to set an example for people to follow," he said. "As a Christian emperor, I have unquestionable family values. You haven't given me much choice about what I must do."

Crispus looked at Constantine. A worried look appeared on his face.

"Divorce her like your father divorced your mother," Crispus said. "But don't expect me to marry her. I want a younger woman who will be faithful."

Constantine grabbed Crispus and threw him to the floor. The guard stood over Crispus. Then Constantine walked away.

Constantine met with Yesus the next day. He seemed uneasy and talked in a soft tone. Yesus had to move closer to him so he could hear what he was saying.

"I have a secret job for you," Constantine said. "We will discuss it later. Just do it."

"Yes, sir," Yesus said. "What is it?"

"I want you to kill my oldest son, Crispus," he said. "He has disgraced our family."

Yesus looked at Constantine and left the office. He realized this wasn't the time to ask questions. He found Crispus, and they walked outside to a new flower garden that had just been built.

"How do you like the new palace and grounds?" Yesus asked. "I like open spaces."

"You didn't bring me here to look at flowers," Crispus said. "What do you want?"

"I have a present for you," he said.

He reached into his waistband, removed a dagger, and stabbed Crispus. Crispus gasped. He leaned forward, grabbed his chest, and fell to the ground. Yesus rolled him over with his foot. Crispus was dead. Yesus removed his royal robes and hid Crispus' body. He returned to the troops and ordered two of them to follow him. They found the body and buried it among the flowers. The soldiers didn't know who they buried and didn't question Yesus.

The following day, Yesus met with Constantine.

"The assignment you gave me is completed," Yesus said. "Eventually, someone is going to ask questions."

"I will take care of that," Constantine said. "If anyone questions you, tell them to see me."

Helena became very curious of Crispus' whereabouts, and she asked Constantine if he had sent Crispus to war. Constantine explained to his mother what he had witnessed between Crispus and Fausta, his discussion with Crispus about the matter, and the order he gave to Yesus. Helena looked directly at Constantine.

"You should also have her killed," she said, unemotionally. "She is a disgrace to you and the empire. I am certain some people know what was going on. We are Christians. You can't condone such behavior."

Constantine was surprised by his mother's cool reaction and hesitated for a few moments.

"I can forgive her," Constantine said. "She didn't choose me. Her father used her as payment for favors."

"She isn't good for us," she said. "Don't be concerned. You don't have to do anything. I will take care of it."

"She has given me three sons," he said. "I love her."

"She doesn't love you," she said. "It will look like an accident. You can have any women in the empire."

Constantine was upset, but he understood his mother's position. He wanted to do what was best for the empire. He put his hands behind him and walked around for a few moments.

"Be careful," he said. "This isn't a good situation. What are people going to think?"

"I am confident their minds will play tricks on their souls," she said. "No one will know for certain. If anyone gives us any problems, have them killed."

Constantine and Helena walked into the flower garden. They were seated at a table, and the servants brought them tea.

The next week, Fausta was found dead in the palace's hot baths. A messenger delivered the news to Constantine. He was heartbroken. When Constantine questioned Helena, she told him the details of Fausta's death. The following day, he saw Judge and requested a proper burial for Fausta. He wanted it to be a burial for the wife of the emperor. A grand ceremony was held at the military auditorium. Many citizens saw this as an opportunity to meet their emperor and attended the ceremony. A marble tomb was built in the town park, and Fausta was put to rest.

Now, without interference from Fausta, Helena began to exert more control over her son. When Constantine was at home, she was with him. She wanted to be involved with every decision.

"Not everyone is treating me with ultimate respect," Helena said. "It is just you and me. Your sons will be emperor, someday."

"It might take them a while," Constantine said. "Our people will understand that you are my mother and must be respected. I will make certain of it."

"I want to help you," she said. "I have many ideas for you to consider."

Constantine looked at his mother and smiled.

"I will always consider your ideas," he said.

"When will the construction be finished?" Helena asked. "I want a church."

"Most of the city's improvements and government building projects are completed," Constantine said. "I will have a church built for you."

"I want a church built on the site of the temple to Aphrodite," she said. "It should be a magnificent church."

"That might be a controversial site," he said. "Must it be built there?"

"Yes," she said. "I want our church to make a statement."

Constantine was not pleased with his mother's insistence on the church's location.

"Building a church will make a statement," he said. "If you are involved, it will be a greater statement."

"I want that site," Helena said. "You owe it to me. I took care of your problem. No one suspects us."

Constantine bowed his head. He knew he had to comply with his mother's request.

"Don't remind me," Constantine said. "Can't you choose a different site? Why make my life difficult?"

Helena looked at Constantine and smiled.

"No," she said. "Don't you want me to help you? Don't you trust me?"

"Yes," he said. "You are my most trusted ally."

"Then have the temple destroyed," she said. "Design my church."

"I need to think about this." He said. "It is a big decision."

"It isn't that big of a problem. Have a builder see me," she said. "I'll give him some ideas."

"I will have our best master builder design it," Constantine said. "He designed the palace."

"Tell him that I want five domes," she said. "I want it shaped like a cross."

When asked why he wanted the church built at that location, Constantine replied that he had a dream that an angel led him to the spot. He made certain the builder understood all the details that Helena desired. The construction of the church was a spectacle that the people regularly visited and discussed. When the priests, at the Church of the Holy Apostles, commenced with services, so many people attended that some people had to be seated outside on the lawn. The entire town wanted to see Helena's church.

The following week, Helena met with Constantine.

"I want gold coins minted to commemorate the new church," she said. "Make thousands of them. No silver; only gold."

"I like new coins," he said. "I will put a picture of the church on the reverse side of the coin."

"Put your likeness on the front of the coin," Helena said. "I want people to know you are a Christian."

"We will design a beautiful coin," Constantine said. "I will tell Yesus to have them minted."

Constantine secretly worried about making a public statement about being a Christian.

The following day, Constantine saw Yesus and explained Helena's idea.

"Yes, sir," Yesus said. "I will see the manager of the mint."

"I am counting on you. Ensure he understands it is Helena's idea," Constantine said. "Get us a few of the first coins that are minted."

"I will use the gold we take from the pagan temples to make the coins," he said. "Gold is our standard."

"What should we do with the beautiful bronze statues from the pagan temples?" Yesus asked. "They are too nice to destroy."

"The really nice ones we will keep," he said. "The others will become coins."

"That will be a lot of coins," Yesus said. "Do we need that many coins?"

"Don't question me," Constantine said. "I am sending two government officials to each territory to manage the confiscation of bronze, silver, and gold from the temples."

"Yes, sir," he said. "I apologize."

"It is easier to take the metal from the temples than it is to have it mined," he said. "It also sends a statement to the pagans."

"I understand," Yesus said. "I will show you the bronze statues we might want to keep."

"I don't need to see them," he said. "Modify them and have them placed throughout the city. Build another town park. Place them in the public park and include statues of me."

Constantine and Yesus found a large level piece of land and set it aside for a park. They chose the types of trees they desired and instructed the builder to include several gardens. The builder used indigenous plants that would grow bright, colorful flowers. He met with Constantine and Yesus.

"I like the land the city acquired for the new park," he said. "I am having trees and flowers delivered from cities throughout the empire."

"We don't want any plant that won't survive in this climate," Yesus said. "We want things that are beautiful and smell sweet."

"Arrange the trees so the troops can ride their horses between them," he said. "I want everything to be symmetric. I want the park to look like a great amount of planning went into the design."

"I am glad you told me about how you want the trees placed," the builder said. "I will make a drawing indicating where to plant them."

"The master builder has designed an arch for the entrance to the park," Yesus said. "The arch will be decorated with likenesses of you."

"When construction of the park is completed, be certain to tell me," he said. "I am looking forward to visiting it."

"I plan to include fruit and nut trees," the builder said. "They will attract children and other animals."

"Children should not be thought of as animals," Constantine said. "They are just little people."

"Sorry, sir," he said. "I would also like to suggest building a lake."

"A lake will attract birds," Constantine said. "Include the lake. Did mother tell you she wants a museum?"

Constantine smiled at the builder.

"I can build a museum," he said. "I will build the new museum adjacent to her church."

"This city will have everything our citizens could desire," Constantine said. "I want you to build a new market close to the new residential area."

In an effort to retain the interest of the rich, Constantine gave them seats in the Senate. He carefully appointed only skilled horsemen, who were lifelong soldiers, to positions of military leadership. This was a good decision and seemed to satisfy most of his followers.

"You are making many changes to the government," a senator said. "It is important that you retain us and allow us to advise you."

"You are important to me," he said. "Our military leaders must be willing and ready to fight for the empire."

The old senator understood Constantine wasn't about to change things again at this time. He didn't want to offend the emperor, so he complimented Constantine on the new park.

"Your leaders will bring power and social status to our new government," he said. "The government in Rome is dying. Your ideas will lead us forward."

"I will prepare my sons to lead," he said. "I want this capital and our government to last forever."

"I have an idea that will increase your popularity," the senator said. "No one will oppose it."

"What is your idea?" he asked.

"I think we need a food program for the poor," he said. "It could be a program such as the one in Rome."

"Yes, Rome's program was popular," Constantine said. "It must be administered fairly."

"It will help us be a great city," he said. "Great cities help their poor and their children."

"Choose someone to lead the food program," Constantine said.

"We will start the program immediately."

Constantine smiled at the senator and said, "Ensure everyone knows I was involved with the decision."

"It is a good decision," the senator said. "We will make a public announcement and start distribution of food."

As a Christian emperor, Constantine was always sensitive to those in government who were not practicing Christianity. He appointed both pagan and Christians to the senate. When Constantine thought of additional ideas to make it an even greater city, construction was almost completed. He talked with the leader of the senate.

"I would like you to make a list of programs and building that exist in Rome, but aren't in Constantinople," Constantine said. "I am certain you can help me with making this city greater than Rome."

"I have been to Rome a few times," he said. "I like their buildings, but getting to the city from the Great Sea is a problem. We have a much better location."

Constantine liked what he heard.

"I will talk with the other senators," the senate leader said. "I think you should also ask the military leaders."

Constantine went back to the palace. He requested a body guard for Helena.

"Some people think Helena had Fausta killed," Constantine said. "I want her to have a soldier with her at all times. Post a guard outside her quarters."

Judge thought for a moment.

"Noah is the man," Judge said. "He has served as your body guard on occasion. I will have him assigned to Helena."

"How can we improve the image of our military?" Constantine asked. "Give it some thought. Talk with a few of the officers."

After a week, Judge saw Constantine and approached him.

"We are on the sea," he said. "Have a great ship built. Form a mounted group to parade in functions. Give them beautiful horses and saddles. Place a special guard in the public parks."

Constantine smiled at Judge.

"You are full of ideas," he said. "Get busy putting them in place. Let me know what you are doing. I will take care of the ship."

Constantine sent a message to Captain Gruffus who had visited the harbors and written the detailed report. He asked him to come to his office. When he arrived, Constantine asked him if he thought they needed a new ship.

"Yes, sir," he said. "We haven't had a new ship in many years. The newer ships are much faster than ours."

"Get with a ship designer and bring me a set of plans. We will have a new ship built," he said. "I want it to be impressive. When people visit the harbor, I want them to notice our great ship."

The captain stood and thanked Constantine. He said he would return in a month.

At the end of the month, Constantine met with the senate leader.

"Have you any other ideas?" Constantine asked. "The food program is doing well."

"We have two programs for you to consider," the leader of the senate said. "The first is an organized message system."

"Tell me more," he said. "What do you mean?"

"When we want to send a message," he said. "We don't know how long it will take for it to be delivered. Sometimes it is never delivered."

"You are suggesting the government have a dependable message delivery system," he said. "That is a novel idea."

"You will need someone to be responsible for the program," he said. "He would gather data about troop movement and the schedule of ships. You might even send a troop delivery on a regular schedule."

"I could assign troops," Constantine said. "It would be their military job to deliver messages."

"You could take the messages to the Istrius and have them delivered up the river," the senator said. "You could have messages shipped directly to Rome."

"Yes, I see," Constantine said. "We will set it up. I will have Yesus start working on it."

He looked at the senator.

"I almost hate to ask," he said. "What was your other idea?"

"Rome has a monopoly on religion," he said. "Elevate the status of our local clergy. Set an archbishop aside from the local church and give him regional responsibilities."

"All of the bishops should report to him," he said. "I could build him an impressive office with a small Chapel."

Constantine remembered Helena's suggestion that her uncle, Eusebius of Nicomedia, be elevated to bishop. He reasoned that if he approved of the position for an archbishop, the priest would certainly promote Eusebius.

"Eusebius will bring Arianism to the church," Constantine said. "That should work. It will please my mother. Things are good when she is happy."

Constantine remembered the counsel and those who followed the ideas of John. He hoped no one else would remember his decisions.

"He is a good politician," the senator said. "I think Eusebius has even tutored at the court. He is a well-liked priest."

"Yes, he can be persuasive," he said. "I have heard him."

"I would commission more new Bibles for the church," he said. "It would be a sign of your honor toward Jesus."

"Thank you for your ideas," he said. "You have been a big help."

Captain Gruffus returned. They went to a table in Constantine's office. The captain unrolled a set of plans. Constantine wasn't certain what he was looking at and asked a lot of questions. Gruffus sensed his lack of understanding and carefully described a beautiful ship with several luxury cabins and three large sails. He pointed to the drawing of the finished ship. Constantine said he liked the idea and he wanted it built. The captain indicated that construction would take about one year.

Constantine met with Judge, Yesus, and other military leaders to implement the ideas. He carefully reviewed each idea with them and planned the details. Yesus discussed the message delivery system with a sergeant.

"You want the military to be responsible for messages sent by civilians?" the sergeant asked. "That seems strange."

"Extra messages will allow us to establish a regular delivery," Judge said. "You could charge a fee based on the destination of the message."

"The fee could help pay for the additional troops, horses, and carriages," Constantine said. "Most of the messages will be sent by rich people."

"We could develop a route that stops at all of the major fortification twice a month," Judge said. "Knowing when messages will be delivered is a good thing."

"We will have to establish a separate division of troops just to deliver messages," the sergeant said. "It may work."

"The more we discuss the idea, the more I like it," Constantine said. "Sergeant, work out the details."

"I will post a statement in the public square," Yesus said. "I want everyone to know about our new service. I might even send my mother a message."

"We don't want too many mother messages," Judge said. "I will make sure the fee eliminates all but urgent messages."

The message delivery system proved to be very popular. Constantine built new quarters for the messengers. They also built new separate stables for their horses. Constantine got personally involved with selecting the new horses.

"I like the black one," he said. "Do you think he would make a good horse for the messengers?"

"Color doesn't matter," Yesus said. "I like him because he has thick legs and is tall."

Constantine allowed Yesus and the troops to select the remaining horses.

Constantine chose only Christians to fill the very top level administrative positions. The citizens of Constantinople could take their private messages to a government office and receive an accurate estimate of when it would be delivered. A special fee was charged if the message was delivered by ship. Constantine received a message.

Constantine

Emperor of the Roman Empire
    May God continue to bless you and your mother.
    Emperor Hadrian had a temple built on holy grounds to honor Aphrodite.
    I would like you to use the power of the empire to destroy the temple.
    The burial and resurrection site of our Lord should be preserved and honored.
    I am writing this message with the approval of your archbishop.

His Holiness
Sylvester

Constantine read the message several times. He didn't want to arouse his mother so he didn't tell her about the pope's message. He responded to Sylvester.

His Holiness
Sylvester

May the Lord show us his way.
    I agree with your request.

I will discuss it with our archbishop.

I will have my military man, in Jerusalem,

investigate the temple and site.

He will advise you of any actions taken 6by the government.

Constantine

Emperor of Roman Empire

He sent for the local archbishop, Paul. They met in Constantine's office.

"I have received a message from the pope," Constantine said. "He said you and he have been discussing Hadrian's temple to Aphrodite."

"That is correct," Paul said. "Many of the priests consider the temple an affront to our Lord."

"You should have come to me before you sent a message to the pope," he said. "I have always helped you."

"Before I bothered you, I wanted to be sure the pope was in agreement," he said. "When I sent him a message, he answered he would contact you, and then you would contact me."

"That didn't work exactly the way you had it planned, did it?" Constantine asked.

"No," Paul said. "It didn't."

"I would like you to go with one of my master-builders to the temple," he said. "Gather as much information as possible and when you return we can talk. I will pay your expenses."

Paul looked up and put his hands together. Then he looked at Constantine.

"Tell me when the ship sails," he said. "I have always wanted to visit Jerusalem."

Two weeks later, the archbishop, the master builder, and several troops sailed to Jerusalem. Constantine remained in Constantinople.

"I went to see the archbishop today," Helena said. "He was not home. They told me, he went to Jerusalem."

"Yes, that is correct," Constantine said. "He told me he would be gone for a while."

"Do you know why he went to Jerusalem?" she asked.

"He told the priests he had never been to Jerusalem," Constantine said. "He was going to visit several churches and holy sites."

"That would be a fun trip," she said. "I will talk with him when he returns."

"I will also be interested in talking with him," Constantine said. "I hope he has a good time."

"I am certain he will," she said. "Constans is growing up. Why don't you give him a horse?"

Constantine was puzzled.

"How did we get from the archbishop to Constans?" he asked.

"You told me you were good at choosing horses," she said. "I thought you might like to purchase him a horse."

"I will talk with him," he said. "Did he tell you he wanted a horse?"

"No," she said. "It is time for him to learn to ride. When I was his age, I could ride."

"Not everyone is as good a horseman as you," he said. "I am certain he will learn to ride."

"I am a horsewoman," Helena said.

She dropped the subject and asked the servant to bring them tea. They walked outside into the flower garden.

"I love this garden," she said. "The flowers grow especially well here. You must have a good gardener."

She picked a flower and smelled it. Then, she handed it to Constantine. He held it by his side. He didn't smell it but carried it with him until they went inside. Constantine saw Judge.

"I am going to bed," he said. "You can extinguish most of the candles. I will see you in the morning."

"Good night, sir," Judge said. "That is a beautiful flower; do you want me to put it in water?"

As time passed, many of the ideas provided by the senate and the military were implemented and worked very well. Constantine noted the value of discussing things before making a decision.

CHAPTER 6

CONSTANTINE INVITED BISHOPS TO NICAEA

The Emperor Constantine's Christian belief was greatly influenced by his mother, Helena. He learned to know his mother's religious teacher, Eusebius of Nicomedia, very well. He had also learned to know several Popes due to his popularity in the western part of the empire. He didn't consider himself an authority about Christianity, but because of his desire to learn more about Christianity and please his mother, he noted several differences in the messages that were taught within the church. When he asked his mother about the differences, she seemed indifferent.

"I believe what Eusebius, my priest, tells me," she said. "He is very knowledgeable and even studied in Antioch with the great Lucian."

As time passed, Constantine became more concerned with the disagreements within the church.

In an effort to resolve these differences and bring harmony to the church, he invited eighteen hundred bishops to attend an ecumenical council in the city of Nicaea. The invitations were made during the year of three hundred twenty-four and the council was to convene the following year. Constantine didn't really know the details of the differences and didn't plan to become overly involved with the discussions. He did demand that the bishops reach consensus. His invitation included payment for their travel expenses and each bishop was allowed to bring a few priests to the meeting. The Pope thought it was a perfect opportunity for his orthodox followers to present their beliefs to the emperor. The Pope wrote to each of his bishops and encouraged them to attend the council in Nicaea.

Constantine went to Rome and met with the Pope.

"I would like you to attend the council and oversee the proceedings," he said. "You may take as many priests as you desire. I will pay all the expenses."

Pope Sylvester thought for a moment. He didn't want to attend the conference, but he didn't want to offend the emperor.

"I am busy and can't stay away from Rome for an extended period of time," he said. "You can oversee the meeting, and I will approve the decision."

Constantine took his refusal personally and glared at the Pope.

"I have given the church much land and great wealth," he said. "The least you could do for me is to attend the meeting."

The Pope became worried about Constantine's reaction. He didn't want to lose the favor of the emperor.

"Because it is so important to you, I will send two legates," he said. "I will also recommend an official moderator for the council. If I attend the council, the bishops will be focused on me and not on the purpose of your meeting. I don't want to influence their decisions."

Constantine understood that the Pope wasn't going to attend the council. He wasn't certain that the Pope had revealed his real reason for not attending, but he accepted the Pope's proposal and returned to Constantinople.

When Eusebius of Caesarea received his invitation, he discussed the purpose of the council with his priests.

"It is important that we have a good representation at the council," he said. "Those from Africa will certainly voice their opinion. I don't want my friend, Arius, to find his position in the minority."

They decided to write messages to the bishops that his priesthood knew and encourage them to attend the council. He realized that most of the bishops that would attend the council would probably come from the orthodox eastern portion of the empire. He was concerned that the decision of the council would become a popularity contest instead of a consensus about Jesus' message. He sent a message to the Pope.

Sylvester
Bishop of Rome

Many of your bishops are concerned about the upcoming council at Nicaea.

If the emperor demands a consensus and then forces everyone to teach the same message, I don't believe that God's best interest will be represented.

Consensus are always a compromise and often result in very few being satisfied with the outcome.

I hope you are able to ensure our church is protected from itself and the influence of the Roman government.

Eusebius
The Bishop of Caesarea

Eusebius started to receive answers to the message he sent to the friends of his priesthood. Most indicated that they wouldn't attend the council. They felt if they attended the council, they would be bound by its decision. Eusebius realized that they would be bound by its decision even if they didn't attend, because the emperor would enforce the consensus.

Arius answered Eusebius' message and indicated that he would be at Nicaea, but because he wasn't a bishop he wouldn't be allowed to vote.

Eusebius
Bishop of Caesarea

Thank you for your concern about our religion.

It is a sad day when the emperor decides what priests are allowed to teach.

I look forward to seeing you and my other friends at Nicaea.

It is the outcome of the council that frightens me.

Arius
Priest

Eusebius received a message from Bishop Macarius. Macarius looked forward to the council and supported the church's orthodox view. He guaranteed Eusebius that the proper interpretation of Jesus' message would prevail. Eusebius began to believe his worst fears would come true.

After two months, Pope Sylvester answered his message.

> Eusebius
> Bishop of Caesarea
>
> I share your concerns that the outcome of the council at Nicaea might not be in the best interest of the church.
>
> The emperor has been to visit with me.
>
> I informed him that I am too busy to attend the council.
>
> I have recommended a moderator and will send several priest to represent me and the local churches.
>
> Constantine truly believes he is doing a good thing.
>
> He doesn't understand that the church has survived just fine for three hundred years without everyone agreeing on each point.
>
> Unfortunately, the church has asked the emperor, for his help in church matters in the past.
>
> That might prove to have been a mistake.
>
> Many of us firmly believe in the separation of the church and the government.
>
> I will have my representatives ensure that you have a chance to present your views.
>
> God be with us all.
>
> Sylvester
> The Bishop of Rome.

Eusebius was very disappointed with the Pope's decision not to attend the council and worried about the emperor's presence influencing many of the bishops.

Many in the priesthood through the church's members would be concerned about the upcoming council as they celebrated Jesus' birthday.

Early in the year, before the council in Nicaea, Hosius, an advisor to Constantine, presided over a council in Antioch that condemned Eusebius of Caesarea of being a follower of Arius. This action sent a strong signal to those invited to the council in Nicaea of what they might face.

CHAPTER 7

THE COUNCIL AT NICAEA

The city of Nicaea was located in a fertile valley in northwestern Analolia. Outside its wall hills rose in the north and south and beautiful Lake Askania stretched far to the west. The majesty of its public buildings was noted in history by Pliny the Younger. No one was certain why Constantine chose this rival city of Nicomedia for the location of a very important church council.

Arius and several of his supporters including Eusebius of Caesarea arrived at the palace in Nicaea during April of the year three hundred and twenty-five. When they arrived, they noted Hosius of Cordoba, the moderator of the council, and his team had prepared to conduct the proceeding following official government protocol. Arius was suspicious of Hosius because he had been a religious advisor to Constantine for many years. Each sect, within the church, gathered together and prepared their agenda.

Bishop Eusebius of Caesarea and his priests counted and listed more than two hundred and fifty bishops that arrived before the council officially started on May twentieth. The bishops would be the only attendees that voted. He estimated the total attendance to exceed two thousand members. Eusebius didn't count those that arrived late. Eusebius of Nicomedia gave a lengthy and pointed opening address. He questioned why so few of those invited chose to attend and addressed the importance of each decision that the council would make. He asked for their consideration of the entire church and not their individual interests.

Eusebius of Caesarea explained himself and the council exonerated him of wrong doing. One of the first topics of discussion was the controversy surrounding Arius' teachings. Before the council began, over twenty bishops encouraged Arius to speak about his understanding of Jesus' message. He spoke for two days. Most of the bishops attending the council were from the orthodox east, and they considered Arius' remarks to be blasphemous. Arius continued to address the council for an additional week, before his supporters addressed the bishops. During the middle of June, Constantine arrived and made a grand entrance. The bishops groveled for Constantine's attention for the next two days. Constantine introduced Paphnutius of Thebes to the council; he was an anti-Arian who suffered physical damage under Maximinus. When he stood, with the aid of a cane, a patch covered his missing eye. His appearance and speech for orthodoxy greatly influenced the members of the council. Finally, Constantine insisted that they return to the work at hand. The following day, Arius again addressed the council.

"Jesus, the Son, was created by God," he said. "Jesus was perfect among God's creatures, but when he was about to die he acknowledged he was not equal to God."

He looked at the bishops who mumbled to themselves, then he quoted from a scroll John, Jesus disciple, had written by his scribe, "You heard me say, 'I am going away and I am coming back to you.' If you loved me, you would be glad that I am going to the Father, for the Father is greater than I." (John, 14, 28, NIV)

The debate became very noisy and members stood and jeered Arius. Nicholas of Myra rushed Arius and struck him in the face. He fell to the floor injured. The members became quiet.

"He wants to destroy the Godhead," Athanasius said. "We can't allow his distorted view."

The bishops acted as a mob. It became necessary for Hosius to bring the members to order.

"Please be reverent representatives of the Pope and God," Hosius said. "Come to order and we will vote of Arius ideas."

The vote wasn't close. All of the bishops from the east voted against adopting any of Arius views. The council adjourned for the day.

Constantine spoke to Hosius.

"I'm not pleased that the bishops seem disinterested in discussion and are set on continuing to perform as they presently act," he said. "You failed when you went to Alexandria and discussed the differences with Alexander and Arius."

"That is why it became obvious to me that this council was needed," Hosius said. "That is why I recommend you talk with the Pope and convene this council."

"The council is fine, and maybe we will reach a consensus, but the differences won't be resolved," Constantine said. "Why didn't the many bishops from the west attend the council?"

"I don't know," he said. "The orthodox east and the Pope are very well represented."

"I wanted this council to represent the views of all Christians," he said. "When the empire offers to pay all expensed and people don't attend, something is wrong."

"Certainly the issues will be resolved," he said. "When the Pope signs, and gives his approval of the decisions of the consensus of the council, they will become generally accepted canon."

"I don't think you have a grasp of the situation," Constantine said. "I am disappointed with your advice; I should have listened to Eusebius of Nicomedia and my mother."

"You were wise to follow my advice," Hosius said. "You wanted consensus, and I made certain that you represented the winning side."

"It is worse than I thought," he said. "If we work as sides, we will always be divided."

Hosius was pleased with the progress the council had made and eagerly approached the following day.

The next day, the council discussed the date of celebration concerning Easter. Because the feast of Easter was associated with the Passover meal, many Christians observed Easter on the Jewish time for Passover. Other insisted that Jesus rose from the dead on Sunday, and that Easter should be celebrated only on a Sunday. After a few days of debate, the council voted that Easter would be celebrated on Sunday. It could be any Sunday after March twenty-first, but it must occur before the twenty-fifth of April. The council members hoped and prayed that the almost three hundred year old controversy was ended. It didn't end the controversy. A more exact way of determining the date for Easter was eventually developed.

The council then discussed Meletius of Lycopolis. He was a bishop in Egypt, and after spending time in prison during percussion, he was outspoken about the ease with which Lapses were readmitted into the church. He refused to allow them to take communion or be ordained a deacon. The council disagreed with the bishop, but they decided to be easy with Meletius and allowed him to remain a bishop in Lycopolis. He was stripped of all powers outside his region. He was humiliated and died soon after the council.

During the next month, the council created twenty canons related to church discipline

"I believe a person must do more than request to be baptized," Nicholas said. "They should familiarize themselves with the teachings of Jesus by completing a prescribed study."

"During this period of study, the candidate must accept the writings of Paul," a bishop said.

The council agreed and wrote a canon requiring a minimum term of catechumens.

"Before a bishop is ordained, he must appear before at least three bishops and be ordained by a bishop of a major city," a bishop said.

"I find it offensive when a member of the cleric allows the presence of younger women in his residence," a priest said.

The council established canons concerning standards for the conduct of the clergy.

The council decided it would provide for minimal punishment against the lapsed during the time of severe persecution.

"We should be Christians even when it isn't popular," Eusebius said. "Many have given their lives for God, as he gave his live for us."

"We must be tolerant of our members," Hosius said. "Jesus taught us to forgive. We must also learn to forget."

The council voted against Eusebius and was tolerant toward the lapsed.

A commonly used biblical canon wasn't a matter of formal discussion at the council. Most of the bishops were in agreement with the canon being used by Athanasius of Alexandria.

Constantine urged the council to create a summary of the Christian faith that represented the vast majority of those in attendance. Eusebius of Caesarea read a creed used in his largest church. The priests from Jerusalem objected to Eusebius' creed and read the creed they used in their churches. It was used as a basis for the creation of the council's creed, but it was greatly modified before it was presented to Constantine. After it was modified, Arius read the creed and found it to be totally unacceptable to him and his followers. The council started creating the creed by stating their approved articles of faith

> We believe in one God -
> And in one Lord Jesus Christ -
> The begotten of God the Father -

The council debated for many days about the use of the word begotten. They finally agreed that it best described the eternity of God, and that the Son was the true God. The words one and begotten were used over the objections of those that followed Arius.

The council thought it was important to stress things three times as many were familiar with Origen's use of the word trinity. They reached agreement after words from John's writings were read aloud to the bishops.

Macarius said, "John wrote 'I and the Father are one' (John, 10, 30, NIV)".

Many of the bishops from the western part of the empire hadn't used the idea of Mary being a virgin and debates raged for several days. It clearly signaled, to them, the inclusion of manmade ideas into the statement of faith. It became obvious to many in attendance that the more orthodox bishops had banned together and would not be swayed from their views. The bishops from the west considered departing, but stayed to honor God, the Pope, and Constantine.

The Holy Spirit wasn't debated by the council, but they devoted days concerning the body of Jesus. Many of the bishops by this point in time became disinterested in the events and simply voted yes to each section that was presented for vote. They figured that it could always be modified by their church to suit their congregations.

Toward the end of July, the council voted on consensus of the decisions made during the council. Eusebius of Nicomedia voiced his concern.

"I am not able to sign a consensus unless we continue to refine this creed," he said.

They eventually, out of respect for Constantine's mother, signed the creed. Three bishops signed the creed due to Constantine's presence, but retained their Arian beliefs. Several none bishops who had voiced strong objections were exiled by Constantine. They had no voting power, but were punished by those in authority.

Arius, Bishop Theonas of Marmarica, and Bishop Secundus of Polemais were excommunicated by the clergy, and Constantine exiled them to Illyricum. Constantine anathematized the writings of those who followed the Arian belief and had the scriptures burned.

At the end of the council, Constantine expressed his desire that the church live in harmony and in peace.

When Vitus and Vincentius, two legates of the Pope's who attended the council in Nicaea, arrived in Rome they advised the Pope about the decisions of the council. Due to his desire to please his friend the emperor, he approved the council's decisions. Constantine reacted and confirmed the Bishop of Rome senior to all other bishops.

CHAPTER 8

CONSTANTINE'S MOTHER VISITED THE HOLY LANDS

The results of the meeting in Nicaea weren't to Constantine's mother's liking. Her church priest tried to explain the situation to her, but she had problems understanding that her son, the emperor, didn't produce her desired results. Constantine sensed Helena's displeasure and went about trying to assuage her feelings. The Church of the Apostles' senior priest conducted services each week. The church's main section was completed and the extensions were under construction. The land for the museum, adjacent to the church, had been cleared. The stone cutters were on the construction site. One could visualize how the completed complex would be interconnected. Helena was pleased with the church. She was eager to have it furnished with relics from throughout the Christian world. She was in constant contact with many bishops and hoped they would bring presents for the church when they visited Constantinople. After services, one Sabbath, she talked with Constantine.

"This is a beautiful church," Helena said. "I love it."

"I am glad," Constantine said. "We are ahead of the construction schedule and will probably finish early. I will see you at the palace for dinner."

"I will talk with my friends for a while," she said. "I will see you tonight."

A few days later, Constantine scheduled a meeting with the town's most noted sculptor to commission a statue of his mother.

"It must be grand," he said. "I want her to appear as she looked when she was younger."

"I can do that," he said. "I have carved statues of many women."

"If I like the statue, I might purchase several," he said. "She has been through a lot and has always been faithful to me."

"I will do my best," he said. "My apprentices could probably make the copies for you."

That evening after Constantine's meeting with the sculptor; he returned to the palace and ate dinner with his mother.

"Good evening, mother," he said. "It is good to see you. Did you and your friends straighten out the priest?"

She looked at him.

"I hope your meeting was important," Helena said. "You left this morning while I was talking with a group of our friends."

"It was very important, or I would have stayed with you," he said. "If I embarrassed you, I am sorry."

"I handled it," she said. "In the future, it would be nice if you would let me know if you must leave."

"Sorry mother, I will give you advanced notice next time," he said. "I hope you enjoyed the lesson this morning."

"I like the changes you made concerning the clergy," she said. "I will invite our archbishop to visit with us."

He looked at Judge and motioned for the food to be served.

"That is nice mother," he said. "Do you know the archbishop?"

After dinner, Constantine and Helena retired to the living area. She seized the opportunity to discuss her latest idea with her son.

"Now that I have been given the title of Augusta," she said. "You can send me on a journey to the holy lands."

Constantine thought this request might be forthcoming. Helena exhibited great interested in the archbishop's trip to the Holy Lands.

He looked at his mother.

"It will be very strenuous," Constantine said. "Are you sure you can endure the trip?"

"Yes," she said. "And the treasury is full of silver and gold."

"I will send a military escort with you," he said. "He will protect you and make arrangements to ship your treasures back to our new museum."

"I hope I find something worthwhile," she said. "We need an important Christian relic to attract pilgrims to the new church."

"I am sure you will be able to locate something," he said. "I will have Judge make travel arrangements for you."

"Have him make arrangements for Constantina as well," she said. "I plan to take her along with me."

A smile came to Constantine's face.

"That is great," he said. "I spend a lot of time with my sons, but I neglect her. I am sure she will be a help to you."

"I am going to tell her not to call me grandmother," she said. "It makes me feel old."

"Have her call you mother," he said. "She won't mind."

"No," she said. "That isn't right. I have instructed her to call me Helena."

"What did she say to that?" he asked. "Addressing you by your first name seems impersonal."

One week later, Constantine talked with Judge about his mother's journey.

"I want you to choose guards to escort her and my oldest daughter," Constantine said. "Don't send Constantine II with her. The two of them might purchase the entire Holy Lands."

Judge smiled and nodded.

"I will choose their escorts very carefully," he said. "I will also make certain she travels on a ship with suitable accommodations."

"She will probably remain in the Holy Land for quite a while," he said. "Send a doctor with her. Make certain she receives the best of care."

"Are there any places in particular you want her to visit?" Judge asked. "I am sure she will want to see the sites associated with Jesus' life."

"I am working on the site of Hadrian's temple to the pagan Gods," Constantine said. "We control it. Let her think she is making the decisions on how it should be rebuilt."

"I got it," he said. "We will take good care of her. She will enjoy her time in the Holy Land. I will also ensure your daughter's safety."

"Arrange for them to live in suitable quarters in the old city," he said. "I have a few friends who live there."

"If I have everything arranged within a month's time, would that be satisfactory?" Judge asked. "I want to make certain everything is just right for them."

"Certainly," he said. "I will tell her to be ready to leave in a month."

That evening, Constantine and Helena enjoyed dinner while discussing her upcoming trip. She looked at Constantine.

"We are to leave in a month? I might not live that long!" Helena said. "I'm not getting any younger."

"I want everything to be just perfect," Constantine said. "I don't want to rush things."

"It seems like a long time," she said. "Do you think I should take Constans with me?"

"No," he said. "You and Constantina will be too busy. Leave him with me."

"Take good care of him," she said. "His brothers are always too busy with the military and horses to play with him."

"I will make certain he has plenty to do," he said. "Remember, he is seven years younger than Constantius II!"

"Constantina and I will be ready in one week," Helena said.

She put her hand over her heart and sighed. Then she pointed her finger at Constantine and laughed. He smiled at her. She drank a cup of warm milk and went to bed. Constantine talked with Judge for a few hours and then went to his room.

He arose early the next morning, ate breakfast, and went to his office.

"I have arranged for Samson to be your mother's escort," Yesus said. "He will pick the other escort soldiers."

"I have met Samson," Constantine said. "Tell him to make certain someone is always with Helena and not to leave Constantina alone."

"Yes, sir," he said. "He was told it might be a two year assignment."

Two days later, Samson provided Yesus with a list of the soldiers he wanted to accompany him. Yesus reviewed the list and made one change.

After a month passed, Judge told Constantine everything was arranged for his mother's trip and their ship would take her to Tyre. The ship required one stop for supplies going and returning. The supply stops provided rest and relaxation. From Tyre, they would travel by carriage.

Constantine explained the itinerary to his mother. She added a few more locations she wanted to visit.

The next morning they went to the dock.

"Good morning, captain," Constantine said. "This is my mother, my daughter, and their military aid, Samson."

"Good morning," the captain said. "Your quarters are prepared."

"You can call her Helena," he said. "She and Constantina will keep Samson appraised of their needs. Your mates can check with him."

"Yes, sir," he said. "Samson's quarters are adjacent to hers."

"Very good," Constantine said. "He is responsible for their well-being."

"As soon as the carriages and horses are on board, we will sail," the captain said. "I will transport them to Tyre."

"If she decides she wants you to stop at an unscheduled port, that is fine," Constantine said. "Just send me a message."

"We can be flexible," the captain said. "When will you need the ship?"

"I don't have any trips planned," he said. "If I need the ship, I will send a message."

In the year three hundred twenty-seven, Helena, Constantina, and their military entourage boarded the ship. It slowly moved out of the harbor and hoisted its sails. The sea breeze filled the sails and they headed east. That evening, the captain invited his passengers to dinner.

"Thank you," Helena said. "Constantina and I will join you for dinner."

"Bring your escort," he said. "I am certain my mate would like to talk with him."

The first stop was in Ephesus. Constantina requested they stop so they could search for Christian relics related to Paul or John. Helena found several scrolls written by John and one by Paul. They were pleasantly surprised to find the house that had once been occupied by Mary and her daughter, Salome. They purchased as many of the furnishings as the owner would sell. After they stopped in Cyprus for supplies, it was smooth sailing to the Holy Lands. When they docked in Tyre, the carriages and horses were prepared for their journey. Helena and Constantina visited a shop located next to a tent manufacturing facility. They purchased a few personal items owned by Paul's family. Then they departed Tyre and headed north.

"Our first stop will be on the north end of the Sea of Galilee," Samson said. "We will stay in Capernaum."

"That was Peter's hometown," Helena said. "I want to see if I can find any evidence of Peter."

Constantina ensured her grandmother they would find something for the museum.

Samson always arrived at Helena's destinations before her. He secured lodging and meals. He demanded the best accommodation available. A few days later, Helena shopped in downtown Capernaum. She asked a shopkeeper about Peter.

"Yes, I have heard of him," the shopkeeper said. "He was a follower of Jesus."

"Correct," she said. "His family lived in Capernaum."

"I think the shop down the street claims to have a few of his personal items," he said. "I am sure he will sell them to you."

She thanked the shopkeeper and started toward the next shop.

When she arrived, she saw a knife labeled "Peter's knife". She became very interested. She looked at the shopkeeper.

"Is that really Peter's knife?" Helena asked. "It looks quite old."

"The man who my father purchased it from said it belonged to Peter," the shopkeeper said. "He knew Peter's father."

"I want to purchase it," she said. "The price seems rather high."

The shopkeeper looked at her clothing and military body guard. He knew she was an important person and probably had plenty of money.

"I have to make a living," he said. "How much would you pay for it?"

"I am purchasing the knife for a museum," she said. "You should give a museum a good price."

"Exhibit the name of my shop, with the knife, in the museum, and I will give you a good price," he said.

"I can arrange that," Helena said. "I will give you half of your asking price."

"Half is the best you can do?" he asked. "I could reduce my price by forty percent?"

Constantina was becoming uncomfortable. She looked at Helena. Helena winked at her.

"Do you have anything else that belonged to Peter?" she asked.

"No, I don't think so," he said. "I am glad you appreciate the knife. It has been here a long time."

"We will pay you sixty percent of your asking price," she said.

"It is more than just an old knife," Constantina said. "It is the type of relic we desire to purchase."

"I will treasure it," Helena said. "Do you know where I might purchase other religious items?"

The shopkeeper hadn't thought of the knife as a religious relic.

"There is a shop in Bethsaida," he said. "He has a pair of crutches you might like. Jesus healed a town beggar who abandoned his crutches when he walked away."

"How do I get there?" she asked. "Is it far?"

"No," he said. "A few hours around the north end of the lake. It is a nice carriage ride. The sea is beautiful and the breeze warm."

"The beggar was a friend of John's," Constantina said. "John, the disciple, and his parents' family lived near Bethsaida."

"Maybe we can find something that belonged to them," Helena said. "John's brother was a learned disciple."

Helena looked at Constantina and smirked.

Samson took the knife and stored it in one of the carriages. They rode along the northern edge of the Sea of Galilee.

"He was correct, the sea is beautiful," Constantina said. "It is very blue. I am sure Jesus liked the sea."

Soon they arrived in Bethsaida. When they entered one of the few shops, Helena saw the crutches in a corner of the room. She told Constantina to watch her methods.

"Shopkeeper," she said. "My feet are sore. I see you have a pair of crutches. How much do you want for them?"

"They are special crutches," he said. "I could take two days wages for them. I would like three days wages, but business has been slow."

"I will give you one and a half day's wages," she said. "Please don't take advantage of me."

She limped toward Constantina.

After Helena purchased the crutches, they looked in other shops. They found a few items that might have belonged to James or John. Constantine had asked Samson to retrace Helen's travels and to ensure the shopkeepers were fairly compensated. He talked with the shopkeeper and gave him a few silver coins.

They traveled back toward Capernaum and stayed at an inn. Samson arranged for a hot bath for the women. The next day, they traveled along the west bank of the Sea of Galilee. The sun shine was bright and the weather hot. They stopped and enjoyed wading in the water. After the horses were rested, they continued to Tiberias. Helena commented about the number of Roman soldiers that were in the area.

"This was once a great fortress on the frontier," Samson said. "Now it has a nice town and a major military installation."

As they walked along the shops, Helena spotted a boat in a store.

"The label says that Jesus' disciples used this boat," Helena said. "He probably has other items. I am going in."

Constantina looked at the boat.

"Can we purchase items as large as this?" she asked.

"Constantine said I could have anything I want," she said. "I like the boat. Getting it home will be Samson's problem."

The shopkeeper explained to Helena how Jesus and his followers liked Tiberias. He said they stayed and taught the soldiers. He claimed the boat was used by Jesus on several occasions.

"Samson, can we get the boat home?" Helena asked. "I really like it."

"Constantine told me to ship large items home at once,' Samson said. "I will take care of it. It will go to Caesarea by wagon and then to Constantinople by ship."

"Good," she said. "You can load it with smaller items. I want these fishing nets as well."

After they spent the night in Tiberias, they rode on to Nazareth. Helena was surprised that Nazareth was such a small town and asked Samson about it.

"We might find something here," Samson said. "The parchment the archbishop provided us states Nazareth was Jesus' hometown."

They found a shop that claimed to have several items that belonged to Joseph, Jesus' father. A table and chair that Joseph made were on display.

"Joseph worked in Tyre, but he often came home. He taught many of his boys the skills of carpentry," the shopkeeper said. "All of the items belonged to Joseph. Jesus might have used some of them."

"Some of his brothers were carpenters," Helena said. "Do you know where Jude lived?"

"Just down the road," he said. "All of his items were passed down to the family."

"I think Jude was a very conservative man," Constantina said. "He was a carpenter, but he did write about Jesus' message."

"Let me see those tools," she said. "What do you think, Samson?"

"Certainly, it is possible," Samson said. "They would make a nice display in the new museum. A lot of people like old carpentry tools."

"Very interesting," Helena said. "We will take all of the tools. Samson put them in the carriage."

"I have them," he said. "Where do you want to go next?"

"Do you want the table and chairs?" Constantina asked.

"I didn't see them," she said. "Show them to me. Samson will ship the furniture home."

"I want to go to Cana," she said. "I know Jesus attended a wedding in Cana."

That evening they stayed at the inn in Nazareth. Samson stayed busy most of the evening arranging for the shipment of Helena's relics.

The next day, they visited the synagogue where the wedding had been performed.

"Is this where Jesus turned water into wine?" Helena asked. "This is a lovely building."

"Yes it is," the Rabbi said. "His miracle made our town famous."

"I want to buy your water jars," Helena said. "Are you certain they are original?"

"No," he said. "I have been told that they were sold a long time ago to a professor who was collecting things that were related to Jesus."

Constantina wondered about the professor. She planned to ask Eusebius about who it might have been.

"That is too bad," she said. "I really wanted to purchase them."

"I could sell you one like the old ones," he said. "They haven't changed much."

"No thanks," Constantina said. "We want the real items."

"You should visit the Inn at Sychar," he said. "They have a small shop, and they claim to have many items associated with Jesus' ministry. I think he stayed at the inn."

Helena's eyes widened. She looked at Samson.

"Thank you," she said. "Samson, we are going to stay at the Inn at Sychar."

When they reached Sychar, Samson secured several rooms.

"I want the best room you have," Samson said. "I also need the room next to it and sleeping quarters for five soldiers."

"We don't give soldiers free rooms," the innkeeper said. "They must pay. I have to pay Roman taxes."

Samson glared at the Innkeeper. He walked away and put his hand into his pocket.

He secured a gold coin and then returned to the Innkeeper.

"Excuse me, sir," Samson said. "This soldier wants to pay for all the rooms and all our meals."

Samson handed, the innkeeper, a gold Solidus.

"A solidus," he said. "This will take care of it. I like these coins. The gold in them is quite pure."

"If you can't spend it, you can melt it," Samson said. "It has value either way."

"I don't see many solidi," he said. "Do you have any more?"

"Helena might have a few," he said. "We want to look at the items in your shop."

The innkeeper smiled.

"I have some very interesting things," he said. "People traveling to Jerusalem, during the last few hundred years, have stayed at this inn."

"Prepare your best meal for the emperor's mother and daughter. They will be down as soon as they have rested," he said. "You might tell them about the inn."

The innkeeper looked sheepishly at Samson.

"Emperor Constantine's mother and daughter?" he asked. "No wonder you have solidus."

The troops stored the carriages and stabled the horses. Then they posted a guard and the remainder of the troops went to their rooms. Helena and Constantina joined the innkeeper for dinner. Helena told him that she would look at the items in his shop in the morning.

The next day after breakfast, she and the owner went to the shop.

"You have many items from Paul's family," Helena said. "Paul was an interesting man."

"My ancestors claim that Paul's family stayed here on many occasions," the innkeeper said. "My several greats-grandfathers, Abraham, conducted business with Paul's brother."

"I guess it is possible," Helena said. "The well just down the road is very famous."

"When they traveled to Jerusalem, Paul's family stayed here," he said. "This is a stopping point for many people going to Jerusalem during the holidays."

"Samson, I want to purchase everything in the shop," Helena said. "Will you have it shipped to the museum?"

"Yes, Miss Helena," he said "Anything you want."

Samson looked at the floor and thought, 'I hope Constantine knew what he was doing went he sent Helena on this trip.' He and the innkeeper loaded two wagons full of items and sent them to Caesarea. The items were shipped to Constantine in Constantinople.

After Sychar, they traveled to Jericho. They located a very nice inn. The doctor informed Helena she needed rest before traveling to Jerusalem.

"I want to go to Jerusalem," she said. "I am fine."

"I have to follow the doctor's orders," Samson said. "We will remain in Jericho."

It took Samson a while to convince Helena that the doctor had the final say concerning her level of activity.

After a week of rest, Helena and Constantina went shopping.

"That is a great wall," Helena said. "I thought this wall tumbled down? You know the story."

"This is a new wall," Samson said. "You can ask about the old wall."

"Many of these old cities have several walls," Constantina said. "See, my tutor taught me something."

"I have purchased twenty pieces of the old wall," she said. "Have it shipped. I didn't find anything else of interest."

When they arrived in Jerusalem, they located the house that Constantine had secured for them. The servants took especially good care of the emperor's mother and daughter. The house was filled with fresh flowers and fresh fruit. After they rested, they spent several weeks touring. The streets near the market were lined with shops.

"I think I could fill a museum just with items from Jerusalem," Helena said. "I like that one shop. Did you see all the coins?"

"No, I didn't notice the coins," Samson said. "I am sure Jerusalem is for sale."

"I have a few items you can send to the museum," she said. "I have gathered soil from the gardens, bricks from the road, six olive trees, six date trees, and several pieces of the old temple."

"Are you certain those trees will survive in Constantinople?" Constantina asked. "It gets very cold at home."

"I don't know," Helena said. "I am certain Constantine employs a gardener who will know how to care for them."

Samson joined the women.

"Constantine told me to take you to the site of the temple to Aphrodite," he said. "He is having it torn down and is planning to build a church in its place."

"I would like to see the site," Helena said. "I believe it is where Jesus was nailed to the cross."

"I would also like to see that site," Constantina said. "Most of the buildings around here are new or being repaired."

"The revolutions have been difficult for Jerusalem," Samson said. "The Jewish people were a problem for the Roman military, and finally, Titus destroyed the city."

The following day, Samson escorted Helena to the construction site and introduced her to the site manager.

"I have been hoping Helena would come to see me," Drawus said. "We may have found Jesus' burial cave."

Helena became very interested. She beamed at the builder.

"Show me the cave," she said. "I want to see it."

"Be careful," Drawus said. "This is a construction site."

"What is all that stuff in the back of the cave?" Constantina asked. "Take it out in the sunlight where Helena can inspect it."

"It looks like three crosses and a pile of cloth," he said. "I plan to enclose the cave with the new church."

"Samson, ship the crosses and burial wrappings to the museum," she said. "Now we really have something. We have the cross on which Jesus hung."

"You could hang the cross in the church," Constantina said.

Sampson picked up a handful of nails and showed them to Helena. She smiled.

"That is quite a relic," Samson said. "Constantine will be proud of you. I will make arrangements to ship it home."

A few weeks later, they went shopping in the old city.

"Tell me about this jar," Helena said. "You have it labeled, 'Concerning Jesus.'"

The shopkeeper looked at Helena.

"When he was hanging on the cross," the shopkeeper said. "Jesus was offered a drink from this jar."

"Are you certain of that?" Helena asked.

It sounded like a story she had heard, but she wasn't certain about the shopkeeper.

"It was given to me by my father," he said. "I don't know where he obtained it. It is old."

"Ok, we will purchase it," she said. "What else do you have?"

"I have the spear used to stab Jesus' side," he said. "The spear belonged to the centurion."

"You have quite an assortment of relics," she said. "Show me more of them."

"I have the uniforms worn by the soldiers who guarded Jesus' tomb. I also have the lots that were tossed."

"I would like to see the lots," Helena said. "Are they stones?"

"Yes, they used stones with symbols on them," he said. "They firmly believed that the God controlled the casting of the lots. Here look at this one."

The shopkeeper handed Helena a small stone. She looked at it very carefully.

"What is that symbol?" she asked. "I don't recognize it."

"The lots often contained symbols that were only understood by a few people," he said.

"What about the clothes they wore?" she asked. "Do you have any of Jesus' clothing?"

"I do," he said. "My family has been gathering items for many years."

"I want all the items for my museum," she said. "What else do you have?"

"If I sell you everything I have, I won't have anything to draw customers into my shop," he said. "I need to keep a few things."

"You can get more items," she said. "You live in Jerusalem."

"It isn't that easy," he said. "You have to ensure the items are authentic."

"I thought you were in business to sell," she said. "Was I wrong?"

Samson extended his hand, palm up. It was full of gold solidus.

"I could sell gold coins that belonged to the emperor," he said. "I have a few more items you might be interested in."

"That looks like junk," she said. "Did it belong to a famous person?"

"These are Barabbas' belongings," he said. "You could make a very nice display out of them."

"I am finished for today," she said.

Helena and Constantina returned to the house and Helena rested. The next morning, she complained of not feeling well.

"I will have our doctor talk with you," Samson said. "He has already treated several of our soldiers."

The doctor determined that Helena was suffering from fatigue. He indicated she needed rest and relaxation. He restricted her travel and ordered meals that contained only vegetables and fruits. She was given large cups of date juice. He instructed Samson that she shouldn't leave the house for two months.

Constantine sent a message to Eusebius, the bishop of Caesarea, indicating that Helena, who was visiting Jerusalem, had become ill. Eusebius and his assistant traveled to Jerusalem to visit with and pray with Helena. When she saw the bishop, her spirits were lifted, and her health began to improve. Helena told Eusebius about all of the Christian relics she had collected for the museum in Constantinople. Eusebius was honored to be of service to the emperor's mother.

After several months, Helena was rested and felt well. She wanted to do more shopping. Samson explained to her that he had sent a message to Constantine informing him that she wasn't well, and he had requested a ship to bring her and Constantina home.

"I will have to get busy," Helena said. "I am too old to ever return to Jerusalem. I don't want the ship to return home with an empty cargo hole."

Samson smiled at her.

"Purchase whatever you want," Samson said. "We are going to leave for Caesarea in one week."

"I can probably find items in Caesarea," she said. "Yesterday, I found several items from the disciples' last supper."

"I love the cups," Constantina said. "I especially like the large wine jug."

The servants prepared a special farewell dinner for Helena and Constantina. Samson paid them handsomely for their services.

The following week, they journeyed to Caesarea and waited for their ship. Helena and Constantina went shopping every day.

"This is a very interesting town," Helena said. "This is where Paul was in prison before they sent him to Rome."

"I think Peter had a friend in the Roman army who lived here," Samson said. "It is a hub of activity."

"Being on the Great Sea is a benefit," Constantina said. "I have found several items including some of Peter's. He was here several times."

One soldier, who was traveling with Samson, approached him and whispered in his ear. A frown appeared on Samson's face. He approached Constantina.

"Are you aware your mother purchased a jail?" Samson asked. "She purchased the entire building."

"No," she said. "I knew she was looking at it and talking to the owner. Maybe you should ask her."

Samson walked to Helena.

"A soldier just told me you purchased the old jail building?" he said. "How am I supposed to get it home?"

"Take it apart," she said. "It can be reassembled in the park."

"It is a large building," he said. "We don't need a jail."

"I am certain Constantine will find a use for it," she said. "It is a Christian relic. Paul was incarcerated in that building for two years."

Samson sent a message to Constantine.

> Constantine
> Emperor of the Roman Empire
>
> You will need God's blessing.
> Helena purchased the old jail where Paul was incarcerated.
> I am sending information and a drawing showing its dimensions.
> She would like it reassembled in the park.
> You might want to talk with a builder about a larger museum.
>
> Samson
> Roman Soldier

"The museum is not large enough to hold what you have purchased." Samson said. "We will need a new museum."

Helena looked at Samson and smiled. She ignored his comment.

"I also have a drawing I want shipped home," she said. "It shows an angel at Jesus' tomb. Make sure to protect it."

"I like the drawing," Constantina said. "It will look grand hanging in the church."

"I don't know where I will put it," she said. "When I get home, I will have to inspect all the relics. When is the ship going to arrive?"

"It will be here tomorrow," Samson said. "The dock workers will load our material and some supplies, and we will depart the next day."

Two days later, they went to the dock.

"It looks like they are putting something behind our boat," she said. "I am ready to go home."

"That is a barge," Samson said. "The jail will be stored on the barge and our ship will tow it home."

"Is the barge full?" she asked.

Samson just looked at her. He didn't answer the question.

The ship's captain arrived as Helena walked to her cabin. Constantina sat on the main deck and looked at the town. Soon, Helena joined Samson.

"Are you planning on stopping?" Samson asked. "Maybe we should purchase a few items on Delos."

"No," Helena said. "I want to go straight home. Have you heard from Constantine?"

"Yes," he said. "I send him a message every week. He insisted I keep him informed about you and Constantina."

"How is his health?" she asked. "Sometimes he doesn't look well."

"He still has some problems," he said. "He can function just fine."

"I will be glad to see him," she said.

The next day, Samson, again, mentioned the lions of Delos. Constantine had informed Samson to bring a lion from Delos to assuage the concerns of the pagans.

"I thought you might like the lions of Delos," he said. "They are very large and quite old."

"If you want one of the lions, purchase one," Helena said. "I don't need to see it now. I will see it at home."

Samson arranged with the Captain to stop at Delos. He explained about the lions and indicated that they could put one on the barge. When they arrived at Delos, Samson talked to Helena.

"You can stay on board the ship," Samson said. "Constantina and I will only be gone for a few hours."

Samson and Constantina visited with the government officials on the island. They sold Constantina a lion and helped Samson load it onto the barge. It took thirty slaves to put the lion on the main deck of the barge.

"I loaded a lion for you and Constantine," Samson said. "When you stand next to it, you realize how large it is."

"I will find a home for it," she said. "I hope someone will appreciate it."

"I hope you like it," Constantina said. "We can always put it in the park."

The Captain hoped he didn't need to stop for any more purchases. The barge was a heavy load for the ship and was slowing it down.

"We aren't making any progress," the captain said. "Samson, do your men know how to row?"

"No, but they can learn," he said. "Do you have oars?"

Eight of the soldiers, were given oars and they rowed the barge when the wind couldn't move the ship.

Helena spent the next few days in her cabin. When the sun shone in the afternoon, she would sit on the main deck with Constantina. Samson checked his inventory to determine what he had sent home. The ship's sails found wind, and they finally arrived in Rhodes.

The captain announced that they would stop for supplies and a day of rest and relaxation. Helena and Constantina went shopping. They located a scroll that Paul had written. They dined at the Harbor Restaurant and then returned to the ship.

When they arrived in the harbor at Constantinople, Constantine and Yesus awaited them.

"I had a large barn built on the palace grounds," Yesus said. "You can store the treasures there."

"Welcome home," Constantine said. "I noticed the ship towed a barge. I love the lion you purchased."

"I am so glad to be home. I am not taking any more extended trips," Helena said. "I am glad you had the doctor and Constantina come with me."

"Did you have a good time purchasing items for the museum?" he asked. "We will store the relics until they are prepared to go into the museum."

"The Holy Lands were wonderful," she said. "Everything is for sale. I bought dirt and bricks."

"You purchased dirt?" he asked. "What are you going to do with dirt?"

"It is from Jesus' favorite garden," she said. "You can use the dirt to build a garden."

"Did you see the construction site?" he asked.

"I did. I spent several days with your builder," she said. "I sent three crosses and some other items home. Constantina found them in Jesus' grave."

"I will see them when we start unpacking everything," he said. "First you are going to rest. I have a carriage for you."

He ordered Yesus and Samson to have soldiers help unload the ship and the barge.

Samson had several wagons loaded with items and transferred them to the barn.

"We will stack the building materials for the jail next to the new barn," Yesus said. "When Constantine decides where he wants it, I will have it reassembled."

"I only want to move that lion one time," Samson said. "Yesus, please ask Constantine were he would like to place the lion."

Samson gathered forty soldiers. They made a ramp of logs from the barge to the dock. They carefully rolled the lion down the ramp. Yesus returned.

"He said to put it in the new park," he said. "Put it where the children can play on it. It took Samson and the forty soldiers two days to move the lion to the park. Eventually, they placed it on a foundation made of large rocks. Everyone who visited the park was curious about the lion. It became a topic of conversation.

Helena and Constantina returned to the palace. Helena relaxed for the next few weeks. Her health had declined so severely that she never regained her full strength. She seemed to be staying alive for the dedication of the new capital city. Constantina was now a young woman and was gaining the attention of the young men of Constantinople.

CHAPTER 9

DEDICATION OF CONSTANTINOPLE

Over the next several years, Constantine worked steadily to create the empire's new capital city. He had chosen a city located on the Black Sea, mainly for its large, deep harbor. The construction of the major government buildings was completed and many of the monetary changes were in place. Most of the building were white stone and reflected the sun's rays. The army was housed in a new complex, and the emperor lived in a new palace. The entrance to the largest public park in the city was through an arch whose keystone was carved as a likeness of Constantine. The parks contained a varied selection of tall, evergreen trees whose limbs provided a home for beautiful birds and small animals. Numerous flower gardens were situated throughout the parks. Lakes provided a lovely location for a family to have a picnic. Constantine had a great column built to commemorate the dedication of the city 'Constantinople' as the new capital of the Roman Empire. The residents especially appreciated the wide streets and many open spaces. Eventually, Helena's new church was opened for Sabbath services.

During the early part of the year three hundred thirty, Constantine planned the dedication celebration for his new capital. He and his mother sat in the living area of the palace and talked about the ceremony.

"I want you to invite a great number of people," Helena said. "This should be a grand party."

"I don't want it to appear that we are wasting money," Constantine said. "You can give Yesus a list of those you want to invite."

"If we can afford to give food away to the poor, we should be able to give the rich a little wine," she said. "Are you going to pay for people to attend the dedication?"

"No, I wasn't planning on it," he said. "This celebration is for the local people, those in the government, and those in the army."

"I want you to pay the expenses for twenty of the bishops I invite," she said. "I will only invite twenty."

"You want me to pay all the expenses for twenty bishops?" he queried. "If each of them were to bring an ornament for the church, it would help justify the expense."

"You don't have to justify every expense," she said. "You are the emperor."

"A good emperor will only raise enough money to manage the empire," Constantine said. "I shouldn't raise taxes on the people so we can invite and pay for the expenses of our friends. I am certain an impressive number of people will attend the dedication ceremony."

"Who will be making speeches?" Helena asked. "I am starting to write mine."

Constantine looked at her.

"I will open the celebration, followed by the leader of the Senate, and then the leader of the military. The archbishop will bless the food," Constantine said. "I haven't planned for you to give a speech."

Helena suffered a pang of rejection. She glared at Constantine.

"You weren't planning on me giving a speech?" she stammered. "I made you emperor. I want to give a speech to our people."

"No, father made me emperor," he said. "He made my half-brothers the next emperors."

"No, your sons will be the next emperors," she said. "I am sure they will be great like you."

"I was made emperor in spite of you," he said. "I think that is why I love you so much. They just didn't understand you."

Helena hung her head and gave Constantine her best hurt mother look.

"How can you talk to me like that?" she said. "Don't you love me? I took care of your major problem."

"That is the main reason I am not allowing you to make a speech," he said. "Many of those who will attend the dedication ceremony think you had Fausta killed."

"They may think it, but they can't prove it," she said. "I don't know why they want to blame me."

"You wouldn't be safe," Constantine said. "That is why I have ordered a military guard assigned to you."

She glared at Constantine and frowned.

"That guard watches my every move," she said. "I can't give him the slip. I guess he is a good tracker."

Her face seemed to light up as she gave Constantine a big smile.

"Maybe, I will be sick on dedication day," she said. "That way you won't have to worry about me."

"Now mother," he said. "I want you to sit with me. It will demonstrate how important you are to me."

"I don't know, maybe I will be sick," she said. "We will see. I don't want to cause problems on such an important day."

"I will reserve the seat next to me for you," he said. "I will count on you. Don't disappoint me."

She excused herself and went to bed.

The next day, Constantine talked with Judge about the celebration.

"It sounds like it will be a good time," Judge said. "Would you like me to invite Nickus?"

Constantine thought for a moment and agreed that it was a good idea.

"Send him a message," Constantine said. "Tell him I will meet him with a ship where the Istrius flows into the Black Sea."

Judge spoke with Yesus.

"Tell him to come a week early," Judge said. "Constantine wants him to have time to see the city. Tell him you will provide quarters for him."

When he received the message, Nickus tried to visualize the new capital city. He sent Yesus a message acknowledging that he would meet Constantine at the Black Sea. He arranged to leave his post and boarded his river boat. They made several stops on their journey down the river. Nickus visited many of the towns and met with the town administrators.

It was a goodwill journey to promote his popularity. He planned to meet with Constantine one week before the dedication.

When the time approached for Nickus to arrive, Constantine talked with Judge.

"I will be sailing tomorrow to meet Nickus," Constantine said. "Make sure his quarters are prepared."

"With your approval, I would like to invite him to dinner one evening while he is with us," Judge said. "He would enjoy that."

"Have our cook prepare his favorite meal," he said.

"I am planning a large outdoor dinner in the new park as part of the dedication celebration," Judge said. "It will be available to everyone in town. We are going to give dried dates to all the children."

"That is fine," he said. "Make certain I am well guarded."

"You will be," he said. "I am having tents erected, just in case of rain."

"We will need large tents," Constantine said. "Build a raised platform for those giving speeches."

"I can obtain large tents from the military," he said. "They always have the best tents."

They looked at each other and smiled.

Constantine instructed the ship's captain that they would be meeting his friend, Nickus, at the Istrius River. He impressed upon him that Nickus was the army commander of the empire's western region, and that he wanted everything to be just right.

A few days later, Constantine boarded the new ship, and they sailed. When they arrived, Nickus' boat was waiting for them.

Nickus stood at attention for a moment and then embraced Constantine.

"I am living in Trier," he said. "I have learned to like the area."

"We have been working on the capital city project for several years," Constantine said. "It is mostly completed."

"This is quite a ship," he said. "I don't have much need for a large ship, but I appreciate the river boats."

"The ship is new," he said. "The wood is cedar from Lebanon."

"I am using our old river boat," Nickus said. "They are still the best boats on the river."

"Your quarters are ready for you," Constantine said. "If you would join me for dinner, I would appreciate it."

Nickus took a tour of the ship and then went to his cabin. He was impressed with the intricate woodwork and the elaborate furnishings in his cabin. He took his boots off and rested until dinner. A sailor came to his cabin and escorted him to dinner.

"This is a fine meal," Nickus said. "We need a new cook on the river boat."

"We have accomplished a great deal since you left," Constantine said. "We still have a few things to implement and a few programs to start, but I think we have the beginnings of a great city."

"I have heard that you are trying to emulate Rome," he said. "Don't copy them too closely. Their army lost to ours."

He smiled at Constantine.

"I am trying to use their good ideas and avoid the bad ones," he said.

Nickus took another bite of his dinner.

"Where did you find your cook?" Nickus asked. "Maybe he would teach my cook a few things."

Nickus and Constantine reminisced as they sailed along the southwest coast of the Black Sea.

When they docked in Constantinople, they were met by troops with carriages.

"I see you have increased the number of your guards," Nickus said. "This is your home. I wouldn't think you would need them."

"We are training new guards," Constantine said. "The old troops are not nearly as good as they used to be. We need better trained troops."

"Like the ones you and I had," he said. "They were the best."

"Since my problems with Crispus, we had to increase the number of guards," Constantine said. "I want you to meet my sons. They have grown."

"How is Constantine II?" he asked. "It's been a long time."

"He is now fourteen years old," he said. "He is quite an equestrian. He will make a great warrior. His brother, Constantius II, is thirteen years old."

"Are you training Constantine II in the military manner?" he asked. "It takes time to be a good warrior."

133

"Yes," he said. "I have started training both of them. They are quite busy studying and riding."

"How is the baby?" Nickus asked. "I know he is not a baby any longer. How old is he now?"

"He is seven," Constantine said. "He is still a child."

"I am sure he will also be a warrior," he said.

They boarded the waiting carriages and went to the palace. They were greeted by Judge. They exchanged pleasantries and started into the palace. Nickus was impressed with the new buildings and gardens.

"I am glad you returned to celebrate with us," Judge said. "Wait until you see the new troops' quarters and training grounds."

"I saw the new ship," he said. "It is very grand."

"It is a show piece," Judge said. "The emperor takes many important people sailing on the Black Sea."

Judge showed Nickus to his quarters and allowed him time to shave and clean before dinner. He was told that Helena would be joining them. When Nickus arrived, she was already seated with Constantine.

"Hello, Nickus," Helena said. "It is good to see you. How is the west? We welcome you to our new capital city."

"The west is just as it was. It is home to me and I love it," Nickus said. "It is good to see you."

Nickus was seated across from Helena.

"I understand you have a new church," he said. "I want to see it."

"It is open, but we are still completing the final touches," she said. "How did you hear about it?"

"Everyone in the empire knows about your church," he said. "Most of our bishops have sent ornaments to decorate it."

"I have received so many gifts; I am putting most of them in the museum that was built next to the church," she said. "Some of the scrolls are very interesting. I will escort you to the church."

"You probably have some original writings as well," Nickus said. "I think the bishop in Gaul sent you a scroll from Irenaeus' collection."

Helena looked at Nickus.

"Are you married?" she asked.

"No," he said. "I guess I will never be married. I'm not home long enough to be a father and husband."

"You can always have a wife," she said. "She would give you boys. You could give her attendants and other gifts."

"My woman, Mary, left me," he said. "She married a shopkeeper. I think she is with child."

Nickus frowned and looked at Helena.

"You can find another girl," she said. "I am sure you have plenty of opportunities to meet women."

"Mary was the one," he said. "I blew my chance. No more women for me."

"If you want me to find a woman for you, just tell me," she said. "Constantina has many young lady friends."

Helena smiled at him. After dinner, they adjourned to the living area.

"Judge will show you our new facilities tomorrow," Constantine said. "I will be busy making final arrangements for the ceremony."

"I would like to see the new training grounds for the troops," Nickus said. "Maybe I will have a new training area constructed."

"I must also practice my speech," he said. "I am opening the dedication ceremony."

"How many speeches will I have to listen to?" Nickus asked. "I'll pretend to listen, just don't expect me to say anything."

"There will be a few speeches," he said. "You don't have to listen to all of them. You can enjoy the food and the park."

After a few hours of reminiscing, they said good night and retired.

The next morning, Judge took Nickus on a tour of the military installation. Constantine met with the soldiers who were erecting the tents.

"I hope we don't need the tents," he said. "But it rains a lot this time of year."

"It is better to be prepared," Yesus said.

Six very large tents were erected in the park. Helena met with Constantine.

"Not all of the bishops have arrived," she said. "What should I do? I have reserved places for them."

"They will be here," he said. "If they don't show, have Judge fill the empty places with guards."

Tables were placed for everyone to enjoy picnics with their families.

Constantine hoped that the park would be enjoyed for years after the dedication celebration.

On the morning of the celebration, the air was brisk, but the sun shone brightly. By midmorning, many people had arrived at the park, and by noon, a large number of troops were present. The ceremonies were scheduled to start at two o'clock. Constantine met with all the speakers an hour before the ceremony.

"I will introduce the senate leader, first," Constantine said. "The Commander of the army will be next."

"How long would you like us to speak?" the senate leader asked. "I just want the people to know who I am."

"I would like each of you to speak about twenty minutes," he said. "The archbishop will be the last speaker. After his speech, he will bless the food."

Helena entered the tent. Everyone noticed her. Her Royal Blue gown glimmered in the light. Her military escort was in his dress uniform. Everyone talked about how grand they appeared. She slowly walked to Constantine.

"Welcome, mother," he said. "I am glad to see you are feeling better."

"Thank you," she said. "I have come to be with my people."

The senate leader started to speak. His speech was political and mostly self-serving. Fifteen minutes later, people helped themselves to the food and sat at the tables. A sudden, heavy thunder storm arrived. The people grabbed their food and ran in all directions, seeking cover. One of the tents became unstable in the high winds, but the troops were able to drive the pegs back into the ground. By the time the storm passed, the food was mostly gone and so was the crowd.

Constantine looked at the Commander.

"You might as well tell us about the military," Constantine said. "The senators are still here. I see that mother has already gone home."

"I am wet," the Commander said. "My speech will be very short."

After brief speeches by the military commander and the archbishop, the senators and the high ranking military officer left for the palace. When they arrived, they were greeted by Judge. Due to the rain, a large number of people had already arrived at the palace for dinner. Dinner was served in the grand hall.

"At least it isn't raining in here," the senate leader said. "The food smells very good."

The guests were all served a glass of wine. It seemed like people would never stop arriving. Carriages lined the lane leading to the palace.

"I have ordered some of the troops to remove the tents from the park," Judge said. "They will also clean up the mess."

"I think the crowd was happy," Constantine said. "They got their food and didn't have to listen to any speakers.".

"There was trash and food all over the ground," Yesus said. "It will be clean tomorrow."

"Determine if mother is coming to dinner," Constantine said. "You can check with her guard."

"Yes, sir," Yesus said. "She is changing clothes. She will join us in a few moments."

After Helena made her grand entrance, everyone was seated, and dinner was served. The evening offered a joyful mood. Many gallons of wine were consumed. At ten o'clock, the guests started to depart. Each guest thanked Constantine and talked with him briefly. Then they wobbled to their carriages and waved goodbye. Judge sent a guard with a few of the couples who had too many glasses of wine. He made certain that everyone made it safely home.

"The city is officially dedicated," the senate leader said. "We have built a fine capital. I am looking forward to working with you."

"It is going to take a few days to get the park repaired," Constantine said. "Many of the trees that we had shipped to us have been cut down and removed."

Earlier, Judge explained to Constantine that the local poor didn't know the trees were special and cut them down for firewood. Constantine listened very carefully.

"I liked some of those trees," Constantine said. "I will have a mounted patrol posted in the park. I will see you in the park tomorrow."

"Yes, sir," Yesus said. "I will be there, supervising the cleanup."

The next day, a large number of soldiers began removing all the trash from the park, while Constantine surveyed the trees with Yesus.

"We might as well purchase another ship load of trees," Yesus said. "If we have more than we need, I will have them planted on the palace grounds."

"Have the stumps removed," Constantine said. "Then, post notices so people know not to remove the new trees."

"I could have a load of fuel wood distributed to the poor," he said. "The people would like free wood."

"That is probably a good idea," he said. "It may save us a few trees and put some people to work."

"One of the tents was ripped," Yesus said. "The others were cleaned and stored."

When Constantine returned to the palace, Judge appeared a little nervous.

"What do you want me to do with the two barrels of coins we had minted to give away at the dedication?" Judge asked. "The people departed before we could give them a coin."

"Store them for the next celebration," Constantine said. "They will still make good gifts."

It was time for Nickus to return home. Constantine bid him farewell and Yesus escorted him to the ship and sailed with him to his boat.

Constantine was aware of the value of riverboats and commissioned the shipyard to build two new boats. The ship's designer visited with Constantine.

They exchanged greetings, and Constantine handed the designer a set of sketches.

"The city is beautiful," the designer said. "On the morning of the celebration, many people visited the harbor. Everyone was impressed with the new ship."

Constantine expressed his pleasure with the new ship.

"I want to build two new riverboats," he said. "One will be for me and my guests. The other will be used as a fighting boat. The troops will live on it, and the weapons will be stored on it."

"Do you want them designed like the last riverboats?" the designer asked. "I helped design the boats that Nickus is using."

"The same size," he said. "I want the newest armor and weaponry used on the fighting boat."

"I will include several grand cabins on yours," he said. "How many cabins do you need?"

"I think five will be sufficient," Constantine said. "Three of the cabins can be less grand than my cabin."

"When the boats are about half completed, I will send you a message," the designer said. "You can have someone inspect them to ensure I am building what you desire. They will be built in the boatyard near the Istrius."

"Thank you," Constantine said. "I will send someone to inspect them."

The designer returned home, and a month later, the two boats were under construction. Constantine was at his office when Judge appeared.

"A ship load of new trees has arrived," Judge said. "Do you want me to have them sent to the park?"

"Yes," Constantine said. "I will instruct Yesus concerning where to have them planted."

Constantine wanted to see the trees, and he met Yesus in the park the next morning. They discussed the idea of using day labor to plant them. They reasoned that if the people planted the trees themselves, they might understand the trees weren't meant to be used as fire wood.

"That is a very nice group of trees," Constantine said. "Plant the large nut trees next to the guard house."

"Luckily, we haven't lost any more trees in the park," Yesus said. "The mounted troops have stopped people from stealing them."

Constantine indicated he had a large bin built next to the guard house, and he wanted it filled with firewood.

"A ship loaded with firewood arrived today," Yesus said. "I will put most of the wood in the bin. I was surprised how much wood a ship can transport. It won't all fit into the bin."

Constantine looked at Yesus.

"That was poor planning," he said. "I want the extra wood protected from thieves. When the weather is inclement, the troops can use some of the wood. The rest will be distributed to the poor," Constantine said. "I want these trees in the park to have a long life."

Yesus had the extra wood stored in the barn.

"I want you to plant an orchard," Constantine said. "I also want a vineyard."

"We will patrol them, but won't discourage individual from enjoying the fruit," Yesus said. "We will have them planted just this side of the barracks."

"If a lot of people use the park," Constantine said. "We'll be able to justify the improvements."

Hundreds of trees were planted. They were aligned in rows and were old enough to produce fruit the next year. Before the last tree was planted, birds were perched in them. The park became a weekend family gathering spot. The troops became park fixtures.

One evening at the palace, Constantine II approached his father.

"Father, I want to join the mounted troops at the park," he said. "I like to ride, and the park is close to home."

"I think you are too young to be a soldier," Constantine said. "You can ride in the park."

Constantine II looked at his father.

"I am a good horseman," he said. "I need to improve my military training."

"Study your languages," Constantine said. "That is very important."

"I am studying my languages," he said. "I study every day."

Constantine didn't want to argue with him.

"Why don't you ask Judge?" Constantine said. "He is a soldier."

"Fine," he said. "He will think I am old enough to be a soldier."

The following day, Judge talked with the sergeant at the troop quarters in the park.

"Constantine wants his son to join your troops," Judge said. "He is a good horseman."

"Just what we need," the sergeant said. "Can I send him home at night?"

"No," he said. "It will be his first military post."

"The troops won't like this," he said. "The emperor's son living with us will put a damper on their fun."

"It could be a blessing in disguise," Judge said. "Do a good job training him for a proper military life, and I am certain the emperor will reward you."

"How old is the kid?" he asked. "Does he still have a runny nose?"

"Constantine II is not a kid," he said. "He is the emperor's son. I think his nose stopped running when his brother disappeared."

"Send him to us," he said. "I will make a soldier out of him."

Judge informed the sergeant that he had made a wise decision.

Constantine II was assigned to the troops, who lived in the guard house, in the park. His father insisted that he spend one day per week studying languages with his tutor. The sergeant was surprised that Constantine II was already an accomplished horseman. The sergeant was in his office at his desk when he looked up and saw Constantine.

"Good afternoon," the sergeant said. "Welcome to our home."

"I am pleased that you are working with my son," he said. "I would like to see him. Is he available?"

The sergeant jumped up and went to the quarters. He returned with Constantine II.

"Father, I like my assignment in the park," he said. "I am learning how to be a soldier."

"That is good, son," Constantine said. "Not every assignment is to defend the empire. We also serve the empire in many other ways."

"This is a good way for me to learn about the military," he said. "The sergeant is a good man. He was a little intimidating at first."

"I was told he was not happy that I had you assigned to him," Constantine said. "I put him in the park because he can deal with people."

Constantine and his son continued their walk in the park.

The following month, the boat designer sent a message to Constantine that stated the boats were ready to be inspected.

Constantine visited the sergeant and the troops in the park.

"Good morning, men," Constantine said. "I am going to inspect our new river boats, and I wanted to take my son with me."

"I will change his schedule and make him available to you," the sergeant said. "How long will he be gone?"

"One month," he said. "We will do a little sailing. Do you need a replacement while he is with me?"

"Yes, sir," he said. "We will be short one man. We could cover for him, but we would have to increase our work time."

"I will have Yesus send you a soldier," he said. "I will see you in a month."

The sergeant looked at Constantine and smiled

"Have a good trip," he said. "We will keep the park safe."

The following morning, Constantine II stabled his horse aboard the ship and waited for his father at the dock.

"Good morning, sir," Constantine II said. "Please tell the captain that I am one of your guards."

"Good morning," Constantine said. "Yes, I will take care of that. You will bunk with the other troops."

Constantine explained to the captain that Constantine II was part of the troop and should receive the same treatment as the other soldiers. The captain was a little nervous, but followed his orders. That evening, Constantine dined with the captain.

"This is a fine dinner your mate prepared," Constantine said. "I especially like the fish."

"I am glad you like it," the captain said. "It was caught late last evening. We saved it for you."

"How has the ship been behaving?" he asked. "Many people have commented about her."

"She is a great lady," he said. "She is the most beautiful ship on the sea. I understand you are going to inspect some new riverboats?"

"Yes," he said. "We are having two built."

"I prefer ships," he said. "Living on a ship is a more adventurous life."

Constantine looked at the Captain.

"I prefer the palace," he said. "The boats are nice to travel through the interior of our empire. We need two to provide protection."

The captain of the ship explained the itinerary to the crew.

"After Constantine is completed with his work at the shipyard, we will be traveling north to a fortification at Tyras," he said.

He referred to it as the black fortification because the sea was especially black at that location.

After a few days, they reached the Istrius River. Constantine and Constantine II inspected the boats.

"They have built all the below deck areas except the cabins," the builder said. "Before I have them built, I wanted to discuss them with you one more time."

"The hull is beautiful," Constantine said. "I want a nice cabin with a small cabin next to it for my guard."

"I have some fixtures I want you to look at," he said. "I had them made by a local carpenter."

"That is a beautiful desk," he said. "He is a master. It is as nice as my desk at the palace."

"Would you like him to build you a large desk for your use at the palace?" he asked. "I could ship it to you in about a month."

Constantine inspected the desk one more time.

"Yes," Constantine said. "It will do my carpenters good to see his work. Would he like to move to Constantinople?"

"I don't think he will move," he said. "He is very old. He lives with his oldest daughter's family."

"Tell him to make me a great desk," he said. "I will make him and his daughter very happy."

They finalized the details concerning the boat and set sail for Tyras. The next morning, Constantine talked with his son.

"We have a small fleet stationed in Tyras," Constantine said. "It is a beautiful place for a fortification."

"I have never heard of it," Constantine II said. "Is it a Roman city?"

"It is not much of a city," he said. "It was rebuilt by the Romans a few hundred years ago."

They spent a day in Tyras and then sailed home. The weather was warm, and the wind was steady. Each soldier was allowed to spend a few minutes with the Captain as he commanded the sailors.

When they reached home, Judge met them. He allowed Constantine an opportunity to tell him about the new boats. Constantine explained that a large desk had been built for him by a carpenter in Tyras. It would arrive at the harbor in about one month.

"I will alert the harbor troops to look for it," he said. "How did Constantine II like being your guard?"

"I think he liked the trip," he said. "I guess he is ready to be home. He didn't need the horse."

Yesus joined Constantine and Judge.

"The sergeant will be happy to have him back," Yesus said. "The temporary soldier I sent him is driving him mad."

"Sergeant will handle him," Constantine said. "What is he doing?"

"The last time I saw him, he was stacking wood," Yesus said. "The sergeant was yelling at him."

"Send him back to training," Constantine said. "Constantine II will join the sergeant today."

"I hope the sergeant is ready for your son," Judge said. "I guess he might eventually see more than one."

"He will probably see all three," he said. "Don't tell him or he might ask for a transfer."

Then he looked at Yesus and laughed.

The next day, Yesus found Constantine outside his office building.

"You received a message from Nickus," Yesus said. "I put it in your office, on your desk."

Constantine went to his office and read the message.

Constantine
Emperor of the Roman Empire

Gods speed.
    I hope you like the greeting.
    I wasn't sure about it.
    I wanted to tell you, I have met a lady.
    We are planning to be married.
    I gave up on marriage a few years ago.

Now it seem like I met the woman for me.
Please say a prayer for us.

Your Warrior
Nickus

Constantine grinned from ear to ear as he reread the message.
He immediately sent a return message.

Nickus
Commander of Army of the West

May God bless both of you.
    I am so glad that you have found the correct lady.
    I hope you have many children.
    Married life is good for the soul.
    I enjoy my children very much.
    The young men are all good horsemen.
    When is your wedding?
    I would like to attend.
    I will send along a present.

Constantine
Emperor of the Roman Empire.

Nickus was relieved when he read the message. He replied that they planned on being married in one month, and that he would send the details to Judge. When Constantine read the message, he ordered Judge to plan a trip. Judge requested that the Captain prepare the sailing ship to take them to the Rhone River. The Captain was ordered to make it as rapid a journey as possible. The only cargo would be their horses, carriages, and one barrel of coins.

The ship was loaded with supplies, and they set sail.

"Sir," the captain said. "I have loaded the ship with enough supplies to get us to the Rhone River. I plan to sail with all sails raised. If the journey is too rough, please inform me."

"Keep the sails in the wind," he said. "I don't want to be late for Nickus' wedding. The barrel contains his wedding present."

"That is one heavy barrel," the captain said. "It is safely secured. I noted you posted a guard."

Constantine had Yesus remove the guard.

The ship proceeded quite rapidly. At times the waves splashed over the bow of the ship. The Captain was in his glory. When they reached the Rhone River, Nickus' carriage awaited Constantine. Other carriages carried supplies and the other troops. The barrel and three guards were loaded onto a riverboat. When Constantine arrived in Lugdunum, he went to the church and talked with the priests. He wanted to ensure that his presence didn't interrupt Nickus marriage. The priest thanked him for his concern and took them to his house so they could relax. The bishop informed Nickus that Constantine had arrived. Nickus went to Constantine.

"I hoped you would attend my wedding," he said. "It means a great deal to me. I want you to meet Martha."

"I am looking forward to meeting her," he said. "Where will I be staying?"

"I have had rooms prepared for you and Yesus at the palace," he said. "The troops will stay with our guards."

Constantine ordered Yesus to have the barrel delivered to the palace living area. Yesus talked with Nickus' military attendant about the wedding gift and arrangements were made to secure it in the palace living area. The wedding was scheduled to occur in three days. The coins arrived the day before the wedding. Things occurred on schedule.

On the day of the wedding, Constantine and Yesus awoke early and put on their dress uniforms. Four guards in dress uniforms escorted them to the church. Most of the local townspeople attended the wedding. Some began to recognize the emperor by his uniform, and word spread throughout the church. After the ceremony, Constantine was escorted back to the palace. Nickus and his new wife, Martha, returned to the palace. The guests changed clothes and were seated in the living area of the house. The servants prepared a great meal for twenty of Nickus' friends. It was to be served at seven o'clock.

Martha noticed the barrel.

"I don't remember that being there," she said. "What is it?"

Nickus had the barrel moved to his wife. A guard opened the barrel.

"That is your wedding present," Constantine said. "I thought you might like it better than a silver spoon."

He smiled at the newlyweds. She couldn't believe her eyes. She wasn't sure what she was looking at.

"Is that what I think it is?" Martha said. "Is that real money?"

"He wants you to have whatever you want," Nickus said. "He is our very good friend."

Tears flowed from Martha's eyes, and she hugged Constantine. He remained with them for a few more days and then returned to Constantinople. The return trip was at a more leisurely pace. When Constantine arrived, Judge was at the dock. They talked while they rode to the palace. The following day, Constantine was busy at the office. He completed some work, but everyone wanted to hear about Nickus' wedding and about his wife. Constantine instructed Yesus to post a memo about the wedding celebration.

That evening after dinner, Constantine talked with Constans.

"Your brothers and I think it is time for you to learn how to ride a horse," Constantine said. "Would you like that?"

"I would love to have my own horse," Constans said. "I have been riding for about a year. The tutor taught me how to ride."

"That is very good," he said. "Both of your brothers are good horsemen."

"With a little practice, I could be better than either of them," he said. "May I have a black horse?"

"I will see," Constantine said. "I also like black horses. The horse that I ride in parades is black."

"Yes, I know," he said. "That horse would do for me."

"It really isn't a very good horse," he said. "I want you to have a smaller, well-trained horse."

Thank you, father," he said.

Constans went to sleep that evening with visions of black horses in his mind.

Judge was told to find a well-trained, black horse for Constans. He looked at several horses and selected a medium sized horse. Judge brought the horse to the palace and gave it to Constans. He jumped astraddle the horse.

"It is beautiful and moves like the wind," he said.

Constantine went outside and watched Constans ride his horse.

"Be careful," Constantine said. "Don't let him throw you."

"Judge found a horse for me," he said. "We will have many good times together."

After dinner, Constantine told Helena that Constans had his own horse. She was surprised that he knew how to ride. Constantine also told Helena about Nickus.

"He said he found the right girl and was getting married," Constantine said. "I was surprised."

Helena looked at Constantine and smiled.

"He told me that he had been scorned and would never marry," Helena said. "I knew he would get over it. He just needed a little help."

The following day, Judge came to Constantine's office.

"Your desk has arrived," Judge said. "It is the most beautiful desk I have ever seen. Now I know why you purchased it."

"Have it put in my office at the palace," he said. "It is too nice for my military office. Take my old desk from the palace to my office on post."

"Yes, sir," he said.

"Have you heard any news about the boats?" Constantine asked. "They should be completed by now."

"No," he said. "I will send the shipyard a message and find out what is causing the delay."

Three weeks later, Judge brought Constantine a message indicating the boats were ready for delivery. Constantine had them taken to the Roman fortification near the Istrius River. Constantine summoned Yesus to his office.

"I want you to take Constantine II and inspect the new boats," Constantine said. "Have him write a formal report about your finding."

"Yes sir," Yesus said. "We will leave in two days. I will make sure he does a good job."

"I want him to learn the proper way to document what he sees," he said. "Don't be easy on him."

They briefly discussed his son's future in the army.

Yesus and Constantine II found the boats to be built exactly as drawn and promised. Constantine II wrote an official report to the commander of the military. The report was very well written and Constantine II's maturity was duly noted. He would now be considered for future assignments on his merit rather than his father's orders.

CHAPTER 10

A Larger Museum

Helena acquired such a monumental collection of Christian relics from the Holy Lands that Constantine became concerned that the new church museum would not be able to display all of the relics properly. The church, the palace, and the barn were already full, and she continued to purchase items. Constantine didn't want to discuss the problem with her, but he felt compelled.

"Mother, how many relics have you purchased?" he asked, nervously. "I had no idea that many items from Jesus' life still existed. You must have been extremely busy."

She smiled coyly at him.

"I've found a few items of interest," Helena said. "Our people will enjoy viewing them in their museum."

"I'm afraid we are going to need a larger museum," Constantine said. "Your ability to find these relics far exceeded my expectations."

"I would like to display everything, so people can enjoy them," she said.

"How many more items do you plan to purchase?" he asked. "We have received something from the Holy Lands almost every week since you've been home."

"They will help the local church members," she said. "Christian relics will remind them of Jesus and his friends."

"I hope they aren't offended because you spent so much money," he said.

"We commissioned the construction of the museum so our people could enjoy the relics and be lifted spiritually by them," she said.

"If they can't see them, they won't learn much," he said. "If we don't know how many pieces we will be displaying, how can we plan for a larger museum?"

"I don't know," she said. "I told several people in Jerusalem to ship me everything they could locate."

Constantine stared at his mother. He began to understand the situation.

"You did what?" he asked. "We need to limit the purchases."

She smiled at Constantine.

"I told them the emperor wanted many relics," Helena said.

"That explains it," he said. "We need to send a message."

"The church is so full, I don't like how it feels," she said. "The palace is overcrowded, and the barn is completely filled."

"I will hire a master-builder to survey what you have," Constantine said. "That will be the easy part. Estimating what is still coming will be more difficult."

"The builder won't know what he is looking at," she said. You will need help from Constantina."

"No one will know what some of the pieces are," he said. "They need to be sorted."

"I would make the new museum at least ten times as large as the existing building," she said. "You could remodel the museum into a library for religious scrolls and codices. It's next to the church."

"Did you purchase many scrolls and codices?" he asked. "They need to be protected. This is getting complicated."

"Let's get started," Helena said. "I didn't have my treasures shipped home to sit in a barn and rot."

Constantine met with a master-builder to plan a new museum. The builder liked the suggestion of remodeling the existing museum. The plan was to turn it into a library with a large public reading room. He assured Constantine that Helena had accumulated an adequate number of scrolls and codices to fill the old building. Constantine realized the builder had been talking with Helena. He also knew that the relics had to be sorted before they could be displayed or before construction of a new museum could begin. He assigned the project to Yesus and Constantina. He gave them permission to hire ten workers. He posted four guards with the team.

"I need four men to stand guard at the palace," Yesus said. "This is about a two month assignment."

None of the troops volunteered.

"If you volunteer, I will give you seven days away from work with pay," he said. "If no one volunteers, I will assign four of you and you won't get any extra pay."

He waited patiently.

Ten men volunteered, and Yesus chose four of them. The next day, they started by locating all the scrolls and codices. They created a parchment indicating what was written on each scroll. Then the troops took the parchment and the scrolls to an empty bedroom in the palace. Next, they sorted through the material that had been placed into a fishing boat before the boat was sent home. The day workers cleaned each of the items. The boat was cleaned and placed on blocks. The nets and small items put back into the boat. They looked at the pile of building material stacked next to the barn, but couldn't figure out how to start the reconstruction of the jail.

The following week, they found twenty trees in the back corner of the barn. Most of them were still alive. Constantina quizzed the gardener.

"They won't survive this far north," he said. "I wouldn't bother planting them."

Constantina talked with Constantine about the trees and the gardeners' advice. He told her that the empire owned the island of Patmos. The island was south and didn't have many trees, because they had been timbered. Constantine made arrangements to ship the trees to Patmos. The soldiers, who were posted on the island, were to plant and care for them. He ensured they understood how important the trees were to him. Constantine told the soldiers that he would inspect the trees in two years.

A few days later, one of the guards approached Yesus.

"The worker over there," he said. "Put a small item in his pocket."

The guard escorted Yesus to the worker.

"What did you put in your pocket?" Yesus asked. "We gave you this job to help you, and now you are stealing from us."

The worker looked at Yesus. He was so scared, he was trembling.

"I found a coin," he said. "I planned to use it to purchase food for my family."

Constantina overheard their discussion.

"Let me see the coin," she said. "We need it for my grandmother's collection."

He reached into his pocket, took out the coin, and gave it to Constantina. She motioned for Yesus to take the worker away.

"Pay him his wages and send him home," she said. "You can find us another worker for tomorrow."

The following day, Yesus returned with a new worker. He introduced him to Constantina, and they continued sorting. Constantina knew that Jesus' cross had already been cleaned and hung in the church, so she was surprised when she came across the clothes and the nails they had purchased. She also found the lots and took them with her for safekeeping. Other large items were cleaned, labeled, and stacked. The smaller items were boxed based on where they had been purchased. After two months, the relics were finally ready for the new museum.

The next time Constantine met with the builder, he showed him a drawing. It indicated the location of the museum.

"I would build the museum as a public display," the builder said. "We can always acquire the land next to the park."

"I don't know if those people will relocate," Constantine said. "Living next to the park is a good location. I will have an inquiry made by a government official."

"They don't have to like it," he said. "The new museum might inconvenience a few people, but it is for the common good."

"I like happy people," he said. "I will authorize the town administrator to offer to purchase the property."

The builder looked at Constantine.

"That might delay our project," he said. "You don't have to be so nice. You could evict them."

Constantine glared at the builder, and then he went back to his office. He discussed the problem with Yesus.

A month later, Constantine met with the builder again to update him on the acquisition of the land for the new museum.

"Some of the people who live next to the park have accepted the government's offer to purchase their land," Constantine said. "We want to purchase enough land to make the park at least twice as large. We are having problems with a few families."

"We could build the park around them," the builder said. "Then they would have to sell their property at a very reasonable price."

"I want to start building the park, but I want as many happy people as possible," he said. "We will work with them a little longer. I will send Yesus to talk with them. He can generally get things accomplished."

Yesus met with the families that were reluctant to sell their properties. The first family had a very modest dwelling that wasn't worth much money. As soon as he saw the couple, he understood the problem.

"I represent the city," Yesus said. "I am authorized to offer you a fair price for your home."

"The offer is very fair," the home owner said. "We are old and have lived here for a long time."

"We understand," Yesus said. "We could help you move."

"We don't want to move," he said. "You will have to put us out."

"We would rather not do that," he said. "But you are giving us no choice."

"You are the government, and we are just little people," he said. "All of our neighbors want us to sell. They are very pleased with your offer."

"You have one week to make up your mind," he said. "If we have to move you, the offer will go away. I will come back to see you."

He walked down the street and met with the other family that caused problems. He knocked on the door, and woman answered. She was large with child and held her stomach with both hands.

"I guess you are here about our house," she said. "We have only had this house for a short time, and you can see I am with child."

Yesus wasn't certain what to say.

"It is very difficult for me to walk now," she said. "In a few days, I will have an infant. We can't move."

Yesus wished her well.

The following day, Yesus met with Constantine and they discussed the families. Yesus was certain the older couple could be moved and their needs could be satisfied. He didn't know what to do about the other family. Constantine told him to give the lady whatever it would take to move her.

Yesus returned to the woman's home.

"I want to talk with you and your husband," Yesus said. "When will he return from work?"

"He will be home at sunset," she said. "He doesn't want to sell."

"May I visit with you this evening?" he asked. "I need to talk with both of you."

"Yes, I suppose so," she said. "When he comes home, I will tell him you are coming this evening."

After sunset, Yesus returned to the house. When he knocked on the door, the husband opened it. They greeted each other, and Yesus was seated in the living area with the woman.

"You wanted to talk to both of us," he said. "We are very nervous about our child. This is our first child, and my wife is very large."

"I have talked with the emperor, and he told me to provide the best of care for your wife," Yesus said. "Tomorrow, a doctor will come and check on her. It is important to the city that you sell us your house."

"We don't want to cause problems, but we don't know what to do," he said. "You will have a doctor look at my wife?"

"Yes and that is just a small part of the city's offer," he said. "We will provide you with a larger house, so you have a separate room for your baby."

The couple agreed that they could use more room.

"I will have soldiers move your belongs to your new house, and the city will provide you with an attendant for six months," Yesus said. "I have found a very nice house for you. We want you to move tomorrow while the doctor is here."

The couple looked at each other. They asked Yesus to wait outside for a few minutes, so they could talk in private.

A few minutes later, Yesus joined them again.

"I have to work tomorrow," he said. "Will you stay with my wife during the move?"

Yesus agreed, and the couple relocated the following day.

The other family didn't take the offer and the city had them moved. Yesus didn't reduce the city's offer, and he monitored the entire process. The family was moved to a nice home and made as comfortable as possible.

A week later, Yesus visited with both families. The young woman had delivered her baby. She was happy with her attendant and things were well. Then, he visited the older family.

"Are you getting adjusted?" he asked. "Can I do anything for you?"

"No, we are fine," he said. "It wasn't as bad as we thought it would be. We were just scared."

Yesus smiled at them.

"When the new museum is open, I will take you to see it," he said. "We will ride in a carriage."

Later, Yesus reported his successes to Constantine.

Constantine met with the builder.

"After you purchase the land and increase the size of the park, I will build the museum at the end of the new park," the builder said. "When may I start?"

Constantine cringed at the question.

"The city has acquired the necessary land," he said. "You can get started."

The builder looked at Constantine and smiled.

"Good, we will start immediately," he said. "We have been waiting."

"Have you surveyed my mother's purchases?" he asked. "I was wondering about the largest item."

"She shipped several large items," he said. "She purchased the jail where Paul was imprisoned in Caesarea. It will have to be restored."

Constantine shook his head.

"I shouldn't have told her to purchase everything she found," he said. "I didn't think she would purchase an entire building."

"I also saw a statue of a lion in the park," he said. "It weighed so much, they could barely move it."

"Make the museum fifteen times larger than the old one," Constantine said. "When we run out of room, we will build another one."

Judge, Yesus, and Constantine looked over the building material in storage. After a long day of moving boxes, they had a good idea of the project before them.

Constantine looked at Judge and laughed. Judge controlled his laughter and only returned a large smile.

A month later, Constantine met with the builder again.

"I recommend we build a museum campus," the builder said. "The jail will be a great attraction. I can use the dirt that she sent back in the flower gardens. I will mix it with local soil."

"Make sure to tell her you used it," Constantine said. "It will complement the public park."

"I will start clearing the land," the builder said. "People won't complain about the public areas. I will include playgrounds for the children and picnic areas on a lake."

"Don't start with the jail," he said. "Start with the playgrounds."

"We also have some great doors," he said. "They came from a large temple. I will modify them and use them in the museum design."

"I will tell the troops in the park that their job is about to get larger," he said. "That will probably make them happy."

When Constantine returned to the palace, Judge met him.

"I have bad news," Judge said. "Your mother is very weak. I had the doctor come to see her. He is with her now."

"Come with me. We will go to her," Constantine said. "I want someone with me. Do you know the whereabouts of my sons?"

As they hurried through the hallways to his mother bedroom, Constantine exhibited a worried look.

"No," he said. "Constantine II is probably at his post in the park. I could check on Constantius II."

"Bring Constantius II to me," he said.

"Take good care of your mother," Judge said. "We'll look after things for you."

Judge found Constantius II and took him to his father.

"I am glad you are here, son," Constantine said. "Your grandmother is very ill. The doctor is with her."

"May I see her?" he asked. "I haven't spent much time with her recently."

"Not now," Constantine said. "When the doctor comes out of her room, he will talk with us."

After a long time, the doctor allowed Constantine and his son to visit with Helena. She faded in and out of consciousness. Constantine walked to her, bent down, and kissed her on the cheek.

"You will be fine," he said. "The doctor finished his examination and will find out what is bothering you."

"Tell the doctor I need a bottle of energy," she said. "The trip was too much for me."

Constantine tried to divert Helena's attention from her weakness. He held her hand.

"I am planning a new museum," he said. "It will be large enough to hold everything you've purchased."

"I probably won't live long enough to enjoy it," she said. "You can have the builder describe it to me."

"You will be fine, mother," he said. "I want you to rest. We will be with you."

The doctor didn't find anything unusual. He said she was elderly and had just run out of energy. Helena went to sleep. Constantine sat next to her in a large chair and squeezed her hand every time she coughed. After a few hours, Constantius II went to his room, and Constantine, with tears in his eyes, went to sleep.

That night, Helena died in her sleep. Constantine asked Judge to inform the other children. When they were all in Constantine's library, he explained that their grandmother had died. Constantina cried profusely. The grandsons were stricken with grief. Constantine remained with them. They all stayed at the palace that evening.

The next day, Judge went to see Constantine and discussed the funeral arrangements.

"I want the archbishop to bless her remains," Constantine said. "You can help him plan the funeral service."

"I will take care of it," Judge said. "Everyone in town will want to be at the church."

Judge departed and had a military escort bring Eusebius, the family's priest, to the palace. He prayed for Constantine and the children.

The following day, Constantine provided more details to Judge.

"My two older sons and I will be in dress uniform," he said. "Constans will be with his attendant."

"I will have temporary seating provided in the church and in the church garden," Judge said. "I will post a large number of honor guards and have Samson lead them."

"Thank you, Judge," Constantine said. "I will see you at the service. I am going to be with my children."

It was a sad day for Constantine; it was a sad day for Constantinople. The church was completely filled. Most of the city came to pay their respects to Helena. Constantina had draped black cloth over the cross to honor her grandmother. The cross reminded her of their trip to the Holy Lands. The archbishop spoke of Helena's life. He quoted from the book of John and said a prayer. After the service, the church bell rang for fifteen minutes while the archbishop and the priests consoled the attendees. Over the following weeks, the city mourned Helena's death.

A month passed before Constantine met with the builder.

"I want you to build the new museum as quickly as possible," Constantine said.

"You can count on me," the builder said. "I am ready to start construction."

"I want it named in my mother's honor," he said. The only gold I want used must be part of a display."

"I understand," he said. "I plan on using marble and cedar. It will be a magnificent building."

"Judge, a member of my staff, will inspect the construction, for me," he said. "If you need anything, ask him."

Judge talked briefly with Constantine about the museum. He inspected the construction progress every two weeks. When he thought the construction wasn't on schedule, he would inform Constantine. Judge was especially impressed with the marble the builder had chosen.

"The marble is very white," Judge said. "Our marble contains many more steaks of black. Where did you find it?"

"I had it shipped from Greece," the builder said. "I like the way it looks. It is a nice contrast with the red cedar."

"I am going to take a small piece of marble and show it to Constantine," Judge said. "I am certain he will be impressed with your effort."

"Thank you,' he said. "A good word to the emperor can be very helpful."

"When will the walls be finished?" Judge asked. "I will tell Constantine."

"It will be about another month," the builder said. "We have many interior walls to build."

"Why so many rooms?" he asked. "That would seem to make the construction more difficult."

"I want each room to feature a display," the builder said. "Small rooms hold fewer people, and they aren't as noisy as larger rooms."

"Helena collected many pieces," Judge said. "Will you display all of them?"

"I want to display about ninety percent of the collection," he said. "We will change about ten percent each year. That way people will come back to see the new pieces. Some displays will be different each year."

"That makes sense," he said. "I will see you in a few weeks."

Once a month, Judge wrote a formal site inspection report for Constantine. He mentioned the white marble in the report and attached a small sample. Constantine read the report and summoned Judge.

"I like the white marble," he said. "I also like the idea of contrasting it with red cedar."

"Yes," Judge said. "I think that will look very nice."

"I want you to have a ship load of red cedar trees from Lebanon planted around the museum," Constantine said.

Two months later, when Judge inspected the site, the roof was constructed.

"That is a great amount of wood," Judge said. "Are you going to use it all?"

"All the wood and some stone," the architect said. "The roof is very heavy."

"I like the columns," he said. "How many are there?"

"Twelve," he said. "Each column represents one of Jesus' original disciples.

It will create an impressive entrance."

"I saw a stone carver working on a large piece of marble," Judge said. "What is he carving?"

"I am having Helena's name carved into the marble," he said. "I will have it placed over the large doors. I am also having a disciple's name carved on the base of each column."

"You are doing a great job," he said. "I am sure Constantine will be very pleased."

"I hope he likes it," he said. "We are starting the gardens."

"Helena loved flowers," Judge said. "Create a large garden to honor her. I want something blooming all summer."

"That is my plan," the builder said. "Flowers will fill the garden. Do you know anything about the twenty-five cedar trees that have been delivered?"

"I guess I forgot to tell you about them," Judge said. "Constantine wants them planted around the museum."

"That will be a nice touch," the builder said. "I will have my workers plant them."

It took a year for the museum to be completed. Constantine devised a plan to ensure the people of Constantinople visited the museum. He planned a dedication ceremony. Many families brought their children to the park and visited the museum. The children especially enjoyed the new playground areas.

Judge congratulated Constantine. It was a grand complex. Everyone, who traveled to Constantinople, visited the museum. The dedication ceremony was on a beautiful, warm summer day. Constantine wanted the museum to be recognized as an extension of the church, so he invited the archbishop and several local priests to speak at the dedication. After the speeches, everyone received a commemorative coin and was treated to a picnic in the park.

"That was a fine dedication ceremony," Judge said. "Handing out the coins was a good idea."

"Those were the coins we had minted to give away at the dedication ceremony concerning the city," Constantine said. "It rained and everyone departed early."

"I brought a few barrels of coins to give away today," Yesus said. "Most people will save a coin as a good luck token."

"I hope they hoard them," Judge said. "That would mean they like them."

A few days after the dedication ceremony, Constantine met with the builder.

He complemented the builder on the design of the complex and how the many different items seemed to complement each other.

"I have taken several items from the church and put them into the museum," the builder said. "I hung the drawing that Helena purchased on her trip to the Holy Lands, in the church."

"The church looks much better," Constantine said. "It was too cluttered."

"I am glad you like it," he said. "We have a great church and a great library."

"That is what mother wanted," Constantine said. "I am certain she is happy."

He paused for a moment. "I am having new Bibles made for us."

"You are having new Bibles made for the church?" the builder asked. "Who is making them?"

"Eusebius is taking care of it," he said. "They will contain the twenty-seven books discussed during the Council at Nicaea."

"That is great," he said. "I have a few other questions."

"Let's hear them," he said. "I am a busy man and need to get to my office."

"What do you want me to do with the lion statue?" the builder asked. "It needs a final home."

"Where is it now?" Constantine asked.

"The troops had to remove it from the barge," he said. "They made a temporary pad for it in the middle of the old park."

"Right, I remember now," he said. "It is not a Christian relic. I don't want it near the church."

"I could meet with Constantina," he said. "She must have had something to do with purchasing it."

When the builder met with Constantina, he asked her where she wanted the lion statue to be relocated.

"The statue needs to be in the children's playground," Constantina said. "The children love to play on it."

She smiled at the builder.

"That is a good idea," the builder said. "We will relocate it. It is extremely heavy. I am glad you only purchased one."

Constantine provided twenty troops to move the statue. They built a rolling platform constructed of logs and used water and olive oil to help relocate the lion.

"The logs are sinking into the ground!" the builder yelled out. "Look out! It is going to turn over."

The lion fell over onto its side. The men worked the remainder of the day cutting more logs and building a lever to lift the statue. The logs were moved and the statue was placed on them again.

"Slowly, this time," the builder said. "It isn't far to the new platform. Easy, take it easy. We don't want to turn him over again."

Eventually, the lion was erected at its new location.

"I hope everyone likes this location," a soldier said. "I spent three weeks on the end of an oar getting that lion to our park, and I don't want to have to move it again."

He pointed at the lion and laughed.

A few days later, Constantine visited the park. The builder waved to him.

"Did you notice the gardens?" the builder asked. "They help blend the museum into the park."

'Yes I did," he said. "What about them?"

"I mixed the dirt your mother sent with our local soil to create the gardens," he said. "The walk from the museum to the garden is made of the bricks she sent home."

"That is wonderful," he said. "I am certain she would have loved the garden."

Constantine and the builder moved to the older part of the park.

"I thought long and hard about what to do with the jail," the builder said. "Putting it back together was a difficult project."

He explained that a small portion of the walls was new construction, but he had it built with used lumber.

"When the roof was installed, it leaked," he said. The repair took longer than building a new roof."

He looked at Constantine.

"I like what you did with the jail," Constantine said. "It looks like it belongs with the troop's quarters."

"That was on purpose," he said. "It causes fewer questions."

"I think the troops like the statement it makes," he said. "I don't expect them to ever use it."

They continued to walk.

"Your mother found a great number of scrolls," the builder said. "I tried to arrange them by author. I will need some help with that."

"Where did you place them?" Constantine asked. "I would like to see them. I will have the archbishop help identify the author of each scroll."

The builder indicated they made a large room in the old museum into a reading room for the new library. The second largest room contained scrolls and codices written by Christians. The smaller rooms contained other scrolls and written materials. He showed Constantine a drawing of the remodeled building.

"That is fine," he said. "I don't want the religious material that isn't orthodox placed with the material that correctly describes Jesus' life."

The builder agreed to put the non-orthodox material in a separate room and clearly label it as such. Constantine thought for a moment. He tugged on the builder's arm.

"How are you going to display the boat?" he asked. "It is not large, but inside it appears very large."

"We are designing a display," he said. "We still have several rooms that haven't been completed."

"You could create a fishing display," he said. "My mother sent back a great number of fishing nets."

"We will come up with something," he said. "I was thinking about a ramp so people could see into the boat. We could display the nets and other smaller items in the boat."

The flow of relics from Jerusalem to Constantinople had slowed dramatically.

"We are still receiving a few items," Constantine said. "I think most of the merchants have received my message to stop sending pieces to us."

"The museum is about full," the builder said. "We don't need any more items."

"I have an empty barn, and the city has a full museum. I like that arrangement."

"I am certain your young men will fill the barn with horses. Then you will need a fenced area for them to practice jumping logs and fences."

"You are probably correct," Constantine said. "I might send them to the military practice area."

The city park was very popular. It was a favorite place for families to picnic on the Sabbath day.

Judge and Constantine relaxed in the living area of the palace.

"I miss my mother," Constantine said. "I want to do more for her."

"I am expecting Eusebius to visit with us," Judge said. "He has an idea for you to consider. He should be here tomorrow."

The next day, Eusebius arrived at the palace.

"It would be a great honor if you changed the name of your mother's birthplace from Drepanum to Helenopolis," he said. "I am certain it would make her very happy."

Constantine wanted to know more, so he quizzed Eusebius.

"People might not like that," he said. "I don't want to alienate my people."

Eusebius explained that everyone loved Helena, and that her museum was the talk of the empire.

Finally, Constantine agreed that renaming her birthplace was a good idea.

"We could remodel the town, and then rename it," he said. "I am sure it needs a park and some new buildings."

"I will visit with the priest there," Eusebius said. "I know him."

"You take care of the details for the ceremony, and I will take care of the reconstruction," Constantine said. "I will build a terminal for our communication system highway."

"Perfect," he said. "That will provide Christians jobs and give them a new building."

A great crowd attended the opening of the new government building, and Constantine renamed the town in honor of his mother.

CHAPTER 11

CONSTANTINE TRAVELED WITH HIS TWO OLDER SONS

Constantine's two oldest sons, Constantine II and Constantius II, were now young men, and he decided it was time for them to experience Rome. He considered the trip to be part of their continuing education. Constantine II had been assigned to the troops posted in the public parks. His brother Constantius II was an accomplished equestrian. Constantine and Judge spent the day at the palace and planned the trip..

"I want them to visit Rome with me as representatives of our capital city," Constantine said. "I also want to take a large contingent of soldiers. If you want to travel, you can go as well."

"No, thank you," Judge said. "I prefer to stay and maintain the palace. I will make arrangements with Yesus. He likes to travel."

Constantine smiled at Judge. He remembered that Judge always got sick when he traveled by boat or ship.

"Determine if Samson wants to travel with me," he said. "He has experience transporting carriages and horses."

"Yes, sir," he said. "I am sure Samson would like to travel with you. I will invite him to dinner."

A week later, Samson came to the capital city to visit Constantine. Judge met him, and escorted him to the palace where they joined Constantine in his office. After they exchanged greetings, Constantine discussed the trip to Rome.

"I want you to accompany me on this trip," Constantine said. "You will command a group of soldiers."

"That sounds fine," Samson said. "How many troops do you want to take with us?"

Constantine held up a hand with his fingers extended.

"Fifty," he said. "I want my two oldest sons to be part of your company. I don't want them to know that I have arranged this. I want them to think of it as a military exercise."

"Yes, sir," Samson said. "I can handle that. Do you want to approve the other soldiers?"

"No," he said. "Choose who you think would be best to represent Constantinople."

"I will need some time to interview the soldiers," he said. "When do you expect to depart?"

"I plan to depart in one month," Constantine said. "I have the ship scheduled. Is that sufficient time for you?"

"Plenty of time," he said. "We will be ready. When the trip's itinerary is completed, have Judge send me a copy. I'll need to do a little planning."

"We are working on it," Constantine said. "We will send it to you next week."

Samson paused and looked at Constantine.

"How is your health, sir?" he asked.

"I am fine," Constantine said. "I planned to have a doctor accompany us. I might take the carriage rather than ride my horse."

"Very good, sir," he said. "I will prepare everything. We will take both black horses."

The following week, Constantine sent the itinerary to Samson and the ship's captain, Windus.

> Itinerary – estimated duration – one month
> We intend to visit the following areas as we journey to Rome.
>> 1. Athens
>> 2. Sicilia

We intend to visit the following areas as we return to
Constantinople from Rome.
1.Delphi
2.Crete
3.Thessalonica

Constantine – Emperor

When Samson and Windus received the itinerary, they planned their
trip. Samson tried to locate matching horses, and Windus ordered supplies
and reserved dock space.

Windus discussed the trip with his first mate.

"Mate, check the docks in Delphi," he said. "I have never docked in
that port. Ensure they know we are bringing the emperor."

"Yes, sir," the mate said. "It isn't on the sea. We will have to dock about
ten miles from Delphi."

The captain thought for a moment.

"That is close enough," he said. "They can use their horses and
carriages."

The day before the ship sailed, Yesus sent everyone a reminder message.
He wanted to ensure everything was ready. The next morning, Samson and
his troops arrived at the dock very early. They wanted to be onboard the
ship and have everything loaded before Constantine arrived.

When Constantine arrived, they greeted one another.

"My troops are aboard and in their quarters," Samson said. "All our
traveling equipment has been stowed."

He stood at attention and smiled at Constantine.

"I should have known that you would have everything ready for me,"
Constantine said. "How are my sons?"

"They are fine," he said. "They are looking forward to this assignment."

Windus saw Constantine talking with Samson and joined them.

"Good morning, Windus," Constantine said. "The troops and I are
ready to sail. How is the wind?"

"It is moderate and steady," he said.

He grinned at Constantine.

"I hope you and Samson enjoy your voyage."

"My two oldest sons are also traveling with us," Constantine said. "They are assigned to the troops."

The captain didn't ask any questions. He surmised he would receive additional instructions.

"I would like you and Samson to join me for dinner," Windus said. "My cook is preparing a special meal for us. Should I invite your sons?"

"No," he said. "They will eat in the galley with the other men."

Windus began to understand the situation.

"I have assigned a mate to care for you and Samson," Windus said. "If you need anything, he will take care of it."

"We will see you for dinner," he said. "Mate, prepare a place on the deck for me to sit in the sun this afternoon. It may do me some good."

The last of the supplies were loaded, and the ship set sail for Athens.

During the second day, a ship started to follow them.

"That ship is not flying a flag," the mate said. "All ships are required to identify themselves. I will keep watch on them."

Windus carefully studied the unidentified ship.

"Reduce speed, lower the main sail," Windus said. "I want them to catch up to us. Tell Samson that I want to see him."

"They are approaching us rather quickly," he warned.

Samson appeared at the captain's side.

"Samson, arm your men and bring all fifty to the main deck," Windus said. "I want our visitors to ascertain that we are a Roman military ship."

"They are coming alongside," he said.

"Man the starboard rail," Samson ordered. "Show them your weapons. Let's see if they really want to get any closer."

"They are turning hard to their starboard," Windus said. "It looks like they've decided not to approach us."

Samson exhibited signs of relief and looked at Windus for instructions.

"Good job, Samson," he said. "I am glad you posted all your men."

"Back to your quarters, men," Samson said. "We must continue our trip. We will fight another day."

"How did you get the name Windus?" Constantine asked. "It is a good name for a sailor."

"My father gave it to me," he said. "He was a sailor and thought it might bring me luck."

"It seems to be working," he said. "You are a captain."

"I like the name," he said. "It is always a topic of discussion."

As their ship approached Athens, Windus ordered his mate to hoist the emperor's flag. Other ships headed to Athens' harbor allowed the emperor's ship to proceed to the dock. Constantine stood on the deck with Samson and looked at the ships.

"I am going to visit the bishop and the governor," Constantine said. "Send ten guards with me. Escort the other men around the town. Be certain to include my sons."

"Yes, sir," Samson said. "We will get the carriage ready."

"Can you see the hills?" he asked. "The Parthenon is located on the top of the highest hill."

"I see them," he said. "I will be with you. My assistant is taking the men on parade."

"Good day, Windus," Constantine said. "I will return this evening. I am dining with the governor."

"Have a good day," Windus said. "We will load a few supplies and clean the decks."

Forty of the troops, including Constantine's sons, enjoyed their day climbing the hills of Athens. They visited historic sites and the great city park. The troops returned to the ship at sundown. Constantine and his guards returned three hours later.

The following morning, Windus escorted Constantine and the troops to a restaurant on the waterfront.

"I think you will like this restaurant," Windus said. "I eat here whenever I am in Athens."

"I like fish and eggs," Constantine said. "When do we sail?"

"We will sail in about two hours," he said. "I talked to the captain of a ship coming from Rome. He told me the weather was good, and we should find plenty of wind."

"Are you enjoying the journey, soldier?" Constantine asked.

"Yes, sir," Constantius II said. "It is a good assignment. It is our honor to travel with you.'

After breakfast, they boarded the ship. Constantine went to his cabin. The ship set sail to Sicilia. The weather was warm and sunny. The sails fluttered noisily in the wind. Samson allowed half of the troops to be on the main deck to enjoy the sun. The other twenty-five were in their quarters, standing by. Windus stood on the main deck and talked with his first mate.

"I was able to secure a good dock in Rome," Windus said. "We are going to take one hundred bags of grain from Sicilia to Rome."

"I will prepare one of the holes," the mate said. "The horses and carriage are in several of them."

"The grain will be waiting for us," he said. "I told them we would load the bags ourselves. Ask Samson to have some of his men help you."

"Yes, sir," the mate said. "Loading won't take them very long."

"I plan to spend the evening in dock," he said. "I think our guests will like Sicilia."

As the ship approached Sicilia, Samson explained the plan to his men. Constantine II and a few of the troops loaded the grain. Half of the troops were allowed to go ashore. The other half of the troops stood guard duty on the ship. Constantine, Samson, and Windus went ashore for dinner.

"Did you give my sons guard duty?" Constantine asked. "I don't want them to receive favors."

"No favors for them," Samson said. "One is ashore, and the other is standing guard."

"You must be keeping them busy," he said. "I have only seen them a few times."

"They are good soldiers," Samson said. "I have made certain they receive good training."

Constantine turned to Windus.

"What do you suggest?" Constantine asked. "I am hungry, I could eat a whale."

Windus tried to recall his last meal in town.

"I like the shell fish," Windus said. "The wine won't disappoint you."

"Samson, order shell fish and good wine," he said. "Give him a solidus."

The owner of the restaurant approached Windus to greet him.

"I see you have an important guest aboard," the restaurateur said. "Welcome to Sicilia."

"This is your emperor, Constantine," Windus said. "Samson is his escort and is responsible for the troops."

"Give us a table full of your best shell fish and a few bottles of your best wine," Samson said. "This should cover the costs."

He handed a gold solidus to the restaurateur.

"Our best is coming your way," he said. "I will have my best server standby your table. If you need anything, just ask."

They were first served bread, cheese and wine followed by shell fish and more wine. It was a very special dinner. They were in a joyful mood when they returned to the ship.

The next morning, the troops stood on the deck of the ship and watched as smoke escaped from the top of a mountain. The captain explained they were looking at a mildly active volcano. The crew maneuvered the ship to the open sea, and they sailed toward Rome.

While seated in Constantine's cabin, he and Samson discussed their plans.

"I will meet with Pope Sylvester the day after tomorrow," Constantine said. "The meeting will require a full dress guard."

"They will be prepared," Samson said. "I plan to have half of the troops on duty each day. I will be with you."

"I'll remain in Rome a week," he said. "Then we will sail to Delphi. If the Pope doesn't seem to be able to cure me, maybe the Oracle will."

He rubbed his elbow and flakes fell from his arm.

"How do you know the Pope will see you?" Samson asked. "He is a busy man. Some people make an appointment a year in advance of seeing him."

"See this gold solidus?" he asked. "This is my reservation."

He waved a solidus at Samson.

"Yes, sir," he said. "That should work."

The next day, Constantine met with the governor of Rome. The governor was very interested in hearing all about the new capital city. He indicated that Rome was now littered with unemployed politicians.

After their meeting, Constantine hurried to his meeting with the Pope. He was informed the Pope was too ill to see anyone. Constantine decided to return the next morning.

"I am sorry I couldn't see you yesterday," Sylvester said. "I am a sick man."

"You were supposed to heal me, and now it is you who is sick," Constantine said.

"You have been sick for many years," the Pope said. "But I think you will outlive me."

"I am sorry you are ill," Constantine said. "Have you seen a doctor?"

"No," Sylvester said. "I know my time is short. I am glad you are still able to travel."

"It is hard to believe," Constantine said. "My skin has been falling off for years, but I am still kicking."

When Constantine rubbed his head, flakes of skin fell to the floor. He smiled at the Pope. The Pope smiled.

"I was too sick to attend your mother's celebration of life," he said. "I would love to talk with you about her church and museum."

"She and my oldest daughter visited many towns in the Holy Lands," Constantine said. "They purchased almost everything related to Jesus' life."

"I am sure they found a great number of relics," he said. "I know you built a large museum for her."

"She actually purchased a jail where Paul was imprisoned," he said. "So now we have a jail in our public park."

"She was a great lady," he said. "Take care of her collections. They are an important part of history."

Constantine spent the remainder of the day telling Sylvester about Helena's journey to Jerusalem, and how the crosses stood guard at the church.

"She wanted to find Moses' rod, but she became too sick to travel," Constantine said. "I had my troops search the world. We found four in Egypt. I purchased all of them for her."

"I know. She threw all four on the ground," Sylvester said. "But none of them slithered away."

They looked at each other and laughed.

The meeting ended with both men in good spirit. Constantine returned to his cabin on the ship. He relaxed and sunned himself until it was time for the ship to depart. Samson joined Constantine on the main deck.

"Did all the troops get to see Rome?" Constantine asked. "It is still a great city with many great buildings."

"Yes, sir," Samson said. "We had a good time. Everything is stowed, and we are ready to shove off."

"You are starting to sound like Windus," he said. "Don't confuse your horse."

Constantine looked at Samson and smiled.

The troops stood on the main deck and waved as the ship sailed from Rome. Their next stop was Delphi. Samson knew the temple was several miles inland. After a few days, Samson motioned to Constantine.

"I see land," he said.

"We will stop for a day," Windus said. "We will be sailing early in the morning. Have a good day ashore."

"This should be interesting," Constantine said. "Get my carriage ready to travel. I will need several guards."

"We are ready," Samson said. "It won't take long to get to the Oracle's complex."

The ship docked, and Constantine and his guards departed for Delphi. The sun appeared as a great ball of fire in the sky. The day was hot. As Constantine's carriage traveled up the mountain, they passed several people walking up the mountain to seek advice from the Oracle. It was a long hard climb. When they arrived at the temple, a guard stopped them.

"I have come to see the Oracle," Constantine said. "Tell him I am here."

"Place your donation here," the pagan priest said. "I will give the coin to him."

"Show this to him." Samson said.

He waved a gold coin at the guard.

"Let me see that," the priest said. "A solidus! I am certain he will see you."

When they entered the room, the priest waved the coin at the Oracle.

"Come in," the Oracle said. "What can I do for you?"

"I have had this skin disease for many years," Constantine said. "I want you to cure it."

"That probably won't shorten your life too much," the Oracle said. "But you will have to live with it."

"You mean you can't cure it?" he asked. "I thought you knew everything."

"I don't know everything," he said. "I do know that your condition can't be cured."

"For some reason, I think you are correct," he said. "I am going to look around your complex."

"Make certain you see the other parts of the temple," he said. "You may like the theater."

Constantine looked at the Oracle.

"Good day," he said. "Next, we will sail to Crete."

"If you are wondering," the Oracle said. "The canal won't be finished for a thousand years."

Constantine was shocked by the Oracle's comment.

"I have two thousand slaves working on it," Constantine said. "They will finish it in just a few years."

"Don't make any plans for the dedication," he said. "The Roman Empire will be finished before the canal."

Constantine didn't know what to say. He excused himself and departed.

Constantine took a tour of the town that afternoon and then returned to the ship. He wasn't in a good mood. People stayed away from him. As the ship sailed, he tried to understand why the canal wouldn't be completed. He was certain two thousand slaves could dig a trench from Corinth to Athens in a few years. He remained puzzled.

A few days later, they docked in Crete.

Windus noted Constantine's aloofness and tried to lift his spirits.

"Good food ahead," Windus said. "We will be Crete for two days. I will have the ship loaded with supplies."

"Sir," the mate said. "Do you remember that ship that followed us into the dock?"

He pointed to an approaching ship.

"Yes, I see it," he said. "It looks familiar. Remove the emperor's flag."

"It is the ship that chased us just after we left Constantinople on our way to Rome," he said. "I am sure of it. I studied it carefully."

"Tell Samson," he said. "Maybe we can surprise them."

Samson conferred with Constantine. The troops were armed and some mounted their horses. After the suspicious ship docked, most of the crew went ashore. The Roman troops quickly boarded the ship. A few hand-to-hand fights erupted. Then mounted troops boarded the ship. The few pirates who remained onboard fought the soldiers.

"Hit them with your clubs and then have them trampled when they are on the deck," Samson ordered. "They chose to sail with the wrong captain."

"We surrender! Don't kill us!" the pirate cried. "When we signed on, we didn't know this was a pirate ship."

Samson didn't believe them and had them bound.

"In the name of the Emperor, I seize this ship," Samson said. "Line up and receive your leg irons. We are going to turn you over to the authorities to be hanged for piracy."

The captain of the pirate ship appeared.

"I demand a trial," the pirate captain said. "You can't have me killed. How do you know we are pirates?"

"Why did you follow us?" he said. "That was a bad mistake."

"We are merchants on a buying trip," he said. "We stopped in Crete for a good meal."

"I will inspect the ship for booty," Samson said. "I better not find anything you can't explain."

"I don't have to explain anything to you. You aren't the emperor," he said. "I sell a great many items."

Samson inspected the ship. He found a pair of candlesticks he recognized. When he returned to speak with the pirate captain, he had the candlesticks under his arm.

He handed on of them to the captain.

"Explain these candlesticks," he said. "I believe our archbishop will identify them as candlesticks stolen from the church in Constantinople."

The pirate captain glared at Samson.

"Ok," he said. "Maybe we can reach some kind of agreement. I have buried treasure."

Constantine joined Samson aboard the pirate ship.

"I will take you and your ship to Constantinople," Constantine said. "Guard, put this man in leg irons and take him to our ship."

"I will guard him," Constantine II said. "I will ensure we get him back to Constantinople. I want to hear more about the buried treasure."

Constantine II took the pirate to their ship and locked him in the brig. As Constantine returned to his ship, he was approached by Constantius II.

"I have captured several of the crew," Constantius II said. "They were drinking in the local tavern."

"Did you have any problem?" Samson asked. "Did they put up a fight?"

"Not much," Constantius II said. "We surprised them. We clubbed a few heads, and they surrendered."

He looked at Constantine for approval. Constantine nodded.

"Put them in irons and take them to our ship," Samson said. "We might have a few more surprises for them."

Several of the pirates escaped into the countryside of Crete. The others were securely bound and held prisoner on the ship. Constantine and Windus dined at a restaurant on the dock.

"You can tell this is a good restaurant," Windus said. "The cook is a very large man."

"How are we going to get the pirate ship to Constantinople?" Constantine asked. "We need another captain."

"My first mate and a few sailors will sail it," he said. "You should have Samson inventory their booty. Relax and enjoy your meal."

"I guess I am a little excited," he said. "Give me a glass of wine."

"What do you want to do tomorrow?" he asked. "It will take us a day to prepare the pirate ship to sail."

"I want to visit the church tomorrow," Constantine said. "Titus, a friend of Paul's, started the church. His family was from this area. Some of them probably still live in the area."

"Good, go visit the church," he said. "It is a beautiful church."

"You could visit the church with me," he said.

"I would love to go with you, but I have to help attend to the pirate ship," Windus said.

Samson assigned soldiers to guard the ship. The captain looked at Constantine.

"Say a prayer for me," he said. "After we prepare the other ship, I will eat some more fish. I really enjoy porting in Crete."

The next day, Constantine visited the church. Constantius II made an inventory of the booty found in the holes of the pirate ship. It appeared it had been stolen from several different ships and towns. Constantine decided to return directly to Constantinople.

"I think we should go directly to Constantinople," Constantine said. "We don't need to visit Thessalonica."

"I have a dock reserved in Thessalonica," Windus said. "It is a nice city and it is not too far from the sea."

"We have pirates to take to Constantinople," he said. "My plans have changed. You need to change yours."

Windus looked at Constantine.

"You have a carriage," he said. "You could ride to town. Thessalonica has a great church and a university."

"What about the pirate ship?" he asked. "When will it arrive in Constantinople?"

"It is no problem," he said. "It is a slow ship. I will go slow enough to observe it until we get closer to home."

"Just get me home. That's an order," he said. "I want to take care of business. You can take me to Thessalonica another time."

Windus understood the conversation had just ended.

"Yes, sir," he said. "I'll change course."

Constantine met with Samson and the troops. He explained it was very important to guard the pirates. They would be paraded through the park and made a public spectacle. When the ship docked in Constantinople, several troops met Constantine and his party.

"We have a present for you," Constantine said. "We have seventeen pirates for you to guard until they are hanged. Take good care of their captain."

"I will have my troops take them directly to jail," the sergeant said. "The troops that sailed with you must have done a good job."

"The pirate ship is following us and should be here this afternoon," he said. "I want to make a public display of the ship."

"I will take care of that," Samson said. "I have several troops who would be interested in doing that."

Each of Samson's soldiers was given a small piece of the booty. They treasured it as a memento more than something of value. The pirate ship was docked, and Windus' mate was hailed as a hero. When the town saw the pirate ship, they marched in the streets chanting, "Constantine! Constantine!"

The next day, Constantine met with his staff.

"Men, when we started for Rome, I didn't plan to capture pirates and their ship," he said. "It was a good trip."

"I will stretch their captain's arms and legs a little," Samson said. "Maybe he will remember where he hid his treasure."

"Don't kill him," Constantine said. "I think he deserves a public hanging. The entire town will probably turn out to see it."

"I think we should put the booty on display," Constantius II said. "I think everyone would be interested in seeing what pirates steal."

Constantine agreed to display the booty.

"Check with Windus and determine if the pirates' ship is any good to us," Constantine said. "Next week, clean it and allow the town's people to walk aboard it."

The pirate captain finally told Samson that he didn't have any buried treasure. He begged for his life. Samson put him in leg irons and returned him to jail. His trial was set for the following week. Constantius II spoke with his father.

"I spoke with one of your builders," he said. "He is going to display the booty in the park for one month."

"After that, melt it and put it in the treasury," Constantine said. "We will give it back to the people as free food."

The following day, Windus came to see Constantine.

"I looked at the ship," Windus said. "It is too old and slow for our use. I could find a buyer."

"Sell it after the people have toured it," Constantine said. "Have the money put in the treasury to be used for navel needs."

"Thank you," Windus said. "Good luck with the trial."

The pirates were tried by Constantine's army and found guilty of piracy. A public hanging was planned. Gallows were erected in the park.

"I don't want to be involved with their hanging," Constantine said. "Samson, take care of that for me."

"Yes, sir," Samson said.

The next day, the captain and his pirates were publicly hanged in the park. A great crowd attended the hangings. After the town's people departed, the bodies of the pirates were placed in unmarked graves outside of the city. The builder replaced the booty display with a stone carving, celebrating the capture of the pirates.

A week later, Constantine's sons visited him at the palace.

"Good evening, father," Constantine II said. "Thank you for inviting us to dinner."

"I hope you enjoyed the trip," Constantine said. "I also hope you learned something."

"It was a great trip," Constantius II said. "I learned a lot, and I am looking forward to more trips with you. Samson is a real soldier. I would serve anywhere with him. You can count on us father. How is Constantina?"

"That is why I asked you to dinner," Constantine said. "She has told me she would like to be married, so I found her a husband."

"Constantina got married?" Constantine II asked. "I guess that is what a woman plans to do when she gets older."

"Did you arrange the marriage?" Constantius II asked. "She is good trading material."

"I guess you could say that," Constantine said. "We are having some problems with a few of the outlying tribes."

"You could send an army to take care of that," Constantius II said. "To whom did you have her married?"

"She was married to your cousin, Hannibalianus," he said. "I gave him the job of ruling the problematic tribes."

He looked at his father and grinned.

"You gave him Constantina and the problematic tribes? That was quite a deal."

"He was agreeable," Constantine said. "It could be the start of a good career."

"What did she think?" he asked. "Did she agree?"

"Yes,' he said. "She loves him, and she told me about him."

"I can understand why she didn't remain in Constantinople," he said. "What's for dinner?"

"Please go to the dining area," Judge said. "We have goat chops and roots for you. Take your wine goblets."

"Did you attend the hangings?" Constantine II asked. "They were gagged and blind folded."

"No, I didn't attend," Constantine said. "They had to be killed, but I didn't want to be involved."

"We understand," he said. "They are buried and will soon be forgotten. They will only be remembered as pirates. No one will think of them as people."

"Someone will remember them as people," Constantine said.

After dinner, they retired to the living area and relaxed. Constantine II suggested that a coin be minted to celebrate the capture of the pirates. Constantine liked the idea and the next day asked the director of the mint to come to his office.

"Good day, emperor," the director said. "Do you need some coins?"

"I had the booty from the pirate ship melted and sent to the mint," Constantine said. "How much gold and silver did you receive?"

"I don't know, but I could check," he said. "I think it was mostly gold."

"I want you to have coins made using that gold and silver," he said. "Send an engraver to see me."

Three days later, an engraver visited with Constantine. The engraver agreed to engrave the pirate ship's likeness on the reverse side of the coin. Constantine's likeness would be on the obverse of the coin. The engraver was thankful for a new challenging job. He spent most of his time engraving dies to replace those broken while minting coins. He explained his job to Constantine.

"Some of the dies break after only fifty coins," he said. "Others last for over a thousand coins, but eventually they all break."

"What do you do with the old dies?" he asked. "They are metal."

"We melt them," he said. "I have probably engraved the same metal many times. I will have the mallet man make a few coins and bring them for your approval."

The following week, the engraver brought six coins to Constantine. He looked at them and smiled.

"I like them all," he said. "Which one is the easiest to produce?"

"This one would be the easiest," the engraver said. "The die will last a long time."

"Make coins until the metal from the booty is used," he said. "Then send the dies to the museum."

"We will start tomorrow," he said. "That was a good choice."

"Bring me about seventy-five silver coins," he said. "I want to give them to my troops."

That evening after dinner, Constantine met with Judge.

"Prepare a ceremony to honor our troops that captured the pirates," Constantine said. "I am having a few coins minted. I will present the coins as a token of the country's appreciation."

"I will talk to Samson and make the arrangements," Judge said. "Do you want to invite anyone else?"

"Invite the head of the senate," he said. "Bring Constans with you."

"I am not a very good babysitter," he said. "Can I bring his attendant?" Constantine looked at Judge.

"He isn't a baby," he said. "He is almost a teenager."

"If he were with his attendant, I would feel better," he said. "She is very good with him."

"Ok," he said. "You can bring his attendant."

"Thank you," Judge said. "I think it will be good for him to see his brothers receive commemorative coins."

The ceremony was held at the military quarters in the park. It was a special ceremony attended by about twenty guests. Constantine invited Windus and his first mate.

"It is an honor for me to make this presentation," Constantine said. "I have invited a few guests and those who traveled with me."

"We took fifty troops as guards and escorts for the emperor," Samson said. "I needed all of them."

"We were able to accomplish my objectives as well as capture the pirates and their ship," Constantine said. "Let me introduce you to the director of the mint."

"We melted the pirates' booty and minted coins," the director said. "The first few coins will be presented today. The others will go into circulation in one week."

"Samson, please come forward," Constantine said. "Take the fifty coins. Please give them to your troops. When you hand them a coin, call their name."

Samson presented the coins to the troops. Then Constantine presented coins to Windus and his first mate.

"Windus is the captain of the ship I use when I travel," Constantine said. "His first mate noticed the pirate's ship and both were instrumental in our apprehending them."

"It is our honor to serve you and the empire," Windus said. "I look forward to our next journey."

"Please take these coins as a token of our appreciation," he said. "I, too, am looking forward to my next journey."

After the coins were distributed, dinner was served. It was a special evening. A spirit of comradery filled the room. The guests mingled for several hours.

"Thank you for inviting me," the head of the senate said. "I see two of the soldiers are your sons."

"Yes," Constantine said. "They work as guards and with the troops in the park."

"My son is also in the army," he said. "He has been away for a long time."

"Is he a Christian?" he asked. "We post Christian soldiers at the church."

"Yes, I think he is a Christian," he said. "His mother insists we both go to church."

"Give his name to Samson," he said. "Maybe he will have a job for him closer to home."

The celebration ended and everyone departed.

Two months later, the head of the senate came to Constantine's office.

"I just wanted to thank you," he said. "My son is now working in the mess-hall at the local military base."

"He must be a good cook," Constantine said. "I am sure Samson will keep him busy. I am glad he is closer to home."

"He is a very good cook," he said. "His mother taught him how to cook. We are very proud of him."

"Tell him to work diligently," he said. "How long has he been in the army?"

"Twelve years," he said. "He is doing well."

"I will tell Samson to take good care of him," Constantine said. "We like soldiers who stay with the army."

"He will remain in the army," he said. "He never wanted to do anything but be a cook for the military."

"Tell him to see Judge," he said. "Have him prepare a meal for me."

Judge and the cook met to plan a dinner for Constantine.

"Make certain everything is just right," Judge said. "I have some special wine you can have served. If the emperor likes his dinner, you might be assigned to cook at the palace."

"This lamb is delicious," Constantine said. "Where did this wine come from? It tastes as good as the wine in Gaul."

The cook was assigned duty in the emperor's kitchen. Constantine especially liked his soups. After a few months, he was promoted to sergeant and cooked full time at the palace.

CHAPTER 12

A TRIP TO THESSALONICA

Constantine had not visited Thessalonica for many years. It was a great city and home to Galerius, one of the co-rulers of the empire before Constantine solidified the empire. It had a great university, an imperial palace, and a hippodrome. Constantine once considered it as a possible capital of his Roman Empire. He had planned to visit there when he traveled to Rome., but capturing the pirates interrupted his plans. He discussed a possible trip with Judge.

"I am considering taking my youngest son, Constans, and his sister, Minera, to Thessalonica," Constantine said. "Please make the necessary arrangements."

"I will check with Minera's attendant," Judge said. "I must ensure Jana is available."

"She can be made available," Constantine said. "I want you to post a military escort for Constans."

"I am certain I will have many volunteers to travel, but escorting Constans is another story," he said. "I will remind them it could be good for their military careers. Do you want to take your other sons?"

"No," he said. "They are busy here. I want them to continue their training at their posts and the military academy."

"I will tell Samson what we have planned," he said. "He will resolve the military issues."

"Please ensure that Minera and Constans eat dinner with me this evening," he said. "Put a small table next to Minera for Jana. I want to talk with them."

"Yes, sir," he said. "Dinner will be served at six o'clock."

Constantine went to the harbor to visit Windus. He found him on the main deck, of the ship, instructing the sailors how to fold the main sail.

Constantine and Windus exchanged greetings.

"Where are we going this time?" Windus asked.

"You said, you would take me to Thessalonica," Constantine said. "I am ready and will be taking a couple of guests."

"Who will be traveling with us?" he asked. "Do I need to make special arrangements?"

"I am taking my son, Constans," he said. "He will travel with a military escort. He is eleven years old."

"That is no problem," he said. "I am looking forward to meeting him."

"I will bring his tutor with him, and I will bring my daughter," he said.

A worried frown appeared on Windus face. He paused for a moment and considered what Constantine had just said.

"Your daughter will be traveling with us!" he queried. "What is her name?"

Constantine looked at Windus.

"Her name is Minera," he said. "She is older than Constans. She will have her attendant Jana with her. They desire to share a cabin."

"Yes sir," he said. "I will have a mate stand guard."

"That won't be necessary," he said. "Samson will provide guards for all of us."

"How many troops will be traveling with you?" he asked. "I will arrange quarters for them."

"We will also be taking two carriages and several horses," he said. "I will have Samson give you our itinerary and a list of our traveling entourage."

"That would be helpful," he said. "When do you plan to travel?"

"I don't know," he said. "When the details are all understood, I will have Judge send you a message."

That evening after dinner, Constantine and his children relaxed in the living area of the palace. Jana was asked to stay with Minera.

"During my trip to Rome, I planned to visit Thessalonica," Constantine said. "The pirates changed our plans."

"Are you referring to the pirates that were hanged in the park?" Constans asked. "You took care of those pirates."

Constantine glanced at his son.

"Now, I want to make the trip to Thessalonica," he said. "Would you like to travel with me?"

"Certainly, I want to go with you," Constans said. "When do we depart? I have to get packed."

"Minera, are you interested?" Constantine asked. "I would like you to accompany me."

"I don't know," she said. "Currently, I am learning about the duties of the emperor's daughter."

"I don't know of a better way for you to learn," he said

"May Jana travel with me?" Minera asked. "I should have a female traveling companion."

"Yes," Constantine said. "You are correct. I want her to travel with you. Both of you will have military guards."

"Are our other brothers going?" Minera asked. "They went with you the last time you traveled."

"No," he said. "They too are busy with their training."

"If Jana can travel with me, I would be pleased to go," she said. "I want her with me at all times."

"Fine," Constantine said. "I will have Judge speak with Yesus."

Minera met with Judge several times and reviewed proper etiquette. She wanted to do everything correctly, so her father would be proud of her.

After much discussion, the group decided they would depart after two weeks. Minera wanted plenty of time to pack.

Yesus went to see Windus. They greeted one another, and Yesus explained Minera's idiosyncrasies.

"Allow me to inform you about Minera," Yesus said. "She will be bringing her attendant and enough clothing for ten women."

'I see," Windus said. "She is going to need extra space."

"Yes," he said. "Both of them will need extra space."

"I will arrange for her to have two cabins," Windus said.

"That would be helpful," Yesus said. "Make certain everything is extra clean. She is very fussy."

"It sounds like she is a little like her grandmother," Windus said. "She was my guest on several occasions."

"Yes, but much younger," he said. "She is about fifteen."

Yesus didn't know her actual age.

"Fifteen," he said. "This is going to be an interesting journey."

Yesus returned to the palace, and Windus started making plans with his crew.

Two week later, the royal party approached the ship. An extra wagon was needed to carry the women's baggage. Windus greeted the emperor.

"I am afraid my daughter is bringing a wagon full of clothes," Constantine said. "I have never traveled with her before."

"I have everything prepared," Windus said. "I spoke to Yesus. She has been provided two adjoining rooms."

Constantine appeared relieved. He smiled at Windus.

"Good," he said. "Please be attentive to my daughter and her attendant."

"We will take good care of everyone," he said. "Cabin number one is waiting for you."

"I am going to stand by the railing on the main deck," Constantine said. "I want to watch the sailors finish loading the ship."

"We will stow all the clothing," Windus said. "Nothing is ever normal on this ship. We are accustomed to facing a variety of situations."

"We have thirty troops and twelve horses," Samson said. "This is a shorter trip with fewer stops."

"It sure is a nice day," Constantine said. "I like the sunshine."

He removed his hat and ran his fingers through his hair.

"The sea encourages everyone to become invigorated," Windus said. "I especially enjoy the sensation of salty sea breeze on my face."

Constantine looked at Windus and noted his smile.

The crew carefully transported the women's belonging to their cabins. Samson posted a guard at their door. The carriages and horses were loaded, and the ship started to move. The sailors manned oars. The wind was very gentle. After the ship cleared the dock, the sails were hoisted and they filled with wind. They were underway.

"Are we allowed to go on deck?" Minera asked. "I want to stand in the sun."

Jana looked at her and shrugged her shoulders.

"Let's go," she said. "I don't think anyone is going to stop you."

They opened the cabin door and stepped outside.

"Good day," the guard said. "May I help you?"

"Where can we enjoy the sun?" Minera asked.

"This way, please. Watch your step," he said. "We will go to the main deck. If you would like a chair, I will get one for you."

Jana smiled at Minera.

"See, I told you," Jana said. "This is going to be a good trip."

"It might be fun," Minera said. "Did you see all the soldiers?"

"Yes and I saw your father," she said. "He is going to make sure we don't have too much fun."

"He loves us," she said. "Hold on. That was a big wave."

The women stayed on the main deck a short time and then returned to their cabin. They were excited about traveling and talked for an hour in their room before the guard knocked on the door.

"The captain has invited you and Jana to dine at his table this evening," the guard said. "Dress will be formal this evening."

"Jana, get some of my nice clothes and put them on the bed," Minera said.

"I am glad you gave me some dresses to wear," Jana said. "I've never been a guest at a formal dinner. This is going to be fun."

The women spent the remainder of the afternoon dressing for dinner. A few minutes before dinner, two guards appeared and escorted the women to the captain's table.

Constantine saw his daughter. He was surprised how mature she appeared.

"Good evening, Minera," Constantine said. "We dressed just for you. On the return trip, we will have one additional formal dinner."

"What should I wear on other occasions?" Minera asked. "I want to dress properly."

"Just dress like you are at the palace," he said.

The women looked at each other and were seated.

"May I bless the food?" Minera asked.

"Yes," Constantine said. "Go ahead, we are waiting."

After the prayer, dinner was served.

"You look very handsome," Minera said to her brother. "I like your cadet uniform."

"You look handsome also," Constans said. "Both of you look handsome."

"You mean they look beautiful or charming," Constantine said. "Men look handsome."

"You and Jana look charming," he said.

Constans paused and looked at Constantine.

"I am going to learn a lot on this trip."

After dinner, the younger people were escorted back to their cabins. They talked about the dinner until they went to bed.

Constantine and Windus smiled at one another and enjoyed a glass of wine.

"I appreciate all your extra work," Constantine said. "Constans will probably be emperor someday."

"You have a fine group of children," Windus said. "Have I met all of them?"

"Yes, I believe you have," he said. "These are the only two still living at the palace."

"I remember Constantina," he said. "She traveled with your mother."

"She is married now," he said. "Her husband is a warrior."

The moon shown in the sky, and the ship cast an eerie shadow on the sea as they sailed toward Thessalonica. The sound of waves breaking against the side of the ship could be heard all night. When the sun rose, they went to breakfast.

"I will probably spend an entire day just at the church," Minera said. "Which days are free for us to explore the city?"

"Tell Samson what you would like to do, and he will provide guards and transportation," Constantine said. "He will work with your schedule."

"The apostle Paul was in Thessalonica on his second missionary journey," she said. "That is what the archbishop told me."

"I know that Paul wrote several important messages to the church that he founded," Constantine said. "The members always needed his direction."

"I also want to visit the university," Minera said. "I understand it is impressive."

"I looked closely at making Thessalonica the capital of the empire," Constantine said. "I wanted a deep harbor, and Thessalonica's docks are several miles from the town."

The women enjoyed the sun and the breeze as they stood on the main deck. They pretended not to notice the sailors that stared at them. The afternoon passed quickly. The next day, they arrived at Thessalonica. Samson directed the offloading of the horses and carriages.

"Keep a tight hold on them and don't slow when you reach the ramp leading to the dock," Samson said. "You have to let the horses know you are the boss. After they understand you are in control, they will follow you."

"Yes, sir," the mate said. "We will get the carriages in a few minutes."

"Good morning," Constantine said. "I have a meeting at the university at noon."

"We are taking Minera and Jana to the church," Samson said. "Constans wants to see the hippodrome."

"Fine," he said. "Send several guards with them."

Constantine and his body guard departed for the university. Constans rode his horse to the hippodrome. Minera and Jana rode their carriage to the church.

Minera met with the senior priest.

"Good morning miss," he said. "I notice you have a soldier with you."

"Yes," Minera said. "Several of them are waiting outside."

"May I help you?" he asked.

"I am Minera," she said. "Emperor Constantine is my father. He will visit with you while we are here."

"The emperor is here?" he asked.

"He has a meeting at the university," she said. "I think the bishop is with him."

The priest paused for a moment. He considered what he should say.

"We like soldiers," he said. "Thirty years ago, Demetrius of Thessalonica was martyred by Galerius."

191

"Was he a soldier?" Minera asked. "I don't know about him."

"He protected us from the Slavic people," the priest said. "Galerius had him killed because he was an orthodox Christian. His family belonged to this church."

"I am very sorry," she said. "My father was not friendly with Galerius."

"We all love your father," he said. "Maybe he will build a church to honor Demetrius."

"He has helped many towns build churches," she said. "I understand Paul sent several messages to this church."

"Yes, he did," he said. "He wrote to us at least three times."

"Would you like to donate one of Paul's messages to my mother's museum?" she asked. "I could put in a good word for your new church with my father."

The priest smiled at Minera.

"I might be able to give you one scroll," he said. "It doesn't address any particular problem like his other messages."

"When my father visits you tomorrow, please talk with him," she said. "Mother collected many scrolls."

"Who is the lady you brought with you?" he asked. "Is she your traveling companion?"

"She is more than that to me," she said. "Jana is my attendant. She is always with me. I have learned a lot from her. She is a good Christian."

"Welcome, both of you," he said. "Please pray at the rail."

Minera and Jana said a prayer and departed to meet Constans at the hippodrome. When they arrived, they didn't see Constans. They also weren't impressed with the chariot races, and decided to return to the ship.

At seven o'clock, a guard knocked on their door and announced dinner was being served in the captain's dining area. When they arrived, Constantine greeted them.

"No dress uniforms tonight," he said. "You young ladies look charming. Good evening Constans."

Minera blessed the food, and everyone started eating.

"After dinner, I want to hear about your day," Constantine said. "Mine was very interesting."

Soup was served first, followed by hot bread and fish. Wine was available for the adults. Goat's milk was served to the ladies and Constans.

Minera looked at her father.

"I think Jana and I should be allowed to have one glass of wine with our dinner," she said. "We are young adults."

"I don't think so," Constantine said. "Constans is too young."

"I wasn't talking about Constans," she said. "I am much older than Constans, and Jana is much older than me."

"Mate, serve the ladies each one glass of wine," he said.

The mate nodded.

After dinner, the table was cleared and they talked.

"The bishop and I discussed the writings of Thomas," Constantine said.

"You mean the saying written by Jesus' brother?" Minera asked. "I thought some of them were interesting."

"The bishop felt that Thomas didn't consider Jesus equal to God," Constantine said. "Thomas considered God to be greater than Jesus."

"I guess it would be difficult to acknowledge that someone you grew up with is God," she said. "I understand that."

"How was your day, Minera?" Constantine asked. "Did you spend all day at the church?"

"Jana and I talked with the senior priest for a long time," she said. "When you see him, he might want to discuss a new church."

"You didn't promise him a new church, did you?" he asked. "They probably want to honor Demetrius."

"No, I didn't promise him anything," she said. "You are correct about the church. He has something to trade."

"What does he want to trade for a new church?" he asked. "It must be unique."

"It is a scroll written by Paul," she said. "It would make a great addition to grandmother's museum."

Constantine smiled at Minera.

"I will talk with him," he said.

"We also stopped by the hippodrome," she said. "We didn't stay very long. There were a bunch of chariots going around the track."

"They were racing," Constans said. "It is easy to find someone who will wager. Everyone thinks he knows who is going to win."

"It is a silly sport," she said. "The horse does all the work."

"You have to know how to drive," he said. "A good driver with an average horse can win some of the time."

"It sounds like you watched many races," Constantine said. "Did you pick any winners?"

"I did pick several winners," he said. "My guards wouldn't allow me to wager."

"Good," he said. "We don't wager."

"Samson, how was your day?" Constantine asked. "You are quiet tonight."

"I had a little problem," he said. "Two of our guards were put into the local prison."

"What did they do?" Constantine asked. "Did you have them released to your custody? Do you have them in our prison?"

"Yes, they are in our prison," he said. "Two half-drunk patrons made a derogatory statement about them being baby sitters. The patrons are lucky they are still alive."

"Your soldiers deserve medals," Constans said. "They were defending me."

"They have to learn that they represent the empire," Constantine said. "Keep them in jail until we leave town. No more time on shore for them on this trip."

"Yes, sir," Samson said. "I think that is fair punishment."

"I don't think they deserve to be punished," Constans said. "You don't need to punish them. They are my heroes."

"Don't be too hard on them," Minera said. "I might visit them in jail. Jesus visited people in jail."

"He wasn't the emperor's daughter," Constantine said. "Forget the jail visit. Go to another church."

"I think they brought honor to the family," she said. "We should at least visit them."

"I think it is better that you don't visit with them," he said. "If you do, our troops might give them a bad time."

"I didn't think about that. You are probably correct," she said. "After we are home, maybe I will visit them."

The next day they rose early for breakfast. A chariot waited to take Minera and Jana to the university. Constans went to the hippodrome again. Constantine went to the church and found the priest waiting for him.

"I understand you talked with my daughter about a new church," Constantine said. "You know we are scheduled to build you a new church. The bishop approved the final plans yesterday."

"Yes, I know," the priest said. "She was trying to get something for her grandmother's museum. I didn't want to disappoint her."

"She said something about a scroll," he said. "Were you going to give me a scroll written by Paul?"

"It might have been written by Paul," he said. "We aren't sure who wrote it. It is different from the other scrolls we are certain he wrote."

He handed the scroll to Constantine.

"Are you sure it is old enough to be written by Paul?" he asked.

"Yes, the scroll is very old," the priest said. "It has been here in our inventory. We have had it long enough for it to be original."

"Then what is your concern?" he asked.

"Well, Paul generally addresses a problem in his messages," the priest said. "This particular scroll is sort of chatter."

"So, it wasn't a church directive?" he asked. "Paul probably was writing to someone who he knew."

"It is yours," he said. "Have your linguist authenticate it."

"It will make an interesting display in our museum," he said. "Minera will think she contributed a scroll to the museum. Don't tell her we had a deal in place."

"Not me," the priest said. "I will say a prayer for us and for the scroll."

"Let's walk to the site where the church will be built," Constantine said. "It is a nice location."

They spent the remainder of the day talking about the church.

When Minera and Jana were at the university, they talked with the faculty about Constantinople.

"It is a beautiful city," Minera said. "It has a large city park and many new buildings. It is known for its deep port on the sea."

"How large is the university?" a professor asked.

"I don't really know," she said. "The professors come to the palace for my lessons. I have never attended a class on campus."

"And your brothers?" he asked. "Do they attend the university?"

"No, they don't," she said. "They have tutors and attend the military academy."

"What is the military academy?" he asked.

"It is on the military complex," she said. "The army officers are their instructors."

It became obvious to Minera and Jana that the professor was asking too many questions. They reasoned that he might like Minera. They enjoyed the attention and decided to continue the conversation. Minera looked at the professor.

"Can they speak Greek?" he asked. "Do they learn about mathematics?"

"My older brothers can speak Greek," she said. "They are very good horsemen. My younger brother, Constans, is learning Greek."

"If I ever get to Constantinople, will you show me the military academy?" he asked. "I would like to see it."

"I would love to show you the academy," she said. "You could have dinner at the palace with me."

"Your father might not approve of me," the professor said. "He probably has great plans for you."

"He might have plans for me," Minera said. "But I like to make my own decisions. I will expect you to visit with me."

"Thank you," the professor said. "I am sorry, but I have to depart and teach my class."

Minera was enthralled with the professor. She looked at Jana and winked.

Minera and Jana were very popular with the faculty and the students. They spent the entire day at the university. Constans watched the chariot races.

At the end of the day, they returned to the ship. Dinner was served at seven o'clock.

"We have fish soup this evening," the mate said. "Then we will have hot bread followed by chops and roots."

"Don't forget my glass of wine," Minera said. "Jana also wants a glass of wine."

"Yes, miss," he said. "Two glasses of wine for the ladies and one goat's milk for the young man. I will put a decanter on the table with glasses for our other guests."

"That is fine, mate," Windus said. "Make it two decanters of wine for us. We are sufficiently old."

He looked at Constantine and laughed.

After dinner, the table was cleared. They relaxed and talked about their day.

"Tomorrow I am going to the mint," Constantine said. "I don't have anything planned for you."

"I have a city tour planned for the ladies," Samson said. "Your carriage will be ready after breakfast. Lunch is planned on the dock."

"That sounds nice," Minera said.

She spoke very softly and batted her eye lids.

"I met a very nice professor today."

"You met one professor?" Constantine asked. "I thought you might meet many professors today."

"I did," she said. "But I only invited one to have dinner at the palace with me."

Constantine was stunned but pretended not to be overly concerned.

"What is his name?" he asked. "Is he an old man?"

"His name is Morus," she said. "He might be twenty-five years old."

"Samson, find out about our future guest," he said. "I want to know about the men who call on my daughter."

"Jana, did you meet any professors?" Constantine asked. "There seem to be plenty to go around."

"No, sir," she said. "I have a man friend at home. He is in the army."

"What does he do for us?"

"He is a medical assistant," Jana answered.

"We need medical assistants," Constantine said. "Good luck with him."

Constans explained how he spent the entire day at the hippodrome. He loved the chariot races and even met several of the drivers.

The next morning after breakfast, Constantine went to the mint. The ladies went on a tour of the town, and Constans went back to the hippodrome.

When Constantine arrived at the mint, he and two guards went inside.

"I have a meeting with the director of the mint," Constantine said. "Tell him I am here."

"He is expecting you," the aid said. "Follow me; I will take you to his office."

Constantine and the director of the mint greeted and were seated.

"Please have your engraver join us," Constantine said. "I want to talk with him."

The chief engraver for the mint joined them.

"We are planning to build a new church," Constantine said. "We want to sell commemorative coins to help fund the project."

"What do you want on the coin?" the director asked. "We need you to identify two images."

"The obverse will be a likeness of me," he said. "The reverse will be a likeness of Demetrius with the new church in the background."

"I will render a sketch for your approval," the engraver said. "I will return in approximately three hours."

The engraver scurried to his office.

"I have brought two barrels of silver bars," Constantine said. "You can use it to make a barrel of coins for the church."

"Two barrels of silver bars will make several coins," the director said. "It will depend on the size of the coin you desire."

"I have also brought several pounds of gold," he said. "Use it to make coins. Send half of them to me and give the others to the bishop."

"What size coins do you want?" the director asked. "If you have two barrels of silver and want a barrel of coins, the coins will be about this large."

The mint director formed a circle with his index finger and thumb. He held it up for Constantine to see.

"That is about the size I want," he said. "Make the gold coins the same size."

"Do you want the coins shipped to Constantinople?" he asked. "It will take me some time to have the dies carved and the coins minted."

"No, give the barrel of coins to the church," he said. "They are going to sell the coins. The metal bars are the empire's gift to Thessalonica."

"I will mint the coins as our present toward the new church," he said. "Demetrius was a fine man. I knew his father."

"I would like to tell the church when they will receive the coins," he said. "Is one month enough time?"

"Certainly, if you approve the sketches for the reverse today," he said. "We have an obverse die we can use."

"Let go to the dock for lunch," he said. "I will treat you to fresh fish."

They rode to the dock and found a restaurant with a table overlooking the harbor. It was a beautiful day. They sat in the sun and enjoyed the warm weather and sea breeze. The gulls chased the pieces of bread Constantine tossed them. After lunch, they visited with the church priest and then returned to the mint. Constantine approved the sketch of the reverse side of the coin and returned to the ship.

Two hours later, Constans returned.

"I am getting tired of the chariot races," Constans said. "I am ready to go home. Did you have a good day?"

Constantine went into great detail about the coins being minted. He wanted his son to understand the dynamics of business and political agreements. Constans listened carefully. Minera and Jana returned to the ship. Dinner was served at seven o'clock. Constantine announced that they would be sailing the following afternoon.

"We had a wonderful time today," Minera said. "This is a nice town and the people are great."

"We saw a large theater and the market," Jana said. "I like our market better. Their market was dirty."

"It is probably much older than our market," Constantine said. "Our market is very clean and well kept."

"Did you have a good time looking at the mint?" Minera asked. "Is it like our mint?"

"Yes, I had a great time," he said. "It is a lot like our mint. They

199

are going to make some coins for me. When I receive them, I will give you one."

"Thank you, father," she said. "I am ready to go home. Maybe, Jana and I will shop in the morning."

"I will prepare a carriage for you," Samson said. "Please return by noon. I need to stow the carriage and stable the horses."

"We will leave to shop as soon as we eat breakfast," she said. "I hope the shops are open."

"Tell Samson where you want to shop," Constantine said. "He will arrange everything for you."

That evening, the group ate a light meal on the main deck of the ship while they looked at the town. The candles seemed to flicker like fireflies in the evening darkness. They became sleepy and went to their cabins.

Breakfast was served early. The ladies went shopping, Constantine and Constans walked along the dock.

"Samson had this shop opened early just for you," the guard said. "One of us will go in with you."

"We will be fine," Minera said. "I hope they have clothes that I like."

"Good morning," the shopkeeper said. "What may I show you?"

"I want some new clothes for me and my attendant," Minera said. "We are about the same size."

"I have a lot of clothes," he said. "My wife will help you ladies."

The shopkeeper's wife escorted the women to a table full of soap.

"I also have nice lilac soap and leather bags," he said. "I like the smell of lilacs. We will take all the lilac soap."

"You want all of it?" he asked. "I have twenty bars."

"Is that all you have?" she asked. "We have a large ship."

"I could get some more," he said. "When do you sail?"

"After lunch," Jana said. "Give the soap to the guard. He will put it in our carriage."

"I like this hat," she said. "Jana, do you like it?"

"Yes," she said. "I like it."

"I'll take this hat," she said. "I also want these five dresses."

"They may not be a perfect fit," he said. "Do you want to try them on?"

"No," she said. "If alterations are necessary, my seamstress will make the necessary changes."

When Minera went to pay the shopkeeper, she realized she hadn't brought any money. She told the shopkeeper, and he became agitated and asked her to send her guard for some money. She wasn't happy with the shopkeeper. The guard returned to the ship. Samson returned to the shop with twenty soldiers and some money.

"I believe Miss Minera owes you some money," Samson said. "How much does she owe you?"

"Are they your troops?" the shopkeeper asked. "Almost one solidus, she wanted several dresses."

"The troops are hers," he said. "We work for her father, the emperor."

The shopkeeper was stunned.

"The emperor?" he asked. "I didn't know she was Constantine's daughter."

"You should treat all of your customers as if they are the emperor's daughter," he said. "Minera, do you want anything else?"

"No," she said. "I think Jana has found a few things."

"Did you bring enough money?" she asked. "How much is a solidus? I don't deal with money very much."

"I have enough," he said. "Your father gave me twenty solidi, and he told me to take you to another shop."

Samson paid the bill, and they went down the street to another shop. They filled the carriage with dresses.

When they returned to the ship, Constantine met them.

"Are you ok?" he asked. "Did you get everything you wanted?"

"I am fine," Minera said. "Yes, I purchased several dresses for me and a few for Jana."

"Good," he said. "The guard will bring them to your cabin."

"I will have the carriage and horses stowed," Samson said. "Windus, we will be ready to sail in one hour."

As the ship sailed, Minera stood on the deck, in the sun, and waved goodbye to Thessalonica. It was a beautiful day, and the sun was warm. When they reached the open sea, the main sails were hoisted and the ship gained speed. The guard announced that dress for dinner would be formal.

"Pick out a nice new dress for me," Minera said. "Wear one of your new dresses. This will be fun."

"Is it proper if we both wear blue?" Jana asked. "We have several new blue dresses."

"I want to wear my new hat," she said. "I am glad we don't have to wear a uniform. Father loves blue."

When Minera arrived to dinner, Constantine smiled and asked her to sit next to him. The soup was served. When Constans arrived, he had a medal on his cadet uniform.

"What did you do to earn a medal?" Minera asked. "I thought you have to kill someone or something to earn a metal."

"I earned it by traveling with you," Constans said. "It is for hazardous duty."

"Very funny," she said. "Well, it looks nice on your uniform."

"Samson gave it to me," he said. "When a cadet travels with troops, he earns a medal."

"What did you do to have to wear that hat?" Constans asked. "I am sure it wasn't an award."

"Constans, be nice to your sister," Constantine said. "She is sitting at my right side this evening."

He glared at Constans.

After dinner, they returned to their cabins and enjoyed an evening of rest. A few of the troops and mates made music and sang nautical songs. It was a great evening to be at sea.

The next morning when they awoke, the sea was choppy and the ship bounced. You could hear the horses neighing. Some of the travelers went to breakfast.

"The horses don't like when the ground they are standing on moves around," Samson said. "I have posted men with them to calm them."

"I don't like it when it moves this much," Constans said. "I don't think I can eat breakfast."

"This is a nice wind," the mate said. "When the waves wash over the main deck, then we are having a strong wind."

The mate looked at Constans, who had turned green, and he laughed.

"I think I'll have hot tea, hot bread and three eggs," Constantine said.

"Where are you going, Constans? Be careful, stay below decks. When the waves are this tall, it is difficult to swim."

Constans went to his cabin. The ladies didn't come to breakfast, they stayed in their cabin. By noon, the wind calmed and the ship stopped bouncing. Everyone went to lunch.

"I am hungry," Minera said. "The sea was so rough at breakfast, I couldn't eat."

"You weren't the only one who didn't eat breakfast," Constantine said. "Samson and I ate breakfast, with the mates."

"He ate three eggs," Samson said. "I ate bread and hot meal."

"We ate in the ships galley," he said. "We used metal bowls. They don't spill and they don't break."

"You were wise to stay in your cabin," Constans said. "I came to breakfast, but the smell of the food was too much for me. I went back to my cabin."

"What's for lunch?" Jana asked. "I am also hungry."

"Raw eggs and raw shell fish," Constans said. "I think they might even give you a glass of wine."

"Not funny, young man," she said. "Could I have some hot tea and bread?"

"Yes," the mate said. "I will bring it to you. I have some very nice cheese."

"That sounds good," Constantine said. "Bring us a wedge of cheese and some hot bread."

"I learned one thing today," Constans said. "I don't want to be a sailor. I feel much safer on a horse."

They joked about the rough sea and enjoyed their lunch.

When the ship arrived at Constantinople, Judge met them.

"It is good to have you home," he said. "We have a new horse."

"The mare gave birth while we were in Thessalonica?" Constantine asked. "She was getting large."

"It is a beautiful foal," he said. "Constantine II was assigned to care for him."

"We have more things than when we departed," he said. "Minera and Jana made certain of that. We will need at least one extra wagon."

"Did you see the director of the mint? Judge asked. "I don't see any barrels of metal sitting on the dock."

"That went very well," he said. "Thanks for the help. When I receive my coins, I will give you one."

"I earned a medal," Constans said. "Samson gave it to me."

"That is great," Judge said. "It will dress up your uniform."

The family returned to the palace. Constans joked with his sister. After dinner, they relaxed and discussed their journey.

"Thank you so much," Minera said. "We enjoyed our trip."

"I am glad you had a good time," Constantine said. "When should we expect the professor for dinner?"

"I don't know," she said. "When I receive a message, I will inform you."

"She found a husband, and I got to see chariot races," Constans said. "Judge, have you ever seen a chariot race?"

"Yes, I have," he said. "They are a lot of fun."

Constantine looked at Constans. He raised his voice slightly.

"When I met him, Judge was the best chariot driver in Rome," Constantine said. "Now he is my number one military aid."

"He was a chariot driver?" Constans asked. "That sounds like fun."

"Someday, he might give you driving lessons," he said. "When you are thirteen, you can ask him."

Six month later, Minera received her third message from professor Morus. She spoke with her father.

"Professor Morus said he is coming to dinner."

"I don't think he is coming all this way just for dinner," Constantine said. "I want to talk to him."

"Good. He wants to talk to you as well," she said. "I think he wants to marry me."

"You are very young," he said. "In a few years, maybe, you can marry him. I will talk with him."

"He will be here next month," she said. "Trust in me, father."

Constantine sent the professor a message and told him not to visit Minera. Minera told Jana that the professor was coming, and that he wanted to marry her. Jana cautioned her not to get her hopes up.

Professor Morus arrived at the palace.

"I have come to call on Minera," Morus said. "She is expecting me."

"Be seated," Judge said. "I will ask if she wants to see you."

He went to Minera's room and told her that she had a visitor. She said she would be down to see him.

When Minera saw Morus, she embraced him. Judge immediately sent for Constantine.

"I have come to talk with your father," Morus said. "I hope to take you back to Thessalonica with me."

"My father is at work," Minera said. "I am certain Judge sent for him. He will be here as soon as possible. I don't think you understand what you are asking of him."

Minera showed him the palace and explained Constantinople to Morus. She also explained how her younger sister married a warrior. An hour later, Constantine arrived.

"Hello Minera," Constantine said. "Please go to your room."

"Hello, sir," Morus said. "I came to talk to you about your daughter."

"I sent you a message. I know you received it," he said. "She is too young to marry."

"I never received the message," he said. "I have been at the university every day since her visit."

"I sent you a message, and the messenger said he delivered it to you," he said. "In the message I told you not to come."

"She is willing to marry me," Morus said. "I have a good job as an assistant professor."

"She is not getting married. She is staying here until the proper opportunity presents itself," he said. "She will marry a king, prince, or a warrior."

"You don't understand," he said. "We are in love."

"No, you don't understand," Constantine said. "When she gets married, the Roman empire will get larger."

"You can't do that to her," he said. "She wants to live in Thessalonica."

"I have an obligation to Rome," he said. "My sons are warriors, and my daughters marry to expand the empire. It is our duty."

"Ask her what she wants," Morus said. "She wants me."

"If you don't leave the palace and Minera's life, I will have you arrested and jailed," he said. "Do you understand?"

"You are making a mistake," Morus said.

Morus left the palace and returned to Thessalonica. Constantine told Minera that he and Morus agreed that she was too young to marry. He would return in a few years.

One month later, Minera disappeared. Constantine couldn't find her anywhere in the city. It was rumored that she married the professor, and they lived in Egypt.

CHAPTER 13

CONSTANTINE AND THE GOTHS

People from Gaul, who were not loyal to the Roman Empire, slowly occupied lands north of the Istrius River. Eventually, their holdings reached the Black Sea. Many of their villages were located in open lands along river valleys and were not fortified. They farmed using hand tools and were skilled at raising grain. For many years, these people were not considered a threat to the empire. The Roman army slowly withdrew from the area. Many of the native people were dispersed along the river. Their lifestyle was different from the Goths. They expected the empire to protect them. Constantine sent his young son, Constantine II, to help the Sarmatians on the north side of the Istrius River come to an agreement with the Goths. The Roman Empire began to consider the Goths a serious threat.

Constantine discussed the problem with Samson.

"The situation along the Istrius River is getting serious," Constantine said. "The Goths are forcing me to take action."

Samson frowned and nodded.

"We can easily take care of that situation," Samson said. "We have chased them north on several occasions."

"Yes, we have," he said. "But, as soon as the Roman army retreats, they start taking land from the Sarmatians and head south."

"They have to acknowledge our borders," Samson said.

"I want you to have a legion go to the extreme north," Constantine said. "Take another legion to the south. I will use the riverboats to chase them north."

"When the Goths retreat north, they will meet us," Samson said. "We will destroy them."

"The northern legion will also cut off their food supply," he said. "When the Goths are on the move, they aren't very well organized."

"Why do we need a legion in the south?" Samson asked. "The troops on the river will ensure they retreat to the north."

"The southern legion will be a show of power," Constantine said. "After the Goths flee north, we will help the Sarmatians."

Samson swallowed deeply.

"It sounds like a good plan," he said. "When do we deploy?"

"I want Constantine II to lead the northern legion," Constantine said. "I want Constantius II to lead the southern legion."

"They can officially lead, but the troops will do the fighting," Samson said.

"Correct," he said. "The northern legion should have Windus relocate them to our fortification at Tyras."

"The southern legion will march along the river," Constantine said. "I will lead the riverboats."

"I will join you," Samson said.

Samson started to make the necessary arrangements. He began with a meeting with Constantius II.

"You will depart next week and deploy a legion on the southern edge of the Istrius River at the Black Sea," Samson said. "Then, you will post it along the south side of the river."

"Yes, sir," Constantius II said. "I hope we see some fighting."

"You will be the commander and represent the empire," he said. "Your troops will do the fighting. You have been assigned a very capable sergeant."

Next, Samson met with Constantine II. He instructed him to take the northern legion to Tyras. Constantine II and his troops eagerly trained until it was time to sail. With Windus as captain, they sailed two weeks later. When the ship returned, Windus took Constantine, Samson, and troops to the new riverboats docked at the confluence of the Istrius River with the Black Sea. Samson met with Constantine in his office to review the plans.

"I plan to take one hundred and fifty troops with us," Samson said. "We will depart next week and carry the best armor and weapons."

"Will the two legions be in place?" Constantine asked. "Did you talk with my sons?"

"The legions will be in place," Samson said. "Yes, I did speak to them. Constantine II seemed eager to fight."

Constantine shook his fist.

"I hope he is careful," Constantine said.

Judge helped Constantine prepare for his journey. He thought about volunteering to go along, but Constantine ordered him to stay at the palace. He stayed behind and managed the palace and the local legion that provided guards in Constantinople. The troops, Samson, and Constantine went to the dock. He and Windus exchanged greetings.

"We are ready to sail," Windus said. "I just returned from delivering Constantine II and his legion to Tyras."

"Did they take plenty of supplies?" Constantine asked. "I hope they are prepared to fight."

"They will do fine," Samson said. "They took carriages, wagons, horses and plenty of food and clothing."

"I am glad you helped them get prepared," he said. "They are going to be doing most of the fighting."

"We will do a little," he said. "I am sure we will meet with resistance along the river."

"Are we taking any horses?" he asked. "Can the riverboat handle them?"

"Yes, we are taking cavalry," he said. "We will have about twenty mounted troops."

Constantine explained that the new boats were designed to accommodate cavalry soldiers.

Samson helped the mates and cavalry soldiers take the horses aboard and stable them in a ship's hole.

The horses didn't like walking across the ship's ramp. One of the horses became spooked and reared.

"Hold on to him!" Samson yelled. "We might have to blindfold him."

The horse slipped on the ramp and fell. Its leg was broken. The horse neighed and writhed in pain.

"We have a problem," Samson said. "Take him away and kill him. We will need another horse. Hurry, we don't want to keep Constantine waiting."

When the replacement horse arrived, Samson made sure it was blindfolded before it was taken aboard the ship.

The ship sailed for the Istrius River. The day was warm, and the sea was mild. Constantine stood on the main deck and talked with Samson.

"I don't feel as good as when I was younger," he said. "I shouldn't complain. They thought this disease would kill me a long time ago."

"I am still in good shape," Samson said. "I will do the fighting. We can do the planning."

"I hope my sons understand how important these battles could be to their popularity and military future," he said. "I want them both to control part of the empire someday."

"I am certain they will be brave," he said. "They will make good leaders."

When they arrived at the Istrius River, the riverboats awaited them. They disembarked the ship and boarded the boats.

"Good day, emperor," Sailus said. "I am the captain of the riverboats. If you need anything, we will assist you. Your cabin is prepared."

Constantine and Samson greeted the captain.

All of the troops, except the guards, boarded the lead boat. Constantine and Sailus boarded the command boat and talked strategy.

"I thought you would be on the command boat with me," Constantine said. "The cabin next to mine is empty."

"I will spend the nights on the command boat," Samson said. "I will be with the troops during the day."

"That is fine," he said. "I will see you for dinner."

Samson looked at Constantine.

"Not tonight," he said. "With your permission, I would like to eat with the troops tonight."

Constantine looked at Samson.

"I will have to eat with the sailors," he said. "I noted his mates are armed."

"Yes," he said. "They have been trained in hand-to-hand combat. They will help defend this boat."

The boats headed up the Istrius River. That evening, Constantine ate dinner with Sailus.

"How long have you been assigned to the boats?" Constantine asked. "What did you do before riverboats?"

"I have been with this boat since its construction," Sailus said. "And I helped build the troop's boat."

"No, wonder you are the captain," he said. "Did you work on riverboats as a young man?"

"I went to school and worked on riverboats on the Rhone," he said. "Then I was captain of a Roman freighter for five years, making runs from Sicily to Rome."

"I have done a lot of fighting along the river," Constantine said. "Did you ever meet a soldier named Nickus?"

"The name is familiar," Sailus said. "Did he serve along the Rhone?"

"Yes, he did," he said. "I was emperor of the west."

"I met him," he said. "I was just a lad."

The mate knocked on the door of the captain's dining area. He announced two visitors.

"I hate to interrupt your dinner, sir," Samson said. "My scouts have returned with news of a town that we will reach by tomorrow. There are problems there."

"What kind of problems?" Constantine asked. "Are the problems related to the Goths?"

"Yes, the Goths have taken over a Sarmatians town and occupy most of the building and have stolen many items," Samson said. "The townspeople have asked for our help and protection."

"We will help them," he said. "Have the southern legion move west."

"I have already ordered it to move west," Samson said. "We have a bigger problem."

"What is that?" he asked.

"The Goths have built a town with a small fort, about a day up stream," he said. "It is in the open land in the valley. I think we can chase them north."

"That is exactly what I want done," Constantine said. "Be prepared. Tomorrow shouldn't be too difficult."

Samson patted the knife in his belt.

"We will be ready," Samson said. "I think the troops are anxious."

The next morning, the boat carrying the troops docked. The command boat anchored in the river and waited. Constantine watched. Suddenly, a large ramp was placed between the boat and the dock.

"They are going to use the mounted troops," Constantine said. "They are very formidable."

"I have never seen mounted troops," Sailus said. "Did you train them in Constantinople?"

"Yes," he said. "Samson trains the troops and the horses. The horses don't like being on a boat."

"The horses are on shore," Samson said. "I don't expect much resistance."

Some slaves fled to the fortified town. The Sarmatians put the remaining slaves in jail.

By the end of the day, Constantine's troops and the Sarmatians had driven the Goths from the local shops. The shop owners prepared to reopen. As predicted, many of the Goths fled to the fortified town. The troops only rounded up a few Goths. After the skirmish, Samson went to talk to Constantine.

"We didn't have much resistance," Samson said. "Most of Goths walked out of the shops and headed out of town."

"We will see them again in a few days," Constantine said. "They will be better prepared."

"The troops gathered a few stragglers and turned them over to the Sarmatians," he said. "They will be in jail for a long time."

"The horse mounted troops did well," he said. "I am glad you brought them along."

"The legion is marching this way," Samson said. "Before we attack the fortification, I want them in place."

"Keep a few of them along the river and use the others to support the riverboat troops," Constantine said. "The legion is very impressive to look at, but your troops are much better at fighting."

"I want to stay here one more day," he said. "Then, Constantius II will be here with the legion and my men will be ready to attack."

The Goths in the fort didn't understand why they weren't being attacked. Constantine's delay worried them.

"I would keep a few of the legion in this area to help the Sarmatians," he said. "We need to make certain all of the Goths, who leave the area, go north."

The town was a beehive of activity until sunset. Then, the shops closed. The candles flickered in the dark. Constantine sat, on the deck of the command boat, and listened to the water bugs. A scout reported that the Goth village contained fifty houses; many of them were small. He also reported that the fortification was weak and could be easily destroyed. The night was calm.

The next morning, Samson sent out another scout to watch for military activity in the Goth's town. The legion arrived before sundown. They established camp and prepared to fight the following day.

Constantius II and Samson met with Constantine on the command boat.

"When the troops attack the Goths, I want both of you to be here with me," Constantine said. "I want the attack to take place one hour after sunrise."

"I need about two hundred men from the legion to join my troops for the fight," Samson said. "The horse mounted troops will lead our charge."

"I want you to either push the Goths to the north or kill them," Constantine said. "I am not interested in taking any prisoners."

"What about the children and women?" Constantius II asked. "We can disperse them among the Sarmatians."

"You take care of it," Constantine said. "I don't want to take them back to Constantinople."

At sunrise, the legion was in place. One hour later, the ship's ramp was lowered and the cavalry lead the charge. The fortification was easily breached, and the cavalry killed a thousand men. The legion followed, and the Goths retreated north. Samson and Constantine planned their next move.

"That was a lot easier than I expected," Constantine said. "Send a scout to tell Constantine II they are heading his way."

"They didn't even have time to take any food with them," Samson said. "I think they took a few empty wagons."

"Anything that was not destroyed, take it to the Sarmatian's town and give it to them," Constantine said. "Order half the legion to chase them north."

"We will continue up the river," Samson said. "We have a few more situations to resolve."

"Order the other half of the legion to march with us. Keep them on the south side of the river," he said. "Some of the Goths will probably go north before we reach them."

The riverboat continued up river for another week. The troops helped the Sarmatians who had been oppressed by the Goths. Most of the Goths fled north. They were able to keep their distance from the troops, as long as they headed in a northerly direction. The Sarmatians resumed their normal lifestyle. They held trials for the Goths who had been put in jail. Several were hung in the town park. Others were beaten, put in leg irons, and returned to jail. The old men and women were given menial tasks to be completed each day. The river towns were again a good place to live. Once again, the area was deemed safe. The boats headed toward the Black Sea.

A month later, they were joined by Constantine II. Constantine greeted his son.

"How did the battle go?" he asked. "We headed them directly into your trap."

Constantine II grinned at his father.

"We killed about five thousand of their troops," Constantine II said. "They had almost no food and very little leadership. We were on them before they knew what hit them."

"How many prisoners did you take?" he asked. "Not many, I hope."

"I have one to turn over to you," he said. "This is, Ariaricus. He is the son of a dead king."

"You were able to kill their king?" he asked. "That is the kind of statement I wanted to make. Most of our problems with the Goths are solved."

"I will place him in jail and post a guard," Samson said. "I want to get Ariaricus to Constantinople alive."

Samson looked at Constantine and smiled.

"The legion has about twenty prisoners," Constantine II said. "They are chained together and are being marched back to the city."

"I don't want the prisoners," Constantine said.

"Then, I will turn them over to the Sarmatians," Constantine II said. "They will put them on public display and then kill them."

As the riverboats sat at the dock on the Black Sea, the troops enjoyed a spirited evening. They sang songs and drank wine. Constantine, his son, and Samson reviewed their success in driving the Goths from the Istrius River Valley. Samson and Constantine planned long range strategy.

"I am going to keep troops in this area," Constantine said. "It is important to maintain control of the river."

"We could keep the riverboat in constant patrol," Samson said. "You could rotate the troops occasionally."

"I like that," Constantine said. "The fortification at the Black Sea would be the headquarters for the troops. We could keep about half of them at the fortification."

"The boats could go up stream for a month and then return the next month," Samson said. "The boats could be maintained during the third month, and the troops would rotate before the next trip."

"That will work," he said. "They would visit the town along the rivers four times per year."

"I will talk with my sergeant," Samson said. "He might have some ideas."

"I will talk with my sons," Constantine said. "It would be good assignments for them. One son could serve at home. His brother could serve on the river."

That evening, Constantine explained the proposal to his sons. Constantius II volunteered to stay on the river for the next year. He also agreed to send a formal report every three months to the head of the military fortification in Constantinople. Many of his troops volunteered to remain with him. Samson's sergeant stayed and served with Constantius II. Constantine visited the fortification at the Black Sea and explained the changes to its commander.

"My son, Constantius II, is going to be assigned to the river," Constantine said. "He will work with you."

"How is that going to change my job?" he asked. "I have faithfully served the empire. Am I losing my command?"

"No," he said. "This fort is your command. When he needs your help, I will expect you to assist my son."

"What exactly is his job?" he asked. "I want to understand the situation."

"He will be your superior," Constantine said. "You will command the fort, and he will command the troops assigned to the boats."

"I see," he said. "You are assigning more men to the post."

"Correct, he will have about four hundred," he said.

"Half of his troops will be here for two months, and then they will be on the river for one month," he said. "Your command responsibilities are getting larger."

"Will you allow us to have another office for a commander and an additional aid?" he asked. "We need to keep our duties separate."

Constantine looked at the commander.

"Yes, I will make money available for the changes," Constantine said. "See Constantius II for all future questions."

"Your ship will arrive tomorrow," Sailus said. "I will miss you."

Constantine dined with the troops that evening. He invited Sailus to dine with them, and he explained the new routine to the troops.

"That is fine," Sailus said. "I love the river. It is always exciting and never exactly the same."

"Your first mate can manage the maintenance of the boats, and you can take time off," Constantine said. "I would like you to be captain any time the boats are on the river."

"Certainly," he said. "I want to be with my boats. When you help build a boat, she becomes part to you."

"Take good care of my son," he said. "He is a fine young man."

"I think he can look out for himself," he said. "When the troops are fighting, I will keep him in the command boat."

"Thank you,' he said. "I hope I will see you again."

After dinner, Samson inspected the troops. In the morning, Constantine and Samson headed to the ship.

"Do you know a sailor, named Sailus?" Constantine asked. "He did a good job commanding the riverboats for us."

Windus smiled at Constantine.

"I know Sailus," Windus said. "I have known him for many years. He is a very capable captain."

"We are ready to head home," Samson said. "Most of the troops will be returning by ship. The others will march to Constantinople."

"If they have something to sleep on, we can accommodate several hundred in the holes." he said. "I will have my mate help you place them."

"During the day, they can enjoy the sun and exercise on the main deck." Constantine said. "They have earned a little relaxation."

"Constantine II will bring the other troops home," Samson said. "It is a good command for him. He did fine in battle."

"It has been a great experience for my boys," Constantine said. "I hope next year is peaceful."

Constantine II remained with his troops and marched with them to Constantinople. They were in a victorious mood and relived their experiences around the campfire at night. Constantine returned home by ship. In two days, the ship docked in the capital city.

Judge met the ship. He exchanged greetings with Constantine and Samson.

"The boys and the troops did a fine job," Constantine said. "Constantius II is commanding the riverboats for a year. Constantine II is marching the troops back home."

"When they arrive, the town will welcome them home as heroes," Judge said.

"Soon, after they are home, I would like to formally honor them," Constantine said. "I want them to march in a parade, so the people of Constantinople can see them."

"I will make the arrangements," Samson said. "I would like to give each of them a medal."

"I will have the mint rush an order for the medals," Constantine said. "I will have the Istrius River engraved on it."

"You could also have them mint some commemorative coins," he said. "I am certain they would be very popular."

"Good idea," he said. "I will take care of it."

When the troops arrived home, they rested for a few days, and then marched in a parade honoring their victory. Each soldier was given a medal. The park was full of excited citizens, families, and friends. It was a joyous occasion. Constantine II made a short speech.

A month later, the coins were released for circulation. People saved the coins rather than using them as currency. The next year was peaceful. The people along the river continued to intermarry and became more homogeneous. Those that lived along the river became successful and purchased slaves to perform all of their menial tasks.

After eleven months, Constantine received a message from Constantius II. He read the message to Samson.

> Constantine
> Emperor of the Roman Empire
>
> May God guide you so all your decisions are popular decisions.
>
> Constantine II will be here in a month to relieve me.
>
> Please advise, I am sensing uneasiness amongst the slaves.
>
> They have been treated quite well, but they have forgotten that they are property and completely controlled by their owner.
>
> They want the right to own property and have held a meeting without the knowledge of the Sarmatians.
>
> We will have to quiet the mobs of slaves.
>
> I have killed several, but they continue to protest.
>
> I should be home in forty-five days.
>
> Constantius II
> Son of the Emperor

"It sounds like Constantine II might have his hands full," Samson said. "I will inform him."

"He might have to evacuate some of the local people," Constantine said. "We don't want to have any of them killed."

"He could evacuate them, kill the slaves, and then return them to their homes," he said. "Sarmatians love the river."

Two week later, Constantine II prepared to go to his riverboat command. The evening before he departed, he dined with his father.

"It is my turn to command the riverboats," Constantine II said, proudly.

"Take well-trained troops with you," Constantine said. "The troops that have been on the boats last year are returning with Constantius II."

"Samson and I have already picked them," he said. "They have received special training in hand-to-hand combat."

"Good," he said. "I hope they don't need it."

"I am going to sail with my ship tomorrow," he said. "Windus has the ship ready for us."

"He is a good man," Constantine said. "Tell him to visit me when he returns. I'll give him dinner, and it won't be fresh fish."

Constantine looked at his son and laughed.

"I will give him your message," he said. "I hope his body can handle chops."

The next morning, Constantine II went to the ship. The sergeant marched the men to the dock, where Windus met them.

"Samson told me you won't be taking horses," Windus said. "I have prepared quarters for your troops in the holes."

"I will have the sergeant take them to their quarters." Constantine II said. "Which cabin did you prepare for me?"

"Your father told me that his sons could use cabin one," he said. "I am certain you will be comfortable."

"That was very considerate of father," he said. "We now officially represent the empire."

"Yes sir," he said. "It is an honor to serve you."

"I almost forgot," he said. "After you and Constantius II return, father wants you to dine with him."

"I will be certain and visit with him," Windus said. "Mate, raise the ramp and prepare to sail."

The ship headed toward the Istrius River. Constantine II allowed his troops to stand on the main deck and enjoy the sun. When they arrived at the Istrius, Constantius II met his brother. They exchanged greetings. Constantine II informed Constantius II concerning the troops in Constantinople. They discussed their father's health.

"He is still bothered by his disease, but he is doing fine," Constantine II said. "How are things along the Danube, Istrius River?"

"The Sarmatians are constantly complaining about their slaves," he said. "You don't know what to believe."

"I will take care of any problem they are having with the slaves," Constantine II said. "Are the riverboats ready to go?"

"Yes, we have completed the maintenance," he said. "Sailus is always ready to navigate the river. I will see you in a year. Don't forget to send the formal report. Father reads them."

After the formal change of command ceremony, Constantius II boarded the ship and sailed to Constantinople with Captain Windus. Constantine II had Sailus put the boats into the Istrius River and the troops boarded them. They went upstream to the first town. Constantine II met with the town leader. He planned to eliminate any problems with the slaves. He considered it an opportunity to impress his father.

"Greetings," Constantine II said. "I will be the commander of the riverboats this year. I am the emperor's oldest son."

"Welcome to the river. We are glad you are here," the town leader said. "We liked your brother."

"He indicated you are having problems with your slaves," he said. "I will be less tolerant with them. What are they doing?"

"They are refusing to work. Some days, they don't do anything," he said. "The men are difficult to control."

"I will take care of that," he said. "I will return with a few troops. We will explain their jobs to them."

Constantine II returned to the town leader's house with about twenty men.

"Is the problem mostly with the men?" Constantine II asked. "Show me which one is causing you a problem."

The shop owner pointed.

"This one seems to be the leader of my slaves," he said. "He often ignores or laughs at me."

"Kill him," Constantine II said. "Round up the other male slaves."

Constantine II decided to make an example of the leader of the slave revolt. He decided to kill only the young slaves. He instructed the soldiers to club the problem slaves. A soldier hit a slave squarely on the head with an iron tipped club. He fell to the floor, dead.

"Here are the other four slaves he owns," the sergeant said. "Should I kill them?"

"Don't kill the old guy," Constantine II said. "I think he will understand our message."

The soldiers killed the three younger slaves. They were carried out of town and buried in one grave.

"Sergeant, this is how we are going to minimize this problem," Constantine II said. "I am going to post several troops at each end of town. If the slaves try to escape, we will kill them."

"I will go to every house and kill all the young male slaves," the sergeant said. "Some will probably come running your direction."

"Remember don't kill the old men," he said. "If they try to evade us, I'll use mounted troops."

By night, the troops had killed sixty-two slaves. They returned to the boat. Constantine II ordered Sailus to move to the next town. The same routine was followed for seven days. At the eighth town, the slaves had already fled.

"I will remain with the command boat and a few mounted troops," Constantine II said. "I want you to pass by two towns and then stop and kill slaves. If they head back this way, I will have them killed."

The boat slipped through the night and stopped at the third town. They sent a scout to gather information. The scout reported the slaves were gathered about a mile out of town. The sergeant decided to attack at sunrise.

"We will surprise them," the sergeant said. "They think we are two towns down river."

"I will have the mounted troops ready at sunrise," the corporal said. "They won't know what hit them."

At sunrise, the troops raided the slaves' camp. Half of the slaves were still sleeping. The troops killed everyone, two hundred and twenty seven in total. The sergeant sent the scout to report to Constantine II. They used this strategy over the next month. The slaves were subdued and no longer posed a problem. Sergeant and Constantine II dined on the command ship.

"I think we have done everything we can do," Constantine II said. "We will stop and visit several towns on our way down stream."

"I don't think the slaves will cause trouble any time soon," the sergeant said. "I lost one of my soldiers."

"What happened to him?" Constantine II asked.

"He fell from this horse and hit his head on a rock," the sergeant said.

"Accidents will happen," he said. "Riding a horse can be dangerous."

Constantine II looked at the sergeant and smiled.

They buried the soldier in the town's cemetery. The next day, they stopped at one of the larger towns. Constantine decided to talk with a lady slave, who was well liked by her owner.

"Do you think everyone understands now?" Constantine II asked. "Will they obey their owners?"

"Most of the men didn't cause any problems," she said. "They were Christians and refused to do manual labor on the Sabbath."

"That is all they refused?" he asked. "They did everything else they were asked to do?"

"Yes, sir," she said. "I am glad you didn't kill my father. He can help me raise our two children."

Constantine II met with the sergeant that evening. He instructed the sergeant to post notices in every town stating that owners of Christian slaves shouldn't ask them to work on the Sabbath. He signed the notices. The boat stopped at every town, and the troops posted notices. The command boat started toward the Black Sea. On the second day, a lookout on the boat saw a man, a Goth, standing on the shore, waving. The boat anchored, and the man came on board.

"I want to talk to Constantine II," the Goth said. "We want peace not war."

"I am Constantine II," he said. "This is my sergeant."

"We want to sign our allegiance to Constantine and to the Empire," he said. "Draw up a formal agreement, and I will sign it."

Constantine II talked with his sergeant and Sailus.

"What gives you the power to sign for others," Constantine II asked. "Who do you represent?"

"Our town of several hundred people is five miles south of the river," he said. "We have never stolen anything or harmed anyone."

"The sergeant will visit your town," he said. "After he sees your town and people, we will talk."

Several hours later, the sergeant returned and explained that he found everything as the Goth described. Constantine prepared a statement of allegiance for the Goth to sign.

"We are also interested in peace," Constantine II said.

After they signed the papers, they saluted each other.

"I have one more question," the Goth said. "Several of our young men want to join the Roman army. What should they do?"

"Have them report to the fortification where the river joins the sea," he said. "I will tell the troops that they are on their way and to induct them into our army."

Constantine II was a little concerned that his father might be told he had killed Christians. He wrote an explanation concerning the rights of a slave owner. His father never questioned him. He also wrote a large section concerning the alliance with the Goths. The Goth men arrived at the fortification while Constantine II was preparing for his next trip up the river. He asked to speak with the leader of the Goth troops.

"How many men do you have?" Constantine II asked. "Are they all young?"

"We are all young and not married," he said. "We want to be warriors in the Roman army."

"What is your name?" he asked. "What have you been doing for the town?"

"My name is Eric," he said. "We stand watch. We are very good at hiding and scouting. We also practice hand-to-hand fighting."

"Would you like to serve with me on the riverboats?" Constantine II asked. "I could use more scouts and guards."

"We would be honored to serve on the river with you," Eric said. "I will tell my men. Where do we live until we board the boats?"

"The sergeant will show you to your quarters," he said. "He will be your leader. You will follow his command."

"Good day, sergeant," he said. "We will help you as you need us. We are brave."

When the next river journey started, Eric's troops were part of the sergeant's complement of troops. They were assigned guard duty on the command boat and scout duty on the attack boat. Eric was assigned the responsibility to command the guards on the command boat. He dined with Sailus and Constantine II.

"Sergeant must like you," Constantine II said. "Commanding my guards is a responsible position."

"He had a hand-to-hand fighting contest," Eric said. "It was a lot of fun. It was make-believe. We didn't kill anyone."

"You must have defeated all your men," he said. "That was a good job."

"I also defeated the sergeant's men," Eric said. "He promised this job to the winner of the contest. I wanted this job. I am a good guard."

"You will like working on this boat," Constantine II said. "Captain Sailus is responsible for both of the boats."

"If we can help your mates, just ask me," Eric said. "We don't know much about boats, but we can learn."

The boat stopped at several towns during the next forty-five days. Then, the boat changed direction and started down the river. They stopped at the towns they skipped on the way up the river. The scouts found very little activity. It was a peaceful journey. Constantine II was very impressed with Eric and his troops. He wrote his father a message. When Constantine received the message, he read it to Samson.

Constantine
Emperor of the Roman Empire

May God guide you.
    The river is under control.
    During our last river trip, we located a Goth village.
    Forty of their young men joined
    The Roman Army.
    They have proven to be good soldiers.
    We are deploying them as guards and as scouts.
    Our endeavors continue to reap dividends.

Constantine II
Son of the Emperor

Constantine never answered the message. He made it part of Constantine II's report. When it was time for Constantine II to return to Constantinople, Eric found him in his office.

"I have talked with my troops. We wish to go to Constantinople and continue to serve with you," Eric said. "I am sure the city needs more guards."

"Constantinople does have a great number of guards," he said. "My first assignment was with the guards in the large public park."

"I can take you to Constantinople, but your assignment will come from Samson," he said. "He commands the army for my father."

"That is fine," Eric said. "Will you tell him we did a good job for you?"

Constantine II looked at Eric.

"Yes," he said. "I will ask if he needs any guards."

The next day, the ship arrived, and a change-of-command ceremony took place. It was a formal ceremony. Constantius II stressed that things might be different because a different commander would be making the decisions.

"We have solved your problems," Constantine II said. "You should have a peaceful year. How is father?"

"He is getting older," Constantius II said. "He is having some problems getting around."

"I am looking forward to a peaceful year," Constantius II said. "Nice job with the alliance with the Goths. Father made a big deal about it. You will probably receive a medal."

He looked at Constantine II and smiled. The troops marched to the ship. Windus met Constantine II on the shore.

"It is good to see you," Windus said. "This is my last trip. I have thirty-five years of military duty, and they have assigned me to a desk job in Constantinople."

"You are very valuable to the military," Constantine II said. "I am certain you will be helpful from behind a desk. I will come and have lunch with you."

"Thank you, sir," he said. "My ship has given me a sense of security. Being with you will give me the same feeling."

"If you have any problems in Constantinople, just see me," he said. "I know the boss."

He shook Windus' hand.

"Will you and your escort have dinner with me tonight?" he asked. "Who is that with you?"

"His name is Eric," he said. "We will join you at dinner."

Later that day, Eric and Constantine II dined with captain Windus.

"Eric is a Goth," Constantine II said. "He and his troops have been guards of the riverboat. Now they are going to Constantinople."

"Welcome aboard," Windus said. "You will like Constantinople."

"We are looking forward to going to Constantinople," Eric said. "This is a beautiful ship. I have never seen a ship this large or this nice."

They sailed to Constantinople. Eric had never been aboard a large sailing ship. When he couldn't see land, he seemed nervous, but he never said anything. He watched Constantine II and mimicked his actions. When they arrived, Samson met them.

"I will take the troops," Samson said. "You can go to your father."

"This is Eric," Constantine II said. "I have brought Eric and forty of his troops. They are part of the Roman army now and want to serve in Constantinople."

"What did they do for you?" Samson asked. "Where should I assign them?"

"They were guards on the riverboat, and they were scouts," he said. "I would assign them to the troops in the park."

"Do we need more troops at the park?" Samson asked. "I will have to talk with your father."

"That won't be necessary," Constantine II said. "These men have served bravely."

He could see a worried look on Samson's face.

"I will talk with father," he said. "You take them to the park."

"Yes sir, thank you" Samson said.

"Thank you," Eric said. "I hope to see you again."

Constantine II went to his father's office and reviewed the last year. His father was pleased to see him. When he told his father about Eric and his troops, Constantine wasn't concerned. They became part of the park patrol.

CHAPTER 14

THE PERSIAN CAMPAIGN

The Roman troops that patrolled along the Istrius River ensured the river area was a safer place to live. The area flourished, and the Sarmatians were free to live where they wanted. The slaves were now controlled. Constantine II sent his father a message announcing that he planned to be married and wanted the ceremony to take place in the Church of the Holy Apostles. He planned to visit Constantinople while the boats were being maintained. Constantine informed Judge of the news.

"Constantine II is coming home to be married," he said. "Plan a grand ceremony."

Judge smiled at Constantine.

"I didn't know he had a serious girlfriend," he said. "I am glad he has met the proper lady."

"I knew he had met someone," he said. "I am a little surprised that they are ready to get married."

"Who is he going to marry?" Judge asked. "I would like to prepare the announcements."

"Her name is Faustana," he said. "She is the daughter of the commander of the military fortification in Tyras."

"I will make the arrangements," he said. "Do you know when he will be coming home?"

"I expect him next week," he said. "The wedding should be the following week."

"That isn't a lot of time for preparation," he said. "Are they returning to the Istrius River area?"

"Yes," he said. "That is his assignment. Just because he is married, doesn't change his assignment."

Judge understood his assignment and planned it execution.

The next day, Judge consulted with the officers' wives. He secured the use of the church and created a list of things recommended to be included as part of the wedding ceremony.

Constantine II and Faustana arrived in Constantinople and stayed at the palace. Constantine had asked Judge and the servants to make an extra effort to make Faustana feel like she was part of the family. After dinner, they talked with Constantine, Constantius II, Constans, Samson, and Judge.

"We want to start a family, so we decided to get married," Constantine II said. "We don't want to wait."

"I have many of the wedding ceremony details planned," Judge said. "The archbishop will marry you."

Constantine II explained he understood the archbishop was an important man, but he wanted to be married by Eusebius.

"Eusebius is my friend," he said. "I have known him most of my life. He even tutored me."

"We could have both of them take part in the ceremony," Judge said.

Constantine listened to the conservation. He posed his hands in a prayerful attitude.

"That would be interesting," he said. "I will talk with them. Eusebius is family."

"Please invite Captain Windus as well," Constantine II said. "He is a good man and has been my friend for many years."

"I have also invited Eric," Samson said. "He and his men will sit with me during the ceremony."

"My future wife's father will be the only person representing her," Constantine II said. "Be certain to greet him."

Constantine didn't want him to feel out of place. He ordered twenty guards to sit with Faustana's father at the church.

It was a lovely wedding. People from all sections of the city started to arrive early for the ceremony. The church filled quickly. The doors of the church were kept open during the ceremony so the crowd that formed outside could hear the couple's vows. Faustana's father and the troops wore their dress uniforms. Faustana wore a white gown that trailed on the ground. She was followed by three attendants. Constantius II wasn't able to attend his brother's wedding, but sent a carriage as a wedding present.

Constantine made arrangements with Judge to have a celebration at the palace.

The city's best musicians were hired for the affair.

"I want the musicians to play long and loud," Judge said. "If it is necessary, hire two groups."

The first group started to play went the first guest arrived. The second group played until the last guest had departed. It was a successful social event. Constans attended with two of his army friends.

"I am glad I had time to change out of my wedding dress," Faustana said. "It was beautiful, but made it difficult to walk."

"You looked beautiful," Constantine II said. "It was nice of father to arrange this wedding celebration, so we could meet his friends."

Constantine II looked around the room.

"Here he comes," Constantine II said. "Father, we love the music."

"Make certain you introduce yourselves to everyone," Constantine said. "It is important they learn to know you."

The musicians played for several hours. Before the guests went home, everyone was served cake and tea.

Judge met with the servants.

"Don't serve any more wine," he said.

After the supply of wine was terminated, the guests departed.

After a week, Constantine II, his bride, and father-in-law returned to their home on the Istrius River.

Constantine and Samson's attention focused on the situation in Persia. The Persian government had imposed heavy taxes on the Christians.

"They are always causing problems," Constantine said. "They should follow my example and things would remain peaceful."

"They have internal problems," Samson said. "Many of them have problems with Jesus' message. They don't want to understand. They are more interested in being unique. I am surprised they haven't created their own religion."

When Christianity became legal in the Roman Empire, life began to be different in Persia. Persian Christians were thought of as friends of the enemy. Persia had allowed Christianity because of a request from Constantine. Shapur, King of Persia, read a message from Constantine to his advisors.

Shapur II
King of Persia

May God give you favor.

I recommend you be tolerant and even kind concerning those who worship Jesus.

I am certain this will increase your popularity.

You have been at war with Rome for many years, but you need not be at war with the Christians.

They are hardworking, good citizens and an asset to our empire.

There is no reason for us to war over Christians.

Constantine
Emperor of the Roman Empire

Shapur's advisors didn't appreciate Constantine's message. They resented his interfering with their country. As time passed, the government of Persia increased its discrimination against the Christians. In retaliation, to Constantine's interference each Christian was forced to pay an additional severe tax directly to the government of the town in which they lived. If they didn't pay the tax, they were put in prison. When Constantine heard about the new law, he wasn't pleased. He discussed the situation with Samson.

"They are trying to tax the Christians out of existence," Constantine said. "They should have been mindful of my request. I am certain they know I will take action against them."

Constantine realized the tax was a challenge to his influence as the emperor.

"We could teach them a lesson," Samson said. "I will send two scouts to gather information about their military."

"Determine how the Christians are being treated," Constantine said.

The next week, Constantine received a message.

"Constantine II wants to see me and will be coming to the palace for a visit," he informed Judge.

Later that month, Constantine II arrived at the palace to have dinner with his father. Judge and Constantine II exchanged greetings.

"He has been expecting you," Judge said. "I will tell him you are here."

Constantine II greeted his father using proper military etiquette.

"Good evening sir," he said. "It is good to see you."

After dinner, they went to the living area to talk. The servants served them tea.

"I would like you to assign me to the Istrius River as a permanent post instead of rotating with my brother," Constantine II said. "Make me commander of the fortification and the boats."

"Your brother has been serving every other year," Constantine said. "We met and agreed to that arrangement."

"If we continue this arrangement, I will spend my next journey up the river doing what he didn't accomplish the previous year," he said. "Assign him to Constantinople where Samson can train him to be a soldier."

A surprised Constantine stared at his son.

"I'm not sure what you mean," he said. "He sends me very complete reports, much more detailed than the reports you send me. I know what he is doing. I am never sure what you have accomplished."

Constantine was irritated. He resented Constantine II's attitude toward his brother.

"Do you want reports or performance and a secure frontier?" Constantine II asked. "If you want both, send me a scribe. He will create complete reports of what has been accomplished."

"I don't want my sons arguing with each other," he said. "Do you think he would care if you stayed on the Istrius River, and I assigned him permanently to Constantinople?"

Constantine II answered immediately, he didn't hesitate.

"No, he won't care," he said. "He would be happy. He likes living in Constantinople."

"Then, plan to stay on the river, but don't say anything until after I talk with your brother," Constantine said. "If he agrees, I will make your permanent assignment official. I will send you a message."

Constantius II and his father had a long discussion about the Istrius River. Constantius II acknowledged he didn't like the assignment on the river and agreed to allow Constantine II to remain permanently on the river. Constantine sent a message to Constantine II.

The next week, Constantine met with Constantius II at the palace and discussed the Persian problem.

"I hope Shapur doesn't force me to invade," Constantine said. "He has been a ruler for many years."

"The scouts will return in a few months, and we will understand the daily situation," Constantius II said. "I don't think we need to be in a hurry. He isn't going anywhere."

A week later, Constantine received a message from the commander of the military fortification east of the Jordan River. The commander noted he had lost several men to the Persian army and asked for reinforcements.

After they discussed the message, Samson sent two hundred troops, twenty horses, and supplies to the eastern frontier. The area continued to be a battle ground and Constantine decided that it was necessary to send Constantius II to the eastern front. They met in Constantine's office to discuss their plan.

"I think we need to make a show of force," Constantine said. "We are losing men on the frontier."

"What do you plan to do?" Constantius II asked. "I could take some men and force the Persians to retreat."

"Have Samson give you an army, I want you to help our troops at the existing fortification," he said. "They have been fighting for a long time. They will appreciate any help you give them."

Constantius II took an army and marched east to the frontier. They fought alongside the existing troops.

"Together we will drive them from this area," Constantius II said. "We will force them to retreat."

"They won't disappear," Jarus said. "They'll just return with more troops and supplies. I think we should kill them while you and your army are here. Then I won't have to fight them again in three months."

Constantius II didn't agree with slaughtering the enemy. His army was successful in discouraging the Persian army.

After two months, the Persian troops retreated from the area. Constantius II sent his father a message stating he had solved the problem on the frontier; however, the local commander also sent Constantine a message stating his disappointment with Constantius II's follow through. Constantine II sent his father a message, indicating that Faustana had delivered a baby girl. He explained he was sorry it wasn't a boy, and he would try again.

Soon, the Persian army began invading the frontier again. Constantius II had only been home for a short time. Constantine spoke with him.

"This time take more men and don't allow them to retreat," Constantine said. "Get men behind them and destroy them. We are at war with the Persians. You should have done that the last time you were there."

Constantius II stared at his father.

"You want to kill them?" he asked. "We could force them to retreat. They would depart for a while."

"If you need help, I will send Constans," he said. "Your little brother can help you."

Constantius II looked at his father. He thought he was joking.

"He isn't ready to fight a war," he said. "He doesn't have any experience with commanding troops."

"When I first sent you out with the troops, you were young," he said. "That is when you gained experience."

Now Constantius II realized his father was serious. He looked at him.

"Father, I don't need him," he said. "He is too immature."

"That might be a good thing," Constantine said. "Irrational behavior is a very scary thing. The enemy won't know how to react."

Constantius II understood his father's mind was made up.

"Alright, send him with me," he said. "I guess he is old enough."

"I want them killed," Constantine said. "This is war, not a game. If you kill them, they won't return."

At Constantine's request, Judge summoned Samson. He entered the room.

"I will take care of it," Constantius II said.

He turned and looked at Samson.

"Samson, are the troops prepared to fight?" he asked.

"Yes," he said. "I will send a few scouts with Constans to help you trap them."

Constantius II glared at his father.

A month later, the troops arrived at the frontier. After sunset, while they sat around a fire, Constans talked with Constantius II.

"I will take a few scouts. We'll return in a few days," Constans said. "Rest the troops, but be prepared to fight."

"Do you want to take any troops with you?" he asked. "We have several troops that came along especially to assist you."

"After we have scouted their troops, we will cover their retreat path," he said. "Wait three days, and then charge them at sunrise."

Constantius II was worried about his little brother. He hoped his father and Samson knew what they were doing.

Three days later, Constantius II and the Roman troops charged the Persian forces. When the outnumbered Persians decided to retreat, they encountered Constans' troops. The Persian troops were completely surprised.

"Kill them," Constans said. "They are retreating. Turn them around and Constantius II will slaughter them."

When the Persian troops realized their retreat path was blocked, they became confused.

"They are coming back," Constantius II said. "Turn them around again and send them back to Constans' troops."

The Persian troops broke rank, and Constantius II troops killed many of them before they started running toward Constans.

"We have them trapped," Constans said. "They don't know what to do or which way to go."

Constans' troops stood their ground and killed many more of the Persian troops.

The Persian troops stopped fighting. They were slaughtered from both directions. All of the foot soldiers were killed. A few of the Persian officers were killed. The others were taken captive by Constans. He planned to take them to his father in Constantinople. The four officers were stripped of all insignia and their hands were bound. Their horses were given to Constans' officers. Then the army marched to Constantinople. Constans made arrangements for his prisoners and his troops to sail to Constantinople. Constantius II send a detailed formal report to Constantine.

When they arrived at the harbor in Constantinople, Samson and a few troops met them.

"I have four prisoners," Constans said. "I will march them to the jail in the park."

"Did you kill many of their soldiers?" Samson asked. "Your father doesn't want to have to send troops to the front again."

"We killed all, but these four," he said. "One of them is a prince. He is Shapur's grandson."

"That should make your father very happy," Samson said. "Where is Constantius II?"

"He is here somewhere," he said. "I think he is in his office finishing writing the report."

Constans looked at Samson and smiled.

"He didn't capture anyone," Constans said. "His troop did a fine job sending the Persians in my direction."

"You didn't actually fight, did you?" Samson asked. "You were supposed to be removed from the fighting. I expected you to be learning as a spectator. The plan was to post you at a safe, distant location."

"I fought hand-to-hand with the enemy," Constans said. "You should have seen me. I remembered everything you taught me. I even have a few dents in my armor."

Samson had a worried look on his face. He wasn't certain what he should tell Constantine.

"If you want to be emperor, you need to be careful," Samson said. "You might've been killed."

"I want to be an engaged emperor, not an emperor who watches his troops take all the chances," he said. "It was just like you told me it would be."

"I remember when I looked forward to hand-to-hand combat," he said. "Now, I look forward to teaching."

The next evening, Constantius II and Constans dined at the palace.

"Good evening, men," Judge said. "I will tell your father that you are here."

"I understand we have a few prisoners," Constantine said. "One of the prisoners is famous."

"You should be able to bargain for him. That is why I captured him," Constans said.

"How did you know who he was?" he asked. "You are correct. He is a valuable prisoner."

"My scouts captured their scouts, and they decided to talk to us," he said. "I know all about their army."

"What did you do with their scouts?" he asked. "You must have really scared them."

"We executed them one at a time, until one of them decided to talk," he said. "You did say this is war and not a game."

Constantine smiled.

"Good job," he said. "What did you do with the one who talked? Did you turn him loose?"

"We branded him first, and then dismissed him," he said. "I don't think he will return to his country."

Constantine and Samson discussed the new prisoners. They decided to send the King of Persia a message. They demanded two wagons loads of gold. The message was delivered to a government official in the closest Persian town. He read the message and immediately sent the message to the King of Persia. The king knew the prince had been captured and was interested in his return. He made preparations. Two wagons were loaded with gold.

Persian representatives were sent to Constantinople. They asked for peace and hoped to bring their defeated prince home. They spoke to Constantine at his military office.

"We don't wish to continue our wars," Harpus said. "We have two wagons loaded with gold for you."

Constantine rubbed his hands together and then scratched his back.

He sent Samson to inspect the wagons. The gold was so heavy, that special wagons had to be built to move it. Each wagon was pulled by twelve horses. Samson took a sample of the gold to Constantine. He let the gold nuggets tumble through his fingers. Then he looked at Harpus.

"I am glad you came to see me," Constantine said. "We will mint coins using this gold."

"Can we see our prince?" he asked. "He is greatly missed at home."

"You can have him," Samson said. "I had to provide him an extra guard so he wouldn't be killed. We don't want him."

"Thank you," he said. "I will take him home."

"He is a broken man," Samson said. "You might have to protect him from his own weapon."

"We will ensure he is returned to his father," he said. "That is the major purpose of our journey."

"Guard, bring the prisoner," he said. "Release him to these men."

The prince knelt before Constantine.

"Kill me," he begged. "Don't turn me over to them. I am a disgrace to my family."

Constantine motioned to the guards. The prince was released to Harpus. He fell to the ground and trembled.

Samson looked at Harpus and asked, "What would you like us to do with the other three officers we took prisoner?"

"We don't want them," he said. "If they were good officers, they wouldn't be here. I would execute them."

Samson told Constantine of their decision.

"They are probably better off with us hanging them, than being sent home," he said. "The king takes great pleasure in killing those he doesn't like."

A message was delivered to Constantine explaining that he had another granddaughter. Constantine II's wife had given birth to another girl. The message indicated that mother and daughter were well and that Constantine II would be trying for a son in the near future.

A week later, Constantine told Samson to make arrangements with Constans to have a public hanging.

"I want the city to see these officers die," Constans said. "They have caused many Roman soldiers' deaths."

"I will have three gallows built," Samson said. "You can have all three killed at the same time. I think that would make a great impression."

"Make certain to invite my brother to the hangings," Constans said. "I want him to get some of the recognition."

"Do you want me to invite Constantine II?" he asked. "He might enjoy coming home for a visit. I could send him a message."

"Send him a message," Constans said. "I don't think he will be interested."

Samson planned a large celebration in the park. He provided cookies for the children and a picnic lunch for their parents. The gold from Persia was used to mint coins. Constantine helped design a coin, commemorating his pending thirty years of being emperor. No one could remember an emperor who had served the empire that long. He distributed the coins to those that attended the hangings. When the officers were led to the gallows, the park was full of people. The officer's necks were placed in the ropes, and they were dropped.

"Two of them have suffered broken necks and are dead," Samson said. "The third one's neck didn't break, I am glad we gagged them."

The third prisoner kicked and struggled. Finally, his lifeless body hung limply from the rope.

"Wait a few more moments," Samson said. "I want to be certain he is dead."

After the third man died, the bodies were removed and taken outside of town and buried. The celebration lasted all day. Constantius II was assigned command of the guards in the park. Constantine assigned Constans command of the legion at the fortification in Constantinople.

The prince was sent home to face his father. Constantine wasn't surprised he was never heard of or seen again. The representatives penned an alliance with Constantine concerning the treatment of Christians. They agreed to cease their persecution of the Christians in Persia

Constantine received a message from Constantine II. He was sorry he wasn't able to attend the hanging.

"Judge, Constantine II, and his family are going to visit with us," Constantine said. "He wants Eusebius to christen his children,"

"I will contact him," Judge said. "We will have the ceremony in Helena's church."

An announcement was posted in the park. Constantine II and his family boarded the ship and headed to Constantinople. The children didn't like the motion of the ship and became sick.

"She is very nauseous," Faustana said. "I will have the attendant stay with her."

"I thought my children would be good sailors," Constantine II said. "If we ever have any, I hope our sons don't get sea sick."

When they docked in Constantinople, Judge met the ship. The children were fine. They enjoyed the carriage ride to the palace. They greeted Constantine.

The day of the christening, the church was filled with people. It was a beautiful day. The sun shone brightly. Eusebius held each child so the people, in the congregation, could see them. The baby girls exhibited beautiful smiles. After the service, many stayed to see the children.

"She is beautiful," Samson said. "You are lucky to have girls first."

"I am looking forward to sons," Constantine II said. "I know my father wants boys."

"He just likes grandchildren," Judge said. "He talks about them every day."

Constantine II's family stayed and visited for a few days and then sailed back to their home.

Constantine realized he was getting old, and that the end of his life was approaching. He decided it was time to be baptized. One evening, he discussed baptism with his closest friends.

"I want to be baptized in the Jordan River," Constantine said. "Jesus was baptized in the Jordan River."

"Who baptized Jesus?" Samson asked. "When did baptism start? Did Jesus start the tradition of baptism?"

"No, his friend, John, baptized him," Constantine said. "I think John started baptizing people in the Jordan River."

"Yes, father, that is the story," Constans said. "I will take you to the Jordan River."

"I want several bishops and the archbishop to travel with me," he said. "Bring Eusebius. He has never seen the Jordan River."

"I will prepare the troops," Samson said. "Should I take Constans?"

"Yes," he said. "I want this to be a religious journey, not a parade of military troops."

"It sounds like you want a pilgrimage," Constans said. "Many people go to Jerusalem each year."

"The Jews go to Jerusalem several times a year for religious holidays," Constantine said. "The army has to post extra troops during the holy days. Jerusalem is crowded, and thieves are attracted to the festivities."

"Many Christians go to Jerusalem," Constans said. "They celebrate the Passover meal. Then, they celebrate Easter."

"Someday, people will come to our church on a pilgrimage," he said. "My mother made sure of that. We have more relics relating to Jesus than any city in the world."

Planning for the trip to the Jordan River continued for several months. It was clear to everyone, except Constantine, that he was much weaker and would never make his trip to the Jordan River.

CHAPTER 15

CONSTANTINE'S DEATH

When the prince was returned to Persia, the war ended for Constantine. He became focused on his rapidly, deteriorating health. He planned a trip to be baptized in the Jordan River, but weakened each month. He often leaned against the walls to hold himself up, and those who walked with him usually had to support him. He was self-conscious about being unsteady, and Judge purchased a walking stick for him. His friend was very worried.

"How do you feel today?" Judge asked. "May I do anything for you? Would you like to take a short walk?"

"I feel a little weak," Constantine said. "I would like to spend a long time in a hot bath today. Have the slave burn more wood than normal. I want hot water and steam."

"I will take care of the bath for you," he said. "Do you want the doctor to see you?"

"No, he knows I am sick. I have been suffering for years," he said. "He thought I was going to die about twenty-five years ago."

"After the bath, do you want to go to the office or remain at home?" he asked.

"I want to go to the office," he said. "I can't do much work at the palace. Everyone visits and asks how I am doing."

Constantius II stopped by the palace to visit with his father. Constantine was surprised.

"How are you feeling today?" Constantius II asked.

"Why does everyone think I am sick?" Constantine asked. "I am sick of being sick. I am just a little weak."

Constantius II took a long look at his father.

"No, father," he said. "You are very weak. We are worried about you. Would you like the archbishop to baptize you now?"

"Not yet," he said. "I still feel it is important to be baptized just before I die. The shorter the duration of time between my baptism and my death, the fewer sins I will have committed."

"I didn't know you were committing sins," Constantius II said. "When you sin, how do you know?"

"Unfortunately, I don't always know, but I am certain that God knows," he said.

"Don't wait too long to be baptized," he said. "All of your children have been baptized."

"That is good," he said. "Religion has changed since I was young. I have endured many changes."

"You have caused many of them," Constantius II said. "At least you gave the church direction."

"All my decisions haven't been correct," he said. "I've even changed my mind. I never could figure out the trinity issue. I am now certain John was correct."

"Have a nice day," Constantius II said. "Enjoy your bath."

Constantine had heard disagreements for many years concerning trinity. He saw irony in the fact that bishops on both sides of the discussion would quote from the writings of John, the disciple, to bolster their position.

Before he went to the office, Constantine spent an extra hour in the baths. Afterwards, he became so tired that he decided to return to the palace. He asked Judge what he planned to do after he died. Judge looked down.

"I hope to retire someday," he said. "I don't want to work for anyone else. I have been in the army for thirty-five years."

"You don't have long to wait," Constantine said. "I need to make arrangements for the division of the empire. I don't want the senate to do it after I die. Have the head of the senate, Claudius, visit with me."

Judge sent a message to Claudius.

Two days later, Claudius visited with Constantine. Judge was asked to remain in the room to witness their decisions.

"I want the western portion of the empire to be the domain of my oldest son, Constantine II," he said. "It will include the tip of Africa, Gaul, and Britain."

"I am certain he will like Gaul," Judge said. "We liked Gaul."

"I want my youngest son, Constans, to rule from the city of Rome," he said. "His brother will advise him for a few years."

"I will record that," Claudius said. "Constantine II will advise Constans for a few years. Which territories do you want to be under his control? It is a very large empire."

"I want his territory to be adjacent to Constantine II's territory," he said. "It will include Africa from the tip to Alexandria."

"I want my daughter to be included," he said. "I want my more distant relative, Dalmatius, to rule from Athens to Constantinople. That way my daughter and her husband, Hannibalianus, can live in the palace."

"Where will Constantius II live?" Judge asked. "I know he is familiar with the east."

"He will rule the eastern portion of the empire all the way to Alexandria," he said. "His religion is more in tune with the religion of Alexandria."

"I hope you can rule for many more years," Claudius said. "You have done a fine job for us. I will make an official document concerning your wishes. We will all sign it, and I will make it public after your death."

Claudius and Judge were sworn to secrecy concerning Constantine's wishes. They relaxed and were served tea. It was necessary for them to elaborate on a few of the details. Constantine became very tired and the meeting was adjourned.

The following day, he discussed his weekend plans with Judge. He allowed Judge sufficient time to perform his requests.

"I want to visit my villa in the country," Constantine said. "Send a few troops and guards to prepare the villa."

"I will ensure they will leave today," Judge said. "The baths will be ready for your use."

"Ensure Samson is available to go with me," he said. "I have a few things to discuss with him."

"I will ensure he is with you," he said. "Have a nice weekend."

When the weekend arrived, Samson took Constantine to the villa via carriage. It was a beautiful weekend. The weather was warm and dry. They enjoyed the carriage ride.

"I am glad you came with me," Constantine said. "How long do you plan to remain in the army?"

"As long as I can work for you," Samson said. "When you retire, I will retire. Only you know how long that will be."

"I plan to stick around a few more years," he said. "I want to build another great church in Constantinople."

"The Church of the Holy Apostles is often so crowded, I can't find a seat," he said. "We could use another great church."

"Send a builder to see me," he said. "If we start now, maybe I can be here when it is finished."

"The doctors will ensure you live a long time," Samson said. "I will send a builder to see you."

As the weekend came to a close, they returned to the palace. Constantine seemed somewhat revived. A few days later, a builder came to see him.

"Samson asked me to visit with you," Rockus said. "He indicated you were thinking of having another church built."

"Yes," Constantine said. "We need another great church."

"I will start on it at once," he said. "Many great cities have more than one great church."

"How long will it take to build?" he asked. "I have a limited amount of time before I die."

"You will be singing in the pews in two years," he said. "You can count on it."

"Two years," he said. "I might not live that long. I want it completed in six months."

"That isn't sufficient time to build a great church," Rockus said. "I will build the sanctuary first. We will open the church, and then I will finish the project."

"Can you get it open in six months?" Constantine asked. "I am in a hurry."

"I think nine months is the soonest," he said. "Tomorrow, we will start cutting stone. I will purchase all the stones that have already been quarried."

Rockus looked at Constantine and mumbled something about everyone wanting everything yesterday.

"That is better," he said. "I will have more Bibles copied. A new church should have new Bibles."

When the walls of the new church were built, Constantine visited with Eusebius about new Bibles.

"I am having a new church built," Constantine said. "Arrange to have more new Bibles produced."

"The fifty produced a few years ago were very popular," Eusebius said. "I will have another fifty produced."

"The Bibles you place in the church should contain many drawings and be written in Latin," Constantine said. "Those of my people who can read understand Latin."

"I will have a few codices written in Greek," Eusebius said. "I will give them to the bishops."

"All of the bishops and priests are using the newer codices," he said. "Very few churches are still using scrolls."

"What the codices say is the important thing," he said. "We want Matthew, Mark, Luke, John, and Paul's books."

"Yes, I still have the list," he said. "It should never be changed."

Eusebius looked at Constantine.

"I want to talk with you about baptizing me," Constantine said. "I am getting old, and it is time for me to be baptized."

"I would be honored to baptize you," Eusebius said. "You may hurt the archbishop's feelings."

"I didn't think about the archbishop," he said. "You are family. He runs a large business."

"Maybe, he could manage the ceremony, and I could baptize you," he said. "Would you like me to talk with him?"

"Yes, tell him that is what I want you to do," he said. "If he hesitates, have him see me."

"When do you want to be baptized?" he asked. "Do you want to be baptized in the new church?"

"Yes, I would like that, but I don't think I will live long enough," he said. "I wanted to be baptized in the Jordan River, but I waited too long. I couldn't survive the journey now. I will have Judge make plans for using The Church of the Holy Apostles."

"Advise me of the date as soon as possible," he said. "The archbishop and I will prepare."

"Samson will come and talk with you about the details," he said.

"I am glad you have changed your mind about Arianism," Eusebius said. "It is the one thing they didn't understand at the council of Nicene."

"The council was a good start," Constantine said. "We must keep evolving. A static religion is a dying religion."

Constantine returned to the palace. While getting ready, he fell. Judge went to his aid. They talked to each other for a few moments, and then Judge lifted him to a standing position.

"Are you able to walk?" he asked.

"I think so. I don't remember what happened to me," Constantine said. "Suddenly, I was on the floor. I would prefer if you didn't tell anyone about this."

"I wish you would see a doctor," Judge said.

"He would just tell me to use my walking stick and walk slower," Constantine said.

"If you change your mind, please tell me," he said. "We have several good doctors on the army post."

Constantine didn't answer. Judge took him into his bedroom and sat him in a chair.

"Would you like me to remove your shoes?" he asked. "I would be glad to do that for you."

"No," he said. "Good night, I will see you in the morning. Close the door on your way out."

Judge went about securing the palace for the evening.

The next day, Constantine instructed Judge to invite Samson,

Constantius II, and Constans, to dinner. Two days later, they sat in the living area.

"I have decided to be baptized," Constantine said. "I want the ceremony to take place in The Church of the Holy Apostles."

"I thought you wanted to be baptized in the new church?" Constantius II asked. "What changed your mind?"

"I didn't change my mind," he said. "I just don't know if I will live long enough to see the construction of the new church completed."

"You will worship there," Constantine II said. "We will all worship with you."

"I hope you are correct," he said. "I will be baptized by Eusebius, and the archbishop will conduct the service."

"I see you have everything planned," Constans said.

"Constantine II will be home again in three months," Constantius II said. "Can we plan it for then? His family might be larger by then. He could bring all of them."

"Judge, plan my baptism when Constantine II visits," he said. "Samson, visit Eusebius and give him the date."

"Yes, sir," Samson said. "I will visit with him this week. I will also find out what is causing the construction of the new church to take so long."

Eusebius was already planning the ceremony. The Church of the Holy Apostles was prepared and extra chairs were placed outside in the grassy area in front of the church. A large crowd started arriving early in the morning. The procession of Constantine and the clergy was an impressive event.

"Doesn't he look regal in his purple robe?" Constantine II asked. "I wish he would wear his robe more often."

"He is an impressive emperor," Constantius II said. "I hope we will be as great as he is."

"You two will live so long, I will never become emperor," Constans said. "That is fine. I will command the army for you. I am a warrior."

"I am surprised that he finally decided to be baptized," Constantius II said. "I am afraid he thinks he is dying."

"Today is his special day," Constans said. "He wants to set a good example for his people."

"After today's ceremony, I expect the number of baptisms will increase," Constantius II said. "I am sorry he couldn't make it to the Jordan River."

"Constantinople is his Jordan River," Constantine II said. "The Black Sea is his home."

Eric troops erected tents and placed long tables under the tents. He and the guard troops were in dress uniform and marched from the park. After the long ceremony, food was made available to everyone. It was a joyous occasion. When the sun started to set, the park was still crowded. Constantine and his family returned to the palace.

"I enjoyed the day," Constantine said. "I should have been baptized many years ago."

"Thank you for allowing me to stay with the family at the palace this evening," Eusebius said. "I don't get to see you very often."

"We are busy keeping the empire safe for you," Constantine II said. "Tomorrow, I will be departing for the Istrius River."

"When is your family getting larger?" Constantius II asked. "Someday, I might get married."

"I am never going to get married," Constans said. "I am too busy to raise a family."

"I haven't found the secret," Constantine II said. "We have two girls. I am trying for a boy. Check with me next year."

He looked at his brothers and smiled.

"I baptize babies, you know," Eusebius said. "You can't be too young to be baptized."

"I will send for you when my wife and I are ready for our son to be baptized," he said. "Have you ever seen the Istrius River?"

Eusebius smiled.

"Yes," he said. "But it was a long time ago. I will look forward to visiting with you."

Constantine II bid him farewell.

The next day, the guests journeyed home. Eusebius thought about baptizing Constantine II's son. Constantine II and his family were excited and had hired an attendant to help when the next baby arrived. Constantine and Samson went to the villa to relax.

"I enjoy visiting the villa," Constantine said. "The hot baths feel soothing. The salts make me tingle."

"They are good for you," Samson said. "Being away from the army and the palace is also good for you."

"I am afraid, I don't have long to live," he said. "I would like very much to talk to my sons."

"Are you going to make Constantine II emperor?" he asked. "I think they would like to divide the empire and each rule a portion."

"He will be the emperor," Constantine said. "I think he will give his brothers specific territories to rule."

Constantine didn't disclose that he had made official plans for the division of the empire.

"I hope they have large families," Samson said. "Your family could rule for a very long time."

Constantine looked at Samson.

"How many of your sons are in the army?" Constantine asked.

"I have two sons. They are both in their twenties and in the army."

"Is your oldest son a Christian?" Constantine asked. "Make sure you have him baptized."

"Yes, he is a Christian," he said. "He and I have both been baptized."

"Promote your oldest son to sergeant," he said. "Do you think he ready to command?"

"I believe he is," he said. "Let's give him some on the job training."

The sun set and they went to bed. The nights at the villa were especially quiet. One could see an occasional ripple in the water of the lake as a fish jumped into the air and caught a bug.

After a week at the villa, Constantine and Samson returned to the palace. Constantine continued to grow weaker. He encountered severe problems walking. He decided to see a doctor.

"Contact the doctor," Constantine said. "I need him to look at me. Maybe, he can give me some energy. I know he can't cure me."

"I will send a messenger," Judge said. "He will come to see you as soon as possible."

The doctor arrived two hours later.

"Hello, Constantine," the doctor said. "Remove your clothes."

"It is the same old thing," Constantine said. "It has gotten a lot worse, and I am seeping all the time."

"You are correct," he said. "You still have leprosy, and it is a lot worse. There is not much we can do for you."

"I am lucky to have lived this long," he said. "I remember the first time a doctor told me I was dying. That was twenty-five years ago."

"You were dying," he said. "We all are dying but at different rates. He didn't know when you would die, and I don't know when you will die."

"How long do you think I will live?" he asked. "I think my leprosy is serious this time."

"When you die will depend on your attitude," he said. "You might live a few months. Not much longer."

"I am glad my house is in order," Constantine said. "I am at peace. I wish the world was at peace."

"It is time for you to turn the empire over to your sons," he said. "They are very capable."

"The empire is lucky. I still have three sons," he said. "They are all serving in the army."

As the church went up, Constantine's health declined. It was a race to the finish. The church was completed just in time for Constantine to dedicate it.

"I want every Christian in Constantinople to be able to sit in a church pew," Constantine said. "The Church of the Holy Apostles was too small. Many had to stand outside. Some just didn't attend."

"Now everyone can attend," the archbishop said. "I want to see both churches full on every Sabbath."

"I am honored to dedicate this church," Constantine said. "I was afraid I would die before it was completed. It is a beautiful church in a beautiful city."

"God bless all of us," Eusebius said. "Jesus has prepared a place for you. 'In my father's house are many rooms, if it were not so, I would have told you. I am going there to prepare a place for you. And if I go and prepare a place for you, I will come back and take you to be with me that you also may be where I am. You know the way to the place where I am going.'[(John, 14, 2 – 5, NIV)]"

After the ceremony, the crowd went to the park. Food and drink were provided for all who attended the dedication. Eusebius spoke with Constantine.

"The archbishop has your funeral service planned," Eusebius said. "I will have a part."

"It is good of you," Constantine said. "Family members are important. I want you to be there with me."

"I want to thank you for all you have done for me," he said. "I work diligently for our God in an effort to help others as you have helped me."

"Goodbye, good friend," Constantine said. "I will see you in eternity."

They embraced each other.

After Eusebius departed, Constantine returned to the palace. He and Judge had a private conversation.

"I want you to create a tomb for me in The Church of the Holy Apostles," Constantine said. "Please don't tell anyone it is for me. If you are questioned, make up a good story."

"Why keep it a secret?" Judge asked. "Everyone expects you to have a large tomb."

"I don't want people to know I am going to die," he said. "They might lose allegiance."

"That wouldn't happen. They all love you," he said. "They will remember you forever."

"Just don't tell anyone," he said. "I want it made using large pieces of rose colored marble."

"That might take me a little time," he said. "I will have the tomb designed, and I will start searching for some nice marble."

"Thank you. When I visited Athens, I saw some marble I liked," he said. "I knew I could count on you. That is why I asked this favor."

After several weekend trips to the villa, Constantine became very ill and returned to the palace. Judge sent a messenger to his sons. Constantius II and Constans stayed by his bedside. He talked with them for several hours, and then he went to sleep and never awoke. His sons had his clean shaven body entombed in The Church of the Holy Apostles during the last week of May in the year three hundred thirty-seven. Samson led the troops.

"Keep the horses steady," Samson said. "Keep the line straight. Don't go too fast."

"Give everyone a chance to look at him before he is entombed," Judge said. "This is a day for history."

"Halt," he said. "Are you ready to place him in the tomb?"

The honor guards removed his body from the wagon. It was placed on a large plank, and the troops carried it to the tomb. They stopped, and Constantius II said a prayer. They paused for a moment of silence. The breeze blew gently through the trees. Constantine was placed in his tomb.

The tomb became a place for prayer and peace for the people of Constantinople. Claudius, the leader of the senate, made a proclamation stating Constantine's desires concerning the division of the empire. Many were surprised that Dalmatius was now a ruler.

Constantius II became concerned about certain members of the family who claimed a right to government power and property. After dinner one evening, he discussed his concern with his brother.

"You solved the empire's problem along the Istrius River," Constantius II said. "I am going to solve our family problem."

He looked at his brother.

"What are you planning to do?" Constantine II asked. "I don't like the tone of your voice."

"I am going to eliminate many of those who might contend for our positions within the government," he said. "I am going to cleanse the side of the family into which our sister married."

"Be careful, brother," he said. "We want to remain popular and live as our father's sons. If you need help, see Eric. I must return to the Istrius."

CHAPTER 16

AFTER CONSTANTINE'S DEATH

Constantine had provided specific instructions for the division of the empire. He planned for his family to rule for many years. That didn't happen, because his family wasn't satisfied with his plan. Constantine II, his two daughters, and his wife relocated to Lugdunum. It was a long journey. A year passed before they were settled. Constans moved to the palace in Rome. He had very little baggage and settled into his new surroundings very quickly. He wasn't pleased that he had to follow the advice of his brother for two years. He realized that his brother hadn't requested the job. Dalmatius, Hannibalianus, and Constantine's daughters moved to Constantinople and enjoyed the grandeur of the palace. However, they found their lives always changing and never became completely settled. Constantius II moved to Antioch and then he made a secret trip to Constantinople to speak with Eric.

"Your brother told me a year ago that you would come to see me," Eric said. I thought you might have changed your mind."

"I haven't changed my mind," Constantius II said. "How is the empire in Constantinople?"

"Dalmatius doesn't rule," he said. "He just entertains. He is always having a party at the palace. He and the women are always dressed in fancy clothing. He does keep my guards busy."

"He is why I came to see you," Constantius II said. "He must be eliminated. He really isn't part of our family. His son married my sister."

Constantius II explained the plan that he and his brother devised to eliminate the unwanted family members. They didn't want anyone, not of blood relations, claiming authority or any part of the empire. The empire belonged only to Constantine's sons. Then, he handed Eric written instructions which he read very carefully.

> Your guards will kill forty members of our family.
>
> Send your best men to complete each execution.
>
> It must happen on the same day in exactly three moons.
>
> This plan is to remain a secret.
>
> I want you to take care of Dalmatius, personally.
>
> If you have any problems, seek my help.
>
> After the family is cleansed, Dalmatius' portion of the empire will be divided between Constans and me.
>
> I will move back to Constantinople.
>
> You and your troops will continue to work for me.
>
> I am returning to Antioch.
>
> Remember, three moons.

Eric nodded that he understood and didn't ask any questions. He escorted Constantius II to his horse, so he could hurry home to be married. His future wife was a member of the family and would be spared. Constantius II's aid planned all the details of the wedding.

"I found a priest you will like," he said. "He will marry you in a very large church."

"How is Martha?" he asked. "Is she excited about being married?"

"I think she is intimidated by the idea of being the emperor's bride," he said. "I am certain she will adjust."

"Bring her to me," he said. "I will talk with her."

When Martha was brought to Constantius II, she was so afraid she was trembling. Constantius promised Martha a good life, and that she could have as many attendants as she would like. He wanted her to have people with her when he was not at home. Martha promised to love, honor, and obey.

Constantius II sent a message to Constantine II.

> Constantine I-I
> Emperor of the Western Empire
>
> I just had a favorable meeting.
>   All is well.
>   In three moons, our problems will be solved.
>   We will all meet in Pannonia.
>   I have a new wife, Martha.
>   You know her.
>
> Emperor of the Eastern Empire
> Constantius II

In four moons, the brothers met in Pannonia. Constans received a small portion of what had been Dalmatius' territory and Constantius II acquired the remainder. The only relatives who weren't killed included three cousins, Nepotianus, Julian, and Gallus. The brothers returned to their palaces and their duties.

Constantius II returned to his troops in Antioch and resumed the war with Persia.

Shapur had gathered a large army and plundered part of the eastern Empire. His army wasn't very efficient and Constantius II's army chased them back towards Persia. Many soldiers in Shapur's army were killed. After Shapur's army commander, his brother, was killed, he ceased his war effort and returned home.

Constantine II became jealous of his "little" brother inheriting a part of the Roman Empire and with Constans' popularity in Rome. He led his army into northern Italy. Constans didn't want to war with his brother and didn't retaliate. Finally, he had no choice. He talked with the leader of his army.

"My brother's army will usurp my territory," Constans said. "They will be marching through this valley."

He handed his commander a drawing. The commander gazed at it.

"We can easily ambush them and destroy the army."

The commander liked the plan and trapped Constantine II's army in the valley near Aquileia. He destroyed his army, but accidentally killed Constantine II. He immediately reported to Constans.

"I didn't mean to have him killed," he said. "We didn't know who we were killing. We had them trapped and they charged us. They didn't have a chance. We didn't have time to do anything except defend ourselves."

Constans grieved for a week. Then, he announced that he was the emperor of the western portion of the empire. Peace was enjoyed throughout the west for many years. Constantius II was in his palace and talked with his sister, Constantina.

"It was unfortunate that your husband was killed," he said. "When you married him, he was useful to us."

She glared at him.

"I am sure you are sorry," she said. "Now, what do you want?"

Constantina knew Constantius II was behind the plot to kill her husband and most of Dalmatius' family.

"Our brother, Constans, is having problems with Magnentius," he said. "I would like you to marry our cousin, Gallus. If you marry him, I will allow him to manage the eastern frontier for the empire. I will rescue Constans."

"Marry my cousin, Gallus?" she asked. "I don't know him very well. He probably doesn't know me."

"You can still be his wife," he said. "You can learn to know each other."

"No," she said. "I am not interested."

Constantius II and Martha never produced any children, so he sought another wife. Martha disappeared and was never heard of again. His second marriage ceremony was a much smaller affair. Constantius II married a lady named Eusebia. It wasn't long before Constantius II could tell they didn't love each other. They were married for several years but didn't produce any children. She died at a very young age.

Three months after Constantina refused to marry Gallus, Constans was killed. Constantius II visited with Constantina.

"Well, Constans is dead," he said. "I guess that is what you wanted."

She looked at Constantius II.

"If you promise to kill Magnentius, I will marry Gallus," she said.

She had tears in her eyes. Constantius II took her hand.

"I will kill him. My army will destroy his army" he said. "Prepare to head east."

Constantina and Gallus were married. Constantius II went to war with Magnentius. Italy switched its allegiance to Constantius II, and his army was victorious. Magnentius was killed, and Constantius II became the sole emperor of the empire. Gallus was not a good leader. The people in the eastern empire didn't respect him. They called on Constantius II for help. When Constantius II questioned Gallus he blamed all the problems on him. Constantius was enraged and ordered his execution. He became aware that he couldn't handle all the problems and sought help. He named Julian to help him control the empire.

Constantius II decided to visit Rome and talked with his aid, Brutus, about his plan.

"I think I would like to speak with the Pope," he said.

"I will make the arrangement for you," Brutus said. "When should I tell the ship's captain you want to travel?"

"I would like to go in about two weeks," he said. "Take ten guards and secure a cabin for you next to me."

"I will send a message to Pope Liberius," Brutus said. "I am certain he will find time to see you."

"I would like to visit some of the great buildings and monuments," he said. "I also want to visit the great church."

"I will take two carriages and several horses," he said.

Everyone prepared to go to Rome.

Two weeks passed, wagons transported the trunks to the ship. It was a beautiful, warm, and sunny day. Constantius boarded the ship and stood at the railing on the main deck. He waved goodbye to those who watched. During the second day at sea, a mate came to Constantius II and informed him that the ship's captain had become sick.

"We are going to have to make an emergency stop and obtain medical help for our captain," the mate said. "Tomorrow, we will stop in Athens."

Later that day, Constantius was informed that the captain had died. The crew planned to bury him at sea. Constantius watched the ceremony.

"Put him in his dress uniform and lay him on the plank," the mate said. "Bring him back topside in one hour."

The plank was put in place and the mates brought the captain topside after one hour.

"Man the plank," the first mate said. "Mate, slide him into the sea."

The mates sang a song of praise for their captain, and then returned to their jobs.

Constantine II inquired who was assigned the duty of the temporary captain.

"The first mate will sail the ship," he said. "When we return to Constantinople, a new captain will be assigned."

After a few days, the ship docked in Rome. Constantius II went to the Pope's church. He was provided quarters. The troops were bunked with the Pope's guards.

The following day, Constantius was informed that Pope Liberius would see him. He was escorted to the pope. They greeted each other.

"Will you tell me your interpretation of the Trinity?" Constantius II asked. "Do you understand the phrase, 'Father, Son, and Holy Ghost' as one entity and eternal?'"

"Yes, that is what we teach," Pope Liberius said. "It is a complicated thought."

Constantius II and Liberius discussed the Trinity and several other topics. The Pope didn't convince Constantius that the son and the father were equal. He knew sons should be subservient to their fathers. He maintained his Arian views. Some, who confronted him about Arianism, were exiled. When he returned to Constantinople, he published several edicts that Pope Liberius had requested. He didn't require the clergy or their sons to serve in the army or to pay taxes.

Constantius II planned to marry again. His wife's name was Faustina. They were a beautiful couple. He finally had found someone he loved and who loved him. After they honeymooned for one month, they planned to visit the western section of the empire.

"Brutus, I want you to plan another trip," he said. "I want to visit the town of Lugdunum."

"Yes, sir," he said. "I will check on the ship. Will your wife be traveling with you?"

"I will check with her," he said.

That evening, Constantius II spoke to Faustina about the trip.

"I am planning a trip to the Rhone River valley," he said. "Would you like to travel with me?"

"I would love to travel with you," she said. "But our baby might not like a bumpy ship ride."

Constantius II looked at Faustina and then hugged her. He took her hand and kissed it. She embraced him.

"I will miss you," he said. "I will make certain everything is taken care of for you. I will have an additional aid assigned to you. When our son is born, you will need more help."

"I hope we have a son," she said. She rubbed her stomach.

Three weeks later, he sailed to the Rhone River valley. When he reached Lugdunum, he became very sick. He spent a few days in the clinic and then requested to be returned to Constantinople. He told Brutus that he had to return home before his son was born.

"I didn't know Faustina was going to have a child," he said. "We will sail as soon as possible."

"When I thought I would spend years with my son, I wasn't in a hurry," he said. "Now I hope I get to see him."

When the ship returned home, Claudius arranged for Bishop Euzoius to visit Constantinople.

"I want to be baptized again as soon as we are home," Constantius II said. "Have the senate leader visit with me."

"I have prepared to baptize you," Euzoius said. "I am surprised you haven't been baptized. I guess you respected your father's example."

"I was baptized," he said. "Thank you for visiting with me. I am glad you are here. I want a proper baptism."

Claudius informed the senate leader that the emperor was very ill and had requested his presence.

"I shouldn't have named Julian as ruler of the western empire," Constantius II said.

"He is a great warrior and a very learned man," the senate leader said.

"He isn't a Christian. Now, he wants to be emperor," Constantius II said. "If I were going to live, he would probably kill me. He won't have that pleasure. I think he will make a good emperor. After I die, name him emperor."

Constantius II never saw his son. Faustina gave birth to a girl. Constantius II died before he saw her.

Julian became emperor.

ABOUT THE AUTHOR

The author served in the U.S. Navy and then went to college. After graduating with an engineering degree, he enjoyed careers (50 yrs.) as an engineer, businessman, and professor. He is now retired but writes novels.

While reading the New Testament for over sixty years and teaching Sunday School Bible classes for twenty years, John Mench Ph.D. has been conflicted by the lack of personality within the testament. He endeavors to add perspective to the message of the testament by creating lives for those who wrote and developed Jesus' message.

Printed in the United States
By Bookmasters